WHO ARE 'WE'?

Methodology and History in Anthropology
Series Editors:
David Parkin, Fellow of All Souls College, University of Oxford
David Gellner, Fellow of All Souls College, University of Oxford

Just as anthropology has had a significant influence on many other disciplines in recent years, so too have its methods been challenged by new intellectual and technical developments. This series is designed to offer a forum for debate on the interrelationship between anthropology and other academic fields but also on the challenge to anthropological methods of new intellectual and technological developments, and the role of anthropological thought in a general history of concepts.

For a full volume listing, please see back matter

Who Are 'We'?

Reimagining Alterity and Affinity in Anthropology

Edited by
Liana Chua and Nayanika Mathur

berghahn
NEW YORK • OXFORD
www.berghahnbooks.com

First published in 2018 by
Berghahn Books
www.berghahnbooks.com

© 2018, 2024 Liana Chua and Nayanika Mathur
First paperback edition published in 2024

All rights reserved. Except for the quotation of short passages
for the purposes of criticism and review, no part of this book
may be reproduced in any form or by any means, electronic or
mechanical, including photocopying, recording, or any information
storage and retrieval system now known or to be invented,
without written permission of the publisher.

Library of Congress Cataloging-in-Publication Data
Names: Chua, Liana, editor. | Mathur, Nayanika, editor.
Title: Who are 'we'? : reimagining alterity and affinity in anthropology /
 edited by Liana Chua and Nayanika Mathur.
Other titles: Who are 'we'? (Berghahn Books)
Description: First edition. | New York : Berghahn Books, [2018] | Series:
 Methodology and history in anthropology ; 34 | Includes bibliographical
 references and index.
Identifiers: LCCN 2017056918 (print) | LCCN 2018014774 (ebook) | ISBN
 9781785338892 (ebook) | ISBN 9781785338885 (hardback : alk. paper)
Subjects: LCSH: Ethnology--Case studies. | Group identity--Case studies. |
 Ethnicity--Case studies. | Other (Philosophy)--Case studies.
Classification: LCC GN495.6 (ebook) | LCC GN495.6 .W5 2018 (print) | DDC
 305.8--dc23
LC record available at https://lccn.loc.gov/2017056918

British Library Cataloguing in Publication Data
A catalogue record for this book is available from the British Library

ISBN 978-1-78533-888-5 hardback
ISBN 978-1-80539-716-8 paperback
ISBN 978-1-80539-903-2 epub
ISBN 978-1-78533-889-2 web pdf

https://doi.org/10.3167/9781785338885

CONTENTS

List of Figures	vii
Acknowledgements	ix
Introduction. Who Are 'We'? *Liana Chua and Nayanika Mathur*	1

Part I. Revisiting the Anthropological 'We'

Chapter 1. Anthropology at the Dawn of Apartheid: Radcliffe-Brown and Malinowski's South African Engagements, 1919–34 *Isak Niehaus*	37
Chapter 2. The Savage Noble: Alterity and Aristocracy in Anthropology *David Sneath*	60

Part II. Alterity and Affinity in Anthropology's Global Landscape

Chapter 3. The Anthropological Imaginarium: Crafting Alterity, The Self and an Ethnographic Film in Southwest China *Katherine Swancutt*	95
Chapter 4. The Risks of Affinity: Indigeneity and Indigenous Film Production in Bolivia *Gabriela Zamorano Villarreal*	128
Chapter 5. Shifting the 'We' in Oceania: Anthropology and Pacific Islanders Revisited *Ty P. Kāwika Tengan*	151

Part III. Where Do 'We' Go from Here?

Chapter 6. Crafting Anthropology Otherwise: Alterity, Affinity and Performance   179
Gey Pin Ang and Caroline Gatt

Chapter 7. Towards an Ecumenical Anthropology   207
João de Pina-Cabral

Afterword   233
Mwenda Ntarangwi

Index   241

FIGURES

3.1. Title card from *1956. A Briton in the Cool Mountains of China* (Swancutt and Jiarimuji 2016). An introductory moment of the film, showing Alan Winnington's book.   119

3.2. Title card from *1956. A Briton in the Cool Mountains of China* (Swancutt and Jiarimuji 2016). Alan Winnington and a group of newly released slaves in Ninglang, circa 1957.   120

3.3. Still from *1956. A Briton in the Cool Mountains of China* (Swancutt and Jiarimuji 2016). A photograph of two former slaves wearing their Nuosu finery, which appears in Alan Winnington's book. Off screen, Nuosu villagers suggest the mountains in the distance are probably the same as those which appear behind these former slave girls, whose portrait was taken sixty years ago.   120

3.4. Still from *1956. A Briton in the Cool Mountains of China* (Swancutt and Jiarimuji 2016). Nuosu villagers try to recall the two former slaves photographed in Alan Winnington's book. My hands support the book, but I am otherwise off camera.   121

3.5. Title card from *1956. A Briton in the Cool Mountains of China* (Swancutt and Jiarimuji 2016). Alan Winnington's map from Lijiang to Ninglang.   121

3.6. Still from *1956. A Briton in the Cool Mountains of China* (Swancutt and Jiarimuji 2016). Part of the film's opening vignette, where I asked nearly a dozen Nuosu persons if they had heard of or seen Alan Winnington before.   122

3.7. Still from *1956. A Briton in the Cool Mountains of China* (Swancutt and Jiarimuji 2016). I introduce Boluo village to our film audience. According to Alan Winnington (1959: 25), Boluo (which he writes as 'Bolo') was the first place in Ninglang that he visited.   122

3.8. Still from *1956. A Briton in the Cool Mountains of China* (Swancutt and Jiarimuji 2016). The staged clip, in which my co-director and I discuss how we will visit a person whom we had just finished interviewing.   123

3.9. Title card from *1956. A Briton in the Cool Mountains of China* (Swancutt and Jiarimuji 2016). The 'sign' indicating the fifth stop in both Alan Winnington's book and our film. Echoing Winnington (1959: 97–119), the film offers local Nuosu reflections on how freed slaves were formed into work teams during the Democratic Reforms.   123

3.10. Still from *1956. A Briton in the Cool Mountains of China* (Swancutt and Jiarimuji 2016). My co-director jokes with a Nuosu woman about my 'foreigner' looks, after she had told us her childhood memories of hiding from Alan Winnington in the highlands of her village. There were local rumours at the time that Winnington was a Tibetan lama who would eat people. As the scene unfolds, this woman confirms that she no longer fears foreigners and is used to seeing them on television. Embarrassed, I laugh at how my alterity, which was often invisible to (or forgotten by) me, surfaces uncomfortably through the 'Orientalism' invoked by my co-director's joke.   124

ACKNOWLEDGEMENTS

This book has been a long time in the making, having originated in a series of conversations between the editors while we were postdocs at Cambridge in the early 2010s. Some of its core ideas were explored in a very stimulating Wenner-Gren funded workshop, *Who are 'We'? Reimagining Alterity and Affinity in Anthropology* (2014), while others were developed as this volume took shape and new contributors joined the conversation. Some of the original workshop participants are now part of this collection, but we would also like to thank Dmitry Arzyutov, Aleksandar Bošković, Richard Baxstrom, Sidney Cheung, Ryan Davey, George Lau, Jeremy MacClancy, Peter Mandler, Mahmut Mutman, Amiria Salmond, Ed Simpson, Nandini Sundar, Alice Tilche and Wazir Jahan Karim for being part of our earlier discussions. We also thank the Wenner-Gren Foundation (particularly the infinitely patient Laurie Obbink), as well as the Royal Anthropological Institute (Esperanza Fund) and the Department of Social Anthropology (Cambridge) for funding the workshop. Further thanks are owed to Brunel University London, Michał Buchowski (World Council of Anthropological Associations), Arturo Escobar, Keith Hart, Sally Lewis and Geoff Moggridge for various forms of support and suggestions, and to all those who contributed to our online discussions on Facebook and the Open Anthropology Cooperative. Last but not least, we are grateful to the series editors, David Gellner and David Parkin, Marion Berghahn and the staff of Berghahn Books for making this volume possible.

Introduction

WHO ARE 'WE'?

Liana Chua and Nayanika Mathur

> While we are very good at analysing how anthropology creates various others such as the 'natives' or the 'locals', we are less adept at rigorously analysing how we create and recreate 'anthropologists'.
> —E. Ben-Ari, 'Colonialism, Anthropology and the Politics of Professionalisation'

This collection interrogates a fundamental but neglected concern in sociocultural anthropology: the articulation of or tacit belief in a collective disciplinary identity, and its relationship to anthropological knowledge and practice. Although anthropology's long-standing 'romance with alterity' (Ntarangwi 2010: xii) has been subject to extensive critical scrutiny, the same cannot be said for presumptions of affinity *between* anthropologists, which, we contend in this volume, are equally instrumental in shaping ethnographic knowledge. As we argue below, the implicit sense of an anthropological 'we' that pervades a great deal of current writing and practice is not only a literary trope but also an epistemologically, morally and politically freighted device that has profound social and theoretical connotations. Yet its influence as such is rarely remarked upon; for the most part it has either remained invisible or unproblematically conflated with a vague image of 'Western' society as a homogenized foil to depictions of 'otherness'.

Our volume seeks to fill this lacuna by exploring how 'we' are imagined and invoked in settings across the global landscape of anthropology, from the anglophone mainstream to various smaller, less influential disciplinary environments. The questions that it poses are: who do 'we' anthropologists think 'we' are? How do our real or imagined affinities with disciplinary and other collective identities shape our methods, theories and analyses? What sorts of 'we's are produced by our scholarly interactions, methodological dilemmas and engagements in the world? Can a discernible anthropological 'we' even be said to exist? And, perhaps more challengingly, what is becoming, and can become, of this 'we' (or 'we's)?

The answers to these questions may seem deceptively simple, particularly for readers already steeped in the postmodernist and postcolonial critiques of the 1980s. These were instrumental in drawing attention to the oppositional quality of much Euro-American anthropology, to the ways that anthropologists often made, and still make, 'an easy living through setting up negativities' (Strathern 1988: 11) between quintessentially 'Western' concepts and various (usually non-Western) ethnographic particularities – between, for example, Western commodity logics and non-Western gift economies, Western individualism and non-Western 'dividuals', or Cartesian dualism and non-Cartesian holism. However well-meaning or heuristic, such dichotomies are premised on, and also reproduce, an assumption of radical difference between 'the West and the rest', one that facilitates the 'double movement' characteristic of much Euro-American anthropology: 'first, and more conventionally, "familiarizing" otherness; second, and more recently, exoticizing sameness' (Restrepo and Escobar 2005: 104–5).

In many of these debates, anthropologists' membership of either Western society or, more encompassingly, a historically Western intellectual framework is frequently taken for granted. Indeed, as we shall shortly argue, it is precisely anthropologists' affinity with a presumed Western readership – and, crucially, their capacity to transcend its ethnocentrisms – that lends much weight to their scholarship. The point that we wish to make, however, is that simply highlighting the imbrication of an anthropological 'we' with a vague image of Western society reveals only part of a more complicated story. For one thing, even those anthropologists who exploit the theoretical cachet of a 'West vs. the rest' approach seldom have an unproblematic relationship with that West. As we explain below, an element of ambivalence, if not outright antagonism, to their 'own' (usually Western) background has frequently characterized the activities of anthropologists, particularly those working within the anglophone mainstream. Another obvious caveat is that despite the global influence of many 'West vs. the rest' theories and concepts, not all anthropologists see themselves as members of that Western, Cartesian, modern 'we'. This applies not only to anthropologists in non-Western contexts, where the lines of alterity and affinity may be drawn quite differently, but also to those in Western anthropological centres who do not easily fit into the implicitly white, male, middle-class mould of the anthropological 'we' – or, for that matter, the very people who do. Finally, we suggest that overplaying the centrality of anthropologists' presumed sociocultural affinities can obscure the many other relations and collective identities that go into the making of anthropological knowledge. Anthropologists are also members of organizations, disciplinary clusters, kinship groups, socioeconomic classes and so forth, who may identify with political movements, regional networks or religious bodies, to name but a few possibilities. All these affiliations – these real and imagined 'we's – are, we argue, as constitutive of anthropologists' thought, practice and disciplinary identities as their presumed membership of a Western 'we'.

In sum, this volume posits that it is not enough to simply critique the anthropological 'we' as constitutively and reductively 'Western'. What is needed, rather, is a concerted interrogation of the multifarious imaginaries and practices through which anthropological 'we's are forged, contested and transformed, as well as the (often oblique but profound) implications of those processes for the forms, politics and ethics of anthropological knowledge production. And it is here that our volume aims to make two key contributions. First, by foregrounding the relational entanglements through which anthropology is enacted, we seek to decentre what in many ways remains the prototype of 'the anthropologist': the individual fieldworker-scholar; the locus of analysis and creativity who mediates between 'the familiar' and 'the strange' (see below). This figure is invested simultaneously with authority, culpability and responsibility; it is s/he who generates anthropological knowledge, but also s/he who is beholden to rectify its wrongs and shortcomings. Its primacy in contemporary anthropology, however, occludes the many collective and relational elements that also constitute anthropology and that anthropological 'I', from socioeconomic or political affiliations to the actions and expectations of non-anthropological parties. By making visible some of these elements, then, our volume seeks to both unsettle and flesh out that anthropological 'I' and its productions by taking seriously its simultaneous, inexorable and sometimes contradictory 'we-ness'.

Doing so, however, demands a second, broader intervention, one that disrupts prevailing disciplinary models and conventions, more specifically those embedded in the anglophone mainstream that currently dominates the global anthropological landscape. Built around the figure of the individual anthropologist, these models and conventions both enshrine and reproduce certain normative prescriptions about what 'good' anthropology entails and thus, by extension, *who* can play the anthropological game. Their exclusionary effects are far-reaching and profound. More than marginalizing other anthropological models and traditions, we suggest that they can also eclipse the very voices that anthropologists have sought to take seriously as collaborators or dialogic partners over the last few decades. Part of the reason for this, as we shall suggest below, is that such efforts (however laudable) tend to be incorporative rather than transformative, drawing 'others' into dominant discursive, epistemological and methodological frameworks without necessarily challenging or transcending any of those frameworks.

Against this tendency, then, our volume asks: how might a reimagination of the anthropological 'we' also provoke a reconfiguration of the very parameters and possibilities of contemporary anthropology? How might new conceptions of who 'we' are, what 'we' do and how 'we' do it reshape currently dominant disciplinary templates and conventions? As will become especially clear in Parts II and III, such a move does not only involve expanding existing anthropological spaces but, crucially, shaking them up and reaching across and beyond them towards other spaces, intersections and possible 'we's. To set the scene for these discussions, our introduction, and the volume as a whole, pursue three main lines of inquiry: *revelation, destabilization* and *(re)imagination.*

We begin in the next section by *revealing* what we argue has become a hegemonic 'we' in the centres of British and North American scholarship that today tower over the global landscape of anthropology. This 'we' is both intellectual and structural, modelled on the figure of an individual, ambivalent Western scholar constantly pushing against his 'own' society, and shored up by various structural mechanisms and inequalities that striate the contemporary academic world system. Such conditions, together with an ongoing captivation with alterity, have enabled the dominant 'we' to retain its tenacious yet subtle grip on anthropological thought and practice, making it difficult for alternative 'we's and models of anthropology to dislodge those of the anglophone mainstream.

Having laid out this problem, we then move on to examine how it – or certain aspects of it – have been challenged or *destabilized* by earlier scholars, notably advocates of the 'writing culture' movement and, more recently, proponents of what are variously called 'world' or 'other' anthropologies. Both constitute important precedents to our project, the first in highlighting the inescapability of the individual anthropologist's subjective presence as fieldworker and author, and the second in drawing attention to distinctive anthropological traditions and collectives around the globe. While building on these insights, however, our project also departs from them in significant ways. As we shall later explain, our aim is not simply to make room in existing anthropological spaces for the inclusion of 'other' voices; neither is it to showcase a plurality of potentially incommensurate anthropologies and anthropological collectives. Instead, by thinking through the question of who 'we' are, we seek to reach across anthropological spaces, to enter new ones and, in the process, to *reimagine* and transform existing forms and spaces of contemporary anthropology.[1] We shall return to these three strategies towards the end of the introduction. But first: some groundwork.

Revelation

Tracing the Anthropological 'We'

This section looks critically at a particular disciplinary 'we' that, we argue, has long occupied a privileged slot in anglophone anthropology as the locus of revelation and knowledge production. In this capacity, it not only serves as an ideal model of disciplinary identity, but is also embedded in highly mobile theories, concepts and analytical frameworks that, for both historical and contemporary reasons, consistently spread to various global centres of scholarship, thereby shaping their parameters and terms of debate. Rather than undertaking a comprehensive survey of the intellectual genealogies of this mainstream – a task that would, in any case, be over-ambitious and unhelpfully reductive – we shall illustrate our point by juxtaposing two key moments at opposite ends of anglophone anthropology's history: Bronislaw Malinowski's *Argonauts of the Western Pacific* (1922), and the 'ontological turn', which has electrified anthropological debates in recent years.

The closest thing that modern anthropology has to a 'mythic charter' (Stocking 1992: 218), *Argonauts* laid out in didactic detail what Malinowski called the 'proper conditions for ethnographic work' (1922: 6). At the centre of this enterprise stood the figure of the 'Ethnographer', a 'scientific specialist' (ibid.: xv) who, unlike his armchair-bound predecessors, engaged in long-term, intensive fieldwork so as to 'grasp the native's point of view, his relation to life, ... *his vision of his* world' (ibid.: 25; italics in original). Such first-hand experience, however, was only part of Malinowski's larger agenda. What added potency to the 'ethnographer's magic' (ibid.: 6) was his unique ability to mediate between the 'natives' and the reader to whom the book was consistently addressed – 'we Europeans'. Discussing Trobriand canoes, for instance, Malinowski wrote:

> We Europeans ... accustomed to our extraordinarily developed means of water transport, are apt to look down on a native canoe and see it in a false perspective – regarding it almost as a child's plaything, an abortive, imperfect attempt to tackle the problem of sailing, which we ourselves have satisfactorily solved. But to the native his cumbersome, sprawling canoe is a marvellous, almost miraculous achievement, and a thing of beauty. . . . (Ibid.: 105–6)

Here, an assumed cultural, historical and philosophical affinity between writer and reader was harnessed, if only to reveal its ethnocentrism and non-universality. This approach both highlighted and sharpened the profound otherness of the book's ethnographic subjects, while advocating – publicly, at least (cf. Malinowski 1967) – a more sympathetic, less high-handed understanding of 'savage humanity' (Malinowski 1922: xv) than had come before.

One of *Argonauts*' chief legacies was thus the articulation and valorization of a recursive dynamic that still characterizes much contemporary anthropology, one summed up by the common axiom, 'making the strange familiar and the familiar strange'. 'Their' social and cultural lives were noteworthy not merely for what they were, but for the way they *differed from* and (potentially) illuminated 'our' own. It was that contrast between 'us' and 'them' that gave Malinowski's ethnography much of its revelatory power and turned his Ethnographer into such a heroic figure – and the basis of an anthropological 'we', made up of numerous such Ethnographer-'I's – for generations to come.

Malinowski's self-alignment with Europeans, however, would only go so far. His Ethnographer was emphatically not like 'other white men' (1922: 6) – missionaries, traders, officials – who lacked the inclination and expertise to understand native society. Indeed, he insisted that it was by avoiding regular contact with his own kind that the Ethnographer could enter into 'natural intercourse' with the natives (ibid.: 7) and gain privileged insight into their lives. Rather than being unproblematically conflated with 'Europeans', the Ethnographer thus inhabited a complex epistemological and ethical triangle consisting of himself, his own society and the sociocultural other. In effect,

Malinowski's Ethnographer was an ambivalent European, constantly pushing against what he defined (rightly, wrongly and certainly vaguely) as the preconceptions of his own society. It was this capacity to transcend the conceptual limitations of his background that gave his descriptions of Trobriand society their distinctive strength and validity.

Let us now track forward to the late 2000s and 2010s, and what has recently been styled as anthropology's 'ontological turn' (see, e.g., Henare, Holbraad and Wastell 2007; Holbraad 2012; Holbraad and Pedersen 2017). Encompassing a diverse body of work, the 'turn' pivots on that perennial anthropological question, which Malinowski answered in his own way, of how to take difference seriously. Pushing against earlier depictions of ethnographic phenomena as culturally specific (mis-)representations of a single reality (Viveiros de Castro 1998), its proponents advocate taking such phenomena at face – that is, ontological – value, as *being* their own irreducible, distinct realities. Earlier incarnations of this movement went so far as to propound that instead of studying different world*views*, anthropologists should think in terms of multiple worlds, or a '*plurality* of ontologies' (Henare, Holbraad and Wastell 2007: 7; italics in original). This ideal of studying and thus bringing into being multiple worlds has since been quietly withdrawn by various advocates of the ontological turn,[2] but not before firing up a whole generation of anthropologists, some of whom have taken up the turn's ethical and methodological call to arms.

Our intention here is not to delve into the many debates surrounding the ontological turn (see Holbraad and Pedersen 2017; Salmond 2014). Rather, what we want to tease out is its enduring ethical and political premise, and more specifically the anthropological 'we' that it implicitly invokes. As Tom Boellstorff notes, the ontological literature never questions the centrality of alterity to anthropology but largely takes it as 'doxic, a pregiven predicate to inquiry' (2016: 391). In this view, the only way to take difference seriously is to approach it ontologically. Such a strategy is not a neutral gesture but a deliberate redemptive act of atoning for the failings of 'us' anthropologists to respect 'our' subjects' alterity. What is thus required, as the closest thing to an early ontologists' manifesto puts it, is a

> humble ... admission that our concepts ... must, by definition, be inadequate to translate *different* ones. This, it is suggested, is the only way to take difference – *alterity* – seriously as the starting point for anthropological analysis. (Henare, Holbraad and Wastell 2007: 12; italics in original)

Accordingly,

> Anthropological analysis has little to do with trying to determine how other people think about the world. It has to do with how *we* must think in order to conceive a world the way they do. (Ibid.: 15; italics in original)

This moral imperative to rejig 'our' conceptions in order to take 'theirs' seriously is a theme that runs through much ontologically inflected literature. Like Malinowski's writing, it first appeals to 'our' shared background – in this case as heirs to a certain anthropological tradition freighted with Western preconceptions – in order to then push against it. But who exactly is this 'we' that is so central to the process of 'ontological breakthrough' (Henare, Holbraad and Wastell 2007: 12)? On this point, ontological writings are reticent, treating 'us' as a self-evident collective comprising both readers and anthropologists at large. A closer reading, however, brings to light a 'we' that appears to be in thrall to various modernist or Cartesian rationalities, with all the dualisms – nature/culture, person/thing, object/meaning and so forth – that come with them. In short, even though it is never explicitly identified as such, the 'we' of the ontological turn is a fundamentally Western one, if not racially or culturally then certainly intellectually (see also Vigh and Sausdal 2014: 69). In this regard, the power of those 'moments of ethnographic "revelation"' (ibid.: 1) to engender new concepts and theories rests primarily on what is assumed to be an a priori difference between an implicitly Euro-American anthropologist (or an anthropologist steeped in an implicitly Euro-American epistemological milieu) and the (usually non-Western) others that s/he studies. Without that contrast and the concomitant opportunity for collective self-castigation and redemption, the ontological turn would lose much of its novelty, recursive potential and creativity, not to mention its moral and ethical force.

Two moments, two 'we's. At first blush, the 'we' of contemporary anthropology could not be more different from the white, male, colonial Ethnographic 'we' that *Argonauts* helped to fashion nearly one hundred years ago. And yet, as the above juxtaposition suggests, they are not entirely disparate either. Both are assumed, more or less explicitly, to be Euro-American, or at least to share a set of Euro-American intellectual baggage; both possess a certain critical, detached perspective on their 'own' kind out of which their ethnographic and analytical revelations about alterity arise; both entrench a mutually constitutive dichotomy between alterity and affinity at the heart of the anthropological enterprise.

These similarities, we argue, are not coincidental but genealogical, reflecting the pervasiveness of a persistent, often unarticulated sense of collective identity that has evolved within anthropology, particularly anglophone anthropology, over the last century. This identity is best thought of not as a fixed entity but as the relational product of that complex triangle between 'our' own society, 'us' anthropologists and 'them' others that underpinned *Argonauts* and the discipline it helped to establish. Even as the composition of each party and the relations between them have shifted, this triangle has remained an important space through which anthropological theory, practice and self-identity have been shaped and negotiated. It is a space in which pushing against, criticizing and even rejecting 'our' own kind has become as instrumental to ethnographic thought and practice as the interactions between anthropologists and 'others'. Here, the revelatory insights afforded by the ambivalent (Euro-American) ethnographer's encounter with (non-Western) alterity are turned into and upheld as the privileged ground of theoretical breakthrough.

It is worth clarifying a few things at this point. First, by positing the existence of this hegemonic disciplinary 'we', we are not downplaying the very real heterogeneity and scholarly fragmentation that has long existed within and beyond the anglophone mainstream of anthropology. Neither are we suggesting that all anthropologists working within these traditions were or are necessarily white, male, Cartesian, middle-class etc. individuals who actually conform to that template of the (neo-)Malinowskian Ethnographer. Having come of anthropological age in Cambridge, where images of what are conversationally and only half-jokingly termed 'the Ancestors' gaze upon staff and students in the main seminar room (recently christened the Edmund Leach Room), we are acutely aware of the vastly divergent biographies, ethnic origins, religious and political affiliations and other different characteristics, not to mention the scholarly spats, that could and can still be found across the anthropological spectrum.

Finally, we are not arguing that there is a clear and unbroken line between the Malinowskian 'we' and that of the ontological turn, or that these two moments can in any sense stand for the whole of anglophone anthropology. Rather, our point is that this 'we' needs to be understood as both a trope and an analytical device that is historically, politically and, increasingly, ethically Western in its constitution. What it generates is an enduring and encompassing *disciplinary* persona with its own orientations and sensibilities that, through a series of historical and other quirks, has come to dominate the anglophone mainstream of anthropology today. In this capacity, it has been adopted, shared and in many ways universalized by disparate anthropologists across the globe, regardless of their national, ethnic, cultural and other origins – with constitutive implications for their conceptual and theoretical projects.

More than being adopted by individual practitioners, however, this anthropological 'we' is associated with a whole set of structural and institutional conditions that, by upholding a certain model of 'good' anthropology, it simultaneously helps to undergird. In this way, it also helps to perpetuate long-standing intellectual and structural inequalities within the dominant centres of anthropology and its wider global landscape. In the next section, we thus turn to the structural and disciplinary bases of anthropology that sustain that textual and theoretical 'we': institutions, global political economy and international models and benchmarks of 'good' anthropology.

Economies, Structures and Politics of 'We'-Production

Institutional Structures

A study of the 'we' of anthropology cannot be bracketed off from its social constitution, in other words the question of *who* this 'we' *is* and *is not*. For one thing, such an omission would be profoundly un-anthropological. Moreover, we contend, the question of *who* gets to occupy privileged positions in the anthropological community has important implications for the benchmarks and forms of knowledge that get produced and perpetuated within it.

Anthropologists in the anglophone mainstream have undertaken the study of class, gender, race and domination in 'other' places right from the inception of the discipline, through sub-fields such as the anthropology of kinship or economic anthropology. Yet, until very recently, they have not turned an ethnographic gaze onto their very own practices as members of university anthropology departments.[3] This was a point made by Hugh Gusterson in his presidential address to the American Ethnological Society, in which he called for anthropologists to undertake their own 'homework' in order to shed light on the changing nature of the public university under conditions of neoliberalism (Gusterson 2017). The need for such 'homework' is borne out by a spate of new publications that have begun to demonstrate, through both quantitative and qualitative research methods, that the Western university system in general remains dominated by male, white and middle-upper-class scholars, many of whom are drawn from a familiar handful of elite universities (Kawa, McCarty and Clark 2016; Ahmed 2017; Savonick and Davidson 2017).

Brodkin, Morgen and Hutchinson, for example, draw on statistics and surveys to demonstrate how anthropology departments in the United States remain 'social spaces that are white owned' (2011: 545). They argue that cultural and discursive praxis, as well as a racialized division of labour, lead to the creation of 'internal others' in departments marked by gender, race and class, thereby ensuring the constant reproduction of US anthropology as what they call a 'white public space'. Likewise, a recent exploration of 'the intersections of race and class for women in academia' (Gutiérrez y Muhs et al. 2012) features interviews with forty women of colour, many of whom recall struggling to overcome deeply embedded presumptions of their incompetence as they worked through the hiring, promotion and tenure-track processes and negotiated relations with students, colleagues and administrators. A similar portrait is painted by Sara Ahmed (2012, 2017) in her groundbreaking work on the exclusionary effects of race, gender and class in higher education. Her discussion of diversity and institutional inclusion moves beyond statistics and online surveys to outline the daily practices that allow for universities in the United Kingdom to reproduce themselves as white male spaces. In her description of how diversity gets done – or rather undone – within seemingly progressive universities, and how institutions clone themselves by hiring and supporting people who do not disrupt the 'white surround' and can easily 'fit in', it becomes clear how universities and departments create their own 'we's (Ahmed 2012: 23–50).

To be clear, our argument is not that only Western, white, middle- and upper-class males have internalized the problematic alterity/affinity dualism outlined above. This problem, we suggest, is prevalent across much of the discipline, regardless of its practitioners' identities or locations. As Dipesh Chakrabarty (2007) notes in *Provincialising Europe*, the task at hand is not related to a place in the world called 'Europe'. Rather, the intellectual project we need to take on is one of questioning anthropology's inheritance of the post-Enlightenment European intellectual tools of thought that many anthropologists, regardless of our location, carry with us. What we wish to underline in this section, however, is that the political economy of knowledge production as well as the generally conservative social composition of anthropology departments make such a project of transformation and critique much more difficult.

Like Ahmed, we argue that gender, race and other forms of exclusion cannot be bracketed off as mere 'problems' of diversity or prejudice. Rather, we contend that these exclusions have a significant role to play in the continual production of anthropological work that is quick to notice alterity in its subject matter while assuming affinity among its fellow practitioners. A recent critique of the construction of a normative anthropological community in the United States offers an initial vantage point on this process. Navarro, Williams and Ahmad (2013) argue that the difficulties faced by women of colour in academia – long documented and publicly bemoaned – have only intensified in recent years, and note an enduring anthropological silence on the issue. Like us, they wonder 'whether anthropology's inability to think beyond dualistic differences and allow for internal diversity may be at the root of some of the difficulties faced by WOC (women of colour)' (ibid.: 445). They highlight a deep-seated problem with which this volume also grapples: the fact that, as a discipline founded on the binaries of subject/object, anthropologist/native, desk/field – or foundational theories of alterity and affinity – anthropology remains fixated on the notion of the Other being found in the (exotic) field. Accordingly, they argue, 'the discipline continues to rely on the assumption of a white, male researcher venturing into the unknown as the neutral anthropological position' (ibid.; see also Ntarangwi 2010). In this intriguing respect, it would seem that there is something specific to the form of othering that occurs within anthropology departments. While some critics attribute this to the inherently Orientalizing and colonial nature of the discipline (e.g. Nyamnjoh 2011), we argue, with Navarro et al., that it also draws sustenance from the manner in which anthropology has always been predicated upon notions of alterity, which in turn feeds back into its own self-composition.

Navarro, Williams and Ahmad (2013) noted that they felt the need to publish their article in a prominent journal like *Cultural Anthropology* in order to push the issue of women of colour in anthropology into the mainstream, as well as to move the discussion beyond the many 'confessional conversations' they regularly had. Similar motivations apply to us – women of colour hailing from Singapore and India respectively, who earned our PhDs at and now work within the overwhelmingly male, white, alterity-centred landscape of British anthropology. Like our peers, we learned to adopt the Malinowskian persona of the ambivalent European and the methodological, analytical and rhetorical conventions, sensibilities and baggage that came with him. Yet, as we later discovered through our own series of confessional conversations, we were also dogged by a persistent, if often inarticulable sense of alienation from this 'I' – and the 'we' to which it spoke – that was routinely invoked in seminars, meetings and theoretical trends. These conversations gave rise to the workshop that inspired this volume, but they are merely a starting point. As noted above, our ambition is to interrogate the persistence of a 'we' in the global landscape of anglophone anthropology, a persistence that requires political and intellectual work – including a genuine democratization and diversification within anthropology departments in Euro-American universities – to be overcome. What is required, we believe, is a foundational transformation of current analytical and theoretical frameworks, many of them built around binary modes of thinking (Navarro, Williams and Ahmad 2013: 447), and the practices and senses of affinity and complicity that they undergird. One way of doing so is by throwing into question the model of 'good' anthropology that is enshrined by the anglophone mainstream and that structures the forms, qualities and inequalities of anthropological conversations across the globe.

Global Inequalities and the Question of 'Good' Anthropology

In August 2012 three leading academic publishers – Oxford University Press, Cambridge University Press and Taylor & Francis – decided to sue Delhi University. The lawsuit was directed at a tiny photocopying shop nestled in the Delhi School of Economics, or D School, as it is fondly called. The shop was accused of copyright violations and piracy due to its practice of photocopying large sections of books that were on D School's reading lists. It is through course material, thus acquired, that generations of Delhi University (and, indeed, all other Indian universities') students have acquired higher education given the woefully sparse public libraries and the exorbitant costs of books and journal articles. The lawsuit set off a series of events, including a campaign called 'Save the D School Photocopying Shop', a letter of protest signed by over three hundred international academics, the wide circulation of critical commentaries, the formation of an Association of Students for Equitable Access to Knowledge (ASEAK), and even the production of a YouTube jingle on the lawsuit.

This case – which D School won in the Delhi High Court on the grounds of equitable access to intellectual goods – draws attention to the persistent inequalities between the global North and South and the manner in which they play out in the international field of anthropological knowledge production. It exemplifies a simple but often overlooked point: the fact that the 'we' of anthropology is largely a product of global inequality, wherein the majority of the world (particularly the global South) does not possess the resources (such as access to journals or books) that would allow it to speak back to or unsettle this 'we'. The continued dominance of the anthropological 'we' is possible not just because of its epistemic hold on and foundational centrality to the discipline, but also because this discipline continues to be practised in increasingly smaller numbers of 'Western' institutions. This is not to suggest, of course, that no seminal scholarship has emerged from the global South. D School, for example, boasts globally renowned anthropologists such as J.P.S. Uberoi, Andre Beteille and Veena Das as students and teachers. However, for the most part, scholars from the global South do not possess the material resources, networks and cultural capital to publish in high-prestige outlets – be they journals or books – and neither is their work cited with the same frequency as that of authors within the anglophone mainstream. The result of this is an incipient marginalization of such scholars that, over time, becomes chronic.

Again, these problems are not confined to anthropology. Ahmed (2017) has documented the citational politics of academia whereby women of colour are systematically dropped and excluded from chains of citation. Wellman and Piper (2017) have worked through a database of articles in leading humanities journals over the past forty-five years to show that authors with PhDs from Yale, Harvard, University of California-Berkeley, Columbia University, University of Chicago, Cornell University, Stanford University, Princeton University, Johns Hopkins University, and Oxford University wrote 2,837 of 5,593 articles. They note the tight correlations between academic prestige and patronage in both publishing and recruitment in the top twenty universities of the world, all of which are based in Europe and North America.

What these studies document is a persistent global imbalance in who gets to write, speak and represent that which counts as 'high-prestige academic knowledge' and that, as we argue, comes to constitute the global anthropological mainstream. While this problem has received minimal attention within anglophone centres, it has been flagged by several important works to have emerged on 'other' anthropologies in recent decades (more on which below). Many of these works seek to lay bare and thus destabilize the epistemic and political dominance of the 'centre' or 'core' of the 'academic world system' (Kuwayama 2004: 9) – that is, the forms of (mainly anglophone) anthropology chiefly associated with the United States, Britain and, to a lesser degree, France (e.g. Buchowski 2012: 29; Gerholm and Hannerz 1982; Mathews 2010: 53; Restrepo and Escobar 2005:

102).[4] These centres' disproportionate power and influence vis-à-vis their peripheries (Gerholm and Hannerz 1982) is commonly remarked upon. Whereas the peripheries tend to adopt the centre's languages (i.e. English), theoretical models and other knowledge practices in order to survive, those at the centre can easily get by with minimal awareness of the peripheries.

Such chronic 'asymmetrical ignorance' (Restrepo and Escobar 2005: 115), however, is only the tip of the iceberg. A more deep-seated problem is the way in which specific theories, methodologies and stylistic devices developed at the centre have become universalized and extolled as epitomes of 'good' anthropology. Many readers will be familiar with this model, which is enshrined in the submission guidelines of major international (read: mainly Anglo-American) anthropology journals, and pithily summarized by the first issue of *HAU: Journal of Ethnographic Theory*, the newest big-hitter in this arena:

> HAU is a call to revive the theoretical potential of all ethnographic insight, wherever it is brought to bear, to bring it back to its leading role in generating new knowledge. . . . The challenge we pose to our fellow anthropologists is therefore to produce ethnographically grounded, theoretically innovative engagements with the broadest possible geographic and thematic range. (Da Col and Graeber 2011: vii)

Characterized by a fine balance between theory and ethnography (usually of alterity), healthy doses of reflexivity and recursivity, and a constant urge (or at least claim) to innovate, this ideal of 'good' anthropology is the historically specific product of the anglophone genealogy that we discussed earlier. In this capacity, however, it has been elevated to the status of a universal benchmark of anthropological merit (see Wellman and Piper 2017).[5] Conversely, scholarship that does not fit that mould is often deemed inferior or less valid, a point illustrated by Kacper Pobłocki's discussion of Western anthropologists' dismissive attitudes towards their Eastern European counterparts (2009). Drawing on specific cases, he reveals how Western anthropology's 'theoretical fetishism' and obsession with 'intellectual discontinuity' (2009: 239) has blinded its members to the particular histories and insights of other anthropologies, while cementing a value system that privileges theory above all else and treats 'positivism' or 'lack of "theoretical content"' as signs of 'backwardness' (ibid.).

Similar arguments are made by Gordon Mathews (2010) and Michał Buchowski (2012), who discuss the often subtle but formidable means by which dominant anthropological modalities are guarded and perpetuated by 'gatekeepers' (Mathews 2010: 54). Critiquing the international peer review system, Mathews argues that regional variations in ethnographic foci, the uses of theory, and styles of anthropological writing and analysis are not always recognized by dominant Anglo-American journals, which, 'like anthropological publications across the globe use referees who essentially share their own values and discursive norms, shutting out, to some extent, those who do not share those values and norms' (ibid.: 54). Conversely, Buchowski's critique of University College London's Marie Curie PhD studentship reveals the caveats of academic inclusivity. Citing its stated mission to 'avail gifted and promising students from eastern and central Europe of the training which will allow them to be as competent and competitive as their western counterparts', Buchowski reflects:

> Thus, it was implicitly assumed that if Eastern European students want to become real anthropologists and as good as their Western peers, they have to be trained in the metropolitan anthropological tradition ... Despite its otherwise commendable goals, this conviction can be read as a case of Categorical Orientalism: post-socialist subjects can be redeemed only if properly trained and transformed into the Western 'us'. (2012: 30)

And so, we return to the anthropological 'we'. As Buchowski's comments suggest, debates about 'other' anthropologies are in many ways debates over what 'defines anthropological citizenship' (Ntarangwi 2010: 16). This is not just a question of who 'we' consist of, but, equally crucially, *how* that 'we' is defined and *who* determines its membership. And it is here that the connection between anthropology's theoretical frameworks, methods, collective identities and 'regimes of value' (Pobłocki 2009: 233) is laid bare. Put plainly, the reluctant Western 'we' of the anglophone canon is not merely a theoretical foil to alterity, but the linchpin of a model of anthropology that can only be undertaken by certain people, predominantly metropolitan academics operating in climates of scholarly autonomy whose freedom to theorize and critique is (relatively) unfettered by governmental dictates, political obligations, fieldsites on their doorsteps. It is no coincidence that such ideal conditions are most closely approximated at specific, mainly Western, academic centres.

Put differently, the ostensibly universal paradigm of 'good' anthropology that continues to structure the academic world system is built around a particular 'we' whose theoretical, methodological and socioeconomic attributes tend to reinforce each other and the structures in which they operate. This vision of who 'we' (ideally) are exerts a strong grip on the anglophone imagination, serving as both an imagined community of peers and the model for what is effectively the elite tier of anthropological citizenship. Anthropologies and anthropologists that deviate from this model – among them the indigenous activists, applied ethnographers and 'native' scholars who participated in our workshop and this volume[6] – are often too easily relegated to the lower rungs of citizenship or excluded from it entirely. These processes of global 'othering', we suggest, are direct offshoots of the same alterizing tendencies that have generated institutional 'others' within the dominant centres of anthropology. What we are looking at, then, is a set of nested inequalities that, far from being removed from the process of anthropological knowledge production, are in fact intimately linked to it.

Although this volume is, to the best of our knowledge, the first concerted attempt to pull together the intellectual, structural and political conditions of anthropological 'we'-production, the problems that we have just raised are not all novel. As we shall now explain, several of the issues that we interrogate here have previously been tackled in different ways and to different ends by various anthropologists. In order to appreciate the distinctive contribution that our collection seeks to make, then, it is worth pausing briefly to consider the precedents on which it builds, chief among them the reflexive 'writing culture' turn of the 1980s and the emergence of 'world anthropologies'.

Destabilization

Unsettling the 'I': Reflexive Challenges

Much of the groundwork for this volume's reflexive agenda was laid by a series of developments in the 1970s and 1980s, which culminated in what became widely termed the 'writing culture' movement. This movement extended a number of thorny questions that had begun to be posed by postcolonial scholars from the 1970s and 1980s – questions, notably, about who speaks for whom, how they speak and on what basis. As groundbreaking works like Edward Said's *Orientalism* (1979) made uncomfortably clear, it was no longer possible for historians, anthropologists and other scholars in the West to discuss the 'other' without a careful self-examination of the lingering prejudices and power structures embedded in their own thought and society. The corollary to this was a concomitant challenge – issued, for example, by the Subaltern Studies collective (1980s) – to the capacity and authority of Western scholars to describe and speak for others. While not itself immune to criticisms of its representational practices (see, e.g., Spivak 1988), the subaltern school, like much postcolonial scholarship, played a critical role in destabilizing the epistemological and authoritative edifices on which earlier depictions of cultural and historical otherness were built. Constraints of space prevent us from delving into these epochal developments, but the point we wish to underscore here is that these constituted an important first step in rendering the anthropological 'we' open to scrutiny and contestation.

This process came to a head in the 1980s, when the critical insights of postcolonial scholarship merged with those of postmodernism, poststructuralism and feminism to culminate in what is now widely known as the 'reflexive turn' in anthropology. While rooted in certain North American quarters, this movement bundled some of the questions and problems listed above into an overtly self-reflexive critique of the practices and politics of anthropological representation. James Clifford and George Marcus's edited volume, *Writing Culture* (1986), which trained anthropologists' critical gaze onto 'the poetics and politics of ethnography', marked a key moment in this turn. Examining what it identified as the principal act of the ethnographer – writing – the collection claimed to signal the crumbling of anthropology's earlier, dominant ideology of 'transparency of representation and immediacy of experience' (ibid.: 2). Disavowing previous objectivist claims to be able to represent empirical realities in the field, Clifford argued that ethnography could only ever produce partial truths due to the inherent situatedness of the anthropologist, her subjects and thus the complex, dynamic relationship between them. Accordingly, he and his colleagues argued, it was now vital to acknowledge ethnography's 'artisanal' nature (ibid.: 6), the fact that ethnography was not a transparent account of some objective reality, but a fiction (ibid.), a representation (ibid.: 7) in which 'natives' also participated as interlocutors.

Underpinning this programme was a specific brand of ethnographic reflexivity that acknowledged the subjectivity of the anthropologist and the power that she exerted in creating – that is, in writing – ethnography. Since then, the act of making explicit the 'I' or the authorial position in anthropological writing has become *de rigueur*, with the ethnographer usually outlining her or his race, gender, age, class, linguistic skills, caste, regional background and/or personal history, and sometimes relating a little anecdote to account for how and what they write. This (putatively) full disclosure of facts is assumed to demonstrate how the ethnography is inevitably partial, profoundly mediated by who the author is. In place of the proverbial fly on the wall, we now have the ethnographer as a fully formed person in flesh and blood with particular sociological characteristics and historical baggage.

If postcolonial and subaltern writings forced anthropologists to confront questions of who wrote and spoke about whom, the reflexive turn made it imperative for them to address questions about who they (individually) were, and how that shaped their fieldwork and writing. To a limited extent, our volume builds on all these projects by asking similarly reflexive, critical questions about the 'we' of anthropology, about how who 'we' (think 'we') are shapes the way 'we' think, write about and even speak for 'them'. However, we also depart from them in a few significant ways. First, our focus is less on interrogating the anthropologist's subject position – the authorial 'I' – than on dismantling the assumption of a shared anthropological community – the 'we' – that is ostensibly made up of all these 'I's, and with which the self-reflexive 'I' imagines itself to be in conversation. While locating the individual anthropologist is an important act, the implicit assumption that there is a collective anthropological community which these 'I's equally belong to, share with and contribute to is, as we suggested above, riven with problems. What is required is a different form and level of reflexive scrutiny than prevalent 'writing culture' conventions allow for.

Second, we argue that despite their best intentions, 'writing culture'-based reflexive projects often fail to challenge the fundamental epistemological parameters of the anglophone mainstream from which they emerged and in which they continue to dwell. The recursive turn is, as Clifford put it, a turn to discourse, to 'a cultural poetics that is an interplay of voices, of positioned utterances' (Clifford and Marcus 1986: 12). In this respect, it revolves around the craft of ethnography, styles of writing and dialogic experimentations, with the added ethical question of who gets to participate in this enterprise. In response, it advocates further discourse and dialogue, but this time with the inclusion of previously repressed or excluded native voices in the ethnographic text. As Mahmut Mutman (one of our workshop participants) muses in his critique of 'writing culture', this entails a 'new "diplomatic" strategy of representation in which this [native's] voice is *marked* as such' (2006: 161; italics in original). Yet, he adds, 'this attempt to repair the exclusion fails to interrogate the very demand that the "other" should speak up – a conventional anthropological/ ethnographic demand' (ibid.).

What reflexive/'writing culture' approaches thus enact, Mutman argues, is a 'recuperative strategy of representation' (2006: 161) that advocates the inclusion of 'other' voices *on anthropology's own terms*, that is, through discourse and writing, and through the universalization of all truths as 'partial' (ibid.: 157). Put differently, these approaches have made it *de rigueur* for 'us' anthropologists to make room for 'them' *within* our existing epistemological and theoretical frameworks, but without necessarily changing those frameworks or reaching beyond them towards other discursive or non-discursive spaces and possibilities of interaction. In order to become heard or visible, then, our subjects (like the Eastern European anthropologists mentioned by Buchowski) have to become like 'us', or, at the very least, learn to speak 'our' language. This process, however, leaves untouched both the theoretical and institutional 'we' of the anglophone mainstream and the fundamentally discursive models of anthropology that 'we' continue to reproduce, now less as ambivalent Malinowskian Europeans than as self-reflexive 'manager[s] of partial truths' (ibid.: 165). But what would happen if this model, its analytical conventions, its implicit 'we's and its parameters of inclusion were shaken up? What if, as the contributors to Part II of this volume ask, 'we' tried reaching across different epistemological and experiential spaces and doing anthropology through different 'we's on different terms?

We shall return to these questions shortly. Before doing so, we turn briefly to another important precedent to this project: various attempts over the years to highlight the existence of 'other' anthropologies.

'Other' Anthropologies, Anthropological 'Others'?

At the time of writing, universities from Cape Town to Oxford are being animated by 'decolonizing' movements, such as 'Rhodes must fall' and 'Decolonise the University'. Older iterations of this need for decolonization and reinvention of knowledge practices in the university are evident not just in Asad's (1973) famous volume on anthropology and the colonial encounter, but also in calls to mainstream 'other' or 'world' anthropologies. In December 1968, for example, there was a feisty discussion by Indian sociologists and anthropologists in the journal *Seminar* on what they termed 'academic colonialism', in which they called for an expunging of the discipline's colonial knowledge practices, both intellectually and institutionally. Most famously, J.P.S. Uberoi derided the 'jargon of international anthropology' (1968: 120) and questioned forms of foreign 'collaboration' that were upholding Western forms of financial and intellectual dominance even as he made a call for '*swaraj*' or autonomy in the workings of the academy in India.

This early work drew attention to the same epistemic problems with anthropology that postcolonialism and postmodern accounts have also tackled head-on. But in the last three decades, the notion that there exist multiple anthropolog*ies* around the world has also begun to receive serious attention, with collections such as Gerholm and Hannerz's issue on 'The Shaping of National Anthropologies' (1982) and Fahim's *Indigenous Anthropology in Non-Western Countries* (1982) constituting some of the earliest discussions on the theme. Their initial focus on nation-based traditions (e.g. Vasavi 2011) has since broadened to include discussions of regional anthropologies (e.g. Mathews 2015; Social Anthropology Forum 2015; Uberoi, Sundar and Deshpande 2007; Vermeelen and Roldán 1995; Yamashita, Bosco and Eades 2004), 'anthropologies of the South' (Krotz 1997), 'peripheral' (Cardoso de Oliveira 1999) or 'other people's' (Bošković 2008) anthropologies, 'indigenous' (e.g. Tengan et al. 2010) and 'native' (e.g. Ohnuki-Tierney 1984; Kuwayama 2004) anthropologies, as well as the more pluralistic, democratizing notion of 'world' anthropologies (Restrepo and Escobar 2005; Ribeiro and Escobar 2006). This period has also seen the establishment of several bodies, each with its own politics and agendas, dedicated to what the World Council of Anthropological Associations (WCAA), for example, describes as 'worldwide cooperation and communication in anthropology' (http://www.wcaanet.org/).[7]

While varying substantially in their scope and agendas, such projects are united by two common aims. First, and most obviously, they draw attention to the distinctive compositions, knowledge practices and theoretical and political concerns of different anthropological collectives, many of which, such as various traditions of ethnology, folk studies and sociology, do not style themselves as anthropologies in the North American and British sense. In so doing, they also complicate the over-simplistic postcolonial depiction of anthropology as 'an "extended arm" of the colonial endeavor' (Bošković and Eriksen 2008: 4), showing how anthropological knowledge in these milieus is shaped by myriad intellectual, political and other circumstances that are often bracketed out of mainstream theory-making.

An edited volume on anthropology in East and Southeast Asia (Yamashita, Bosco and Eades 2004), for example, reveals a number of historically and politically specific influences on the discipline's 'indigenization' in the region, among them its ambivalent relationship with colonialism and the West, its linguistic dilemmas and its imbrication with national(ist), regional and ethnic politics. It shows, among other things, that 'the inward-looking nature of much Asian anthropology' stems in large part from the priorities of government funding agencies, which are 'primarily interested in the contribution that anthropology can make to nation-building and development' (ibid.: 15), and that there are complex differences between 'native' and 'indigenous' anthropologies, which produce distinct kinds of scholarship for diverse audiences. Similarly, a collection of twelve biographical essays on the founding figures in the history of Indian sociology and anthropology from the late nineteenth to the late twentieth century provides another important vantage on what it describes as an 'anthropology in the East' (Uberoi, Sundar and Deshpande 2007). The collection 'seek[s] to give a specific twist to the recovery of disciplinary history by exploring, in and through the lives and writings of their subjects, the linkages between knowledge, institutions, and disciplinary practice' (ibid.: 5).

Second, in highlighting anthropology's global multiplicity, these discussions also underscore the situatedness and particularity of the anglophone mainstream, thereby opening it up to the sort of critique and destabilization that this volume also undertakes. The above section on the definition and universalization of 'good' anthropological models in the anglophone mainstream offer salient examples of this; indeed, it is no coincidence that many critics cited in it are either contributors to 'world anthropologies'-related projects or themselves situated on the 'peripheries' of Euro-American centres (or a combination of both). Their efforts can be read in conjunction with a smaller but important body of work produced by non-Western anthropologists that, not unlike this volume, seeks to 'anthropologize' the anglophone mainstream and its relations with its internal and global 'others'. For example, Mwenda Ntarangwi's 'African ethnography of American anthropology' lays bare those aspects of US anthropology that 'dominant tenets of reflexivity' (2010: 3) often occlude – among them the race- and gender-inflected interactions that take place in universities, classrooms and conferences, and the sorts of relations, knowledges and, crucially, anthropologists that they produce. Another salient example is the work of Japanese anthropologist Takami Kuwayama, who, in an intriguing exercise of 'ethnographic reading in reverse' (2004: 87), reinterprets Ruth Benedict's classic ethnography of Japanese society, *The Chrysanthemum and the Sword* (1946), as a 'self-portrait of Americans by using the radically different culture of Japan as a mirror' (ibid.: 88).

By exposing and critiquing the global hegemony of the anglophone mainstream, these myriad 'other' voices have cumulatively paved the way for a reimagination and transformation of the anthropological 'we' and the models and conventions bound up with it. While acknowledging their seminal influence, however, we also sound a few cautionary notes. First, we argue that it is not enough to simply showcase the existence of multiple anthropological 'we's, a potentially 'auto-provincializ[ing]' (Bošković and Eriksen 2008: 3) move that risks creating 'new centers of power and cartels of exclusion' (Ntarangwi 2010: 137) or 'mutually incompatible national [and other] projects' (Yamashita, Bosco and Eades 2004: 20). Neither is it enough, as the 'world anthropologies' project advocates, to cleave open a pluralistic, heteroglossic space of 'global anthropological scholarship' (Ribeiro and Escobar 2006: 5) in which diversity and incommensurability can thrive – although that certainly is important. Although we share this project's utopian (ibid.: 23) desire to enlarge the horizons of anthropology, we contend that its emphasis on pluralism risks glossing over the many, often uneven interactions, commonalities and overlaps that have long been found *between* anthropologies and anthropologists. Moreover, by focusing on a plurality of voices we also risk losing sight of the alterity/affinity dichotomy that remains at the beating heart of the anthropological mainstream. While we agree that the project of highlighting and bringing centre stage 'other' or 'world' anthropologies and traditions is critical, our volume thus takes a slightly different path. Rather than further foregrounding anthropological diversity, our aim here is to *reach across* multiple anthropological spaces and traditions, to spark new connections, alignments and possibilities in order to reimagine who 'we', and anthropology, could become. The next section expounds further on this agenda.

(Re)imagination
Where Do 'We' Go from Here?

In this final section, we ask how the process of revealing and destabilizing the anthropological 'we' can precipitate a reimagination and transformation of that 'we' – and thus of anthropology. Importantly, our aim is not to simply jettison or replace the hegemonic 'we', although we are keen to raise critical awareness of its ubiquity. Rather, we propose forging a novel, self-transformative form of anthropological scholarship that opens up the space for a new kind – and diversity – of 'we's. In this, we draw partial inspiration from scholars like Ntarangwi and Kuwayama, who, while critiquing existing anthropological hegemonies with unflinching candour, also seek to forge new and productive modes of anthropological practice and scholarship that entail different kinds of 'we'. Such proposals are not just equalizing but expansionary, endeavouring in their own ways to enlarge anthropology's global parameters of inclusion, belonging and visibility. What we wish to pick up on here is not so much their individual programmes for doing so, but their shared impulse to reach across spaces in order to expand, reimagine and transform them.

The contributions to this volume enact this project of reaching across spaces and reimaging and re-presenting the anthropological 'we' in three main ways. In Part I, Isak Niehaus and David Sneath revisit the works of three prominent 'ancestors' of British anthropology: Malinowski, A.R. Radcliffe-Brown and E.E. Evans-Pritchard. In a series of excavatory moves, they delve beneath the surface of these scholars' now canonical writings to reveal the complex dynamic between their scholarly outputs, their individual subject positions and, far less examined, their involvement or identification with various collective affiliations. Opening the collection, Niehaus discusses Malinowski's and Radcliffe-Brown's engagements with the state and funding bodies in apartheid South Africa between 1919 and 1934. He shows how, despite their apparent similarities – both 'cosmopolitan European intellectuals . . . united in their rejection of social evolutionist dogma' – their actions were shaped by their contrasting political opinions on race and segregation, as well as their divergent attempts to negotiate their identities and responsibilities as public intellectuals vis-à-vis the colonial government. In the process, they produced significantly different kinds of anthropology and stances on 'the native question'. Niehaus's analysis complicates the dominant depiction of anthropology in this period as a straightforward 'handmaiden of colonialism' (Asad 1973). While acknowledging the discipline's imbrication with colonial structures of power, he also highlights how different individuals navigated those structures in their own ways, resulting in 'sharp political differences' that mitigated against the emergence of a collective disciplinary 'we' in South Africa.

Malinowski also features in Sneath's chapter, which reinterprets his and E.E. Evans-Pritchard's classic ethnographies through the comparative lens of 'aristocracy'. Sneath argues that these anthropologists' respective visions of the Trobriand Islanders and the Nuer were informed, on the one hand, by the then-prevalence of the notion of 'kinship society' as a hallmark of alterity, and, on the other, by their personal senses of affinity with what were essentially the equivalents of aristocratic classes and ideologies in their fieldsites. Intriguingly, he suggests that these senses of affinity indelibly shaped their fieldwork relations and ethnographic findings, which, he argues, largely reflected an elite perspective. Yet, in a further translational twist, both Malinowski and Evans-Pritchard then recast their findings in the more conventionally alterizing idiom of kinship, then widely seen by their disciplinary peers as the organizing principle of classless 'primitive' societies. But what would emerge, Sneath asks, if these now-canonical descriptions of 'holistic social systems' were reinterpreted in more familiar, less comfortably 'other', terms as 'political orders'?

Both Niehaus's and Sneath's chapters grapple with 'our' disciplinary inheritances at one of the centres of the academic world system – British social anthropology. Together, they constitute a critique from within, revealing the fragility and specificity of the theoretical and ethnographic edifices that structure its disciplinary identity and practices, showing how its 'ancestors'' individual scholarship was indelibly shaped by their political, class-based and other affinities. Although Niehaus and Sneath reach different conclusions about how who 'we' (think 'we') are determines the character of anthropological knowledge, they complement each other in revealing how 'our' theories and concepts always bear the imprint of wider historico-economic pressures and relations, as well as individual biographies. In this respect, conversations between past and present anthropological scholarship are also conversations between different 'I's and 'we's, each entangled in the world in specific ways.

If Part I reimagines the canon by reaching back across time and beyond the scholarly boundaries of early twentieth-century anthropology, Part II reaches across different contemporary spaces of praxis and knowledge-making to reimagine the anthropological 'we' in ways that do not pivot on either the anthropological 'I' (mentioned earlier) or a clear dichotomy between alterity and affinity. Katherine Swancutt's chapter is built around an ethnographic film set in Southwest China (2016) that she co-created with her Nuosu ethnologist interlocutors. Like Niehaus and Sneath, she too foregrounds the indelible 'we'-ness of the anthropological 'I', in this case by inverting the romantic trope of the anthropologist as shape-shifter and examining how her interlocutors – native anthropologists, ethnologists and cinematographers among them – took pains to craft her professional persona for specific ends. Crucially, rather than simply incorporating Nuosu voices into existing anthropological spaces, Swancutt lays bare the (often hidden) processes by which the documentary team collectively produced and sustained an 'anthropological imaginarium', 'assembl[ing] each other through creative acts of alterity-making and affinity-making', and 'co-produc[ing] unique imaginaries that potentially shape their worlds and those of their audiences'.

As a reflexive exercise that transcends the individualism of earlier postmodernist critiques, Swancutt's chapter powerfully demonstrates how anthropologists (native and otherwise) can be transformed by their efforts to reach across different epistemological and other spaces, while also creating new spaces and imaginaria in the process. Her chapter raises a further important question: what happens to the anthropological 'we' when conventional lines between alterity ('them', subjects, cultural others) and affinity ('us', anthropologists) cannot easily be drawn? Although the blurring of such lines has been reflexively discussed in relation to individual 'native' anthropologists (e.g. Narayan 1993), much more could be made, we suggest, of the ways in which anthropological practice and scholarship – usually individual in tone and form – are generated or indeed cross-cut by myriad other divisions and allegiances.

This is a point fleshed out by Gabriela Zamorano Villarreal's chapter on indigenous film in Latin America, which attends to both the benefits and the very real pitfalls involved in reaching across spaces, particularly – as has long been fashionable in anthropology – when claiming affinity with 'marginal' others. Anthropologists, she writes, often laud the emancipatory potential of indigenous media in Latin America, using it to challenge the alterizing tendencies of dominant modes of ethnographic authority. Yet, such challenges – which arguably reflect these anthropologists' own political affinities and ambivalent relationships to disciplinary hegemonies – also risk pigeonholing a whole range of agendas and practices as 'indigenous', thus further essentializing their creators as exotic 'others'. Critiquing anti-hegemonic initiatives such as 'anthropologies of the South' and 'world anthropologies' for their over-optimistic focus on building collaborative bridges, she argues for a simultaneous recognition of the *chasms* that also characterize 'our' engagements with other 'we's beyond anthropology.

Ty Tengan takes a more hopeful view in his meditation on the Oceanic 'we'. Like Zamorano Villarreal, he highlights the stubborn persistence of alterizing frameworks in his reflections on Indigenous anthropologists' efforts to 'unsettle any stable notions of a "we" in Oceanian anthropology'. Drawing partly on personal experience, he notes how, upon entering the academy, indigenous anthropologists continually encounter both institutional and intellectual 'blockage' – 'specifically in the ability and right to freely move from "one being to another" and assert the copresence of multiple ontologies in the practice of Indigenous anthropology'. But rather than responding antagonistically towards a white, Western 'other', Tengan invokes Epeli

Hau'ofa's writings on 'Oceania as a place of expansive possibility', and calls for the creation of a more inclusive 'we' that can 'accoun[t] for the Indigenous and the anthropological together'. Crucially, this move does not involve simply embracing difference and plurality, but a commitment to reaching across spaces. As Tengan puts it:

> It is precisely through tracing the intersections and divergences of Indigenous and anthropological genealogies that we (Indigenous anthropologists and allies) remain active and present in the field, committed to redefining and reshaping a decolonial future for the discipline.

By focusing on the diverse ways in which the contemporary anthropological 'we' is composed, shaped and enlarged through anthropological engagements with/in the world, the chapters in Part II thus push us to re-envisage collective disciplinary identity as consisting of more than just the sum of its individuals. Following on from this, Part III offers two distinct contemplations on where these processes could take 'us'. Gey Pin Ang and Caroline Gatt's jointly authored chapter is itself the product of their ongoing collaboration as a theatre practitioner/scholar and an anthropologist/theatre practitioner respectively. Through an account of their mutually transformative experience of working together, they argue that ethnographic collaborations offer one way of taking alterity seriously, not as a clear-cut dividing line between 'us' (anthropologists) and 'them' (others), but as a means of allowing anthropology to differ within, and from, itself. Central to this is a notion of the anthropological 'we' as heterogeneous, as defined not by its genealogy, 'its alignment with predetermined and rigid criteria', but by engagement and 'affinitive or associative relations', which can in turn produce 'anthropological artefacts that bear little resemblance to ethnographic texts and narratives'. Producing and engaging with them, however, demands a commitment to decolonizing prevalent anthropological parameters of knowledge and inclusion, and to experimenting with ways of 'crafting anthropology otherwise'.

Like Swancutt's and Tengan's contributions, Ang and Gatt's chapter offers an example of how the anthropological 'I' can be decentred, rendering it permeable to various 'we's, 'I's and other elements that are always co-present in anthropological practice and theory (Chua 2015). By making visible such complex intersections of alterity and affinity, their chapters point to some ways in which dominant models and parameters of anthropology can be unsettled and even displaced. A similarly disruptive process is advocated by João de Pina-Cabral, who calls for an 'ecumenical' response to the very real heterogeneity of anthropological 'we's. Criticizing recent anthropology's obsession with 'hypostasizing diversity', he calls for a re-acknowledgement of the world as an 'ecumene' or 'dwelling space of intercommunicating humans'. The 'ecumenical anthropology' that he proposes has the dual effect of dissolving the 'imperial hegemony of the Western "we"' and making room for a diversity of anthropologists, while simultaneously reaffirming anthropology's long-standing mission of explicating the human condition. The 'we' of anthropology, he argues, should consist of both a 'community of information' and, more broadly, membership of a shared humanity to which it is historically and morally committed.

While propounding quite a different vision to Ang and Gatt of where 'we' should go from here, Pina-Cabral sketches a similarly expansive, transformative aim: to 'ope[n] up the path for wider and wider dialogues, broader and broader ecumenes'. Such contrasting visions, however, are not limited to Part III or to Mwenda Ntarangwi's penetrating, reflective Afterword. As we hope will become obvious, each chapter can be seen as foregrounding specific 'we's, understandings of anthropology and hopes for what 'we' – and anthropology – could become. And this is precisely the point of this volume. By putting disparate views and, more unusually, styles and modalities of anthropology in dialogue, we have sought to create a space not just of plurality but of connection and overlap, in which it is possible to think through, play with, contest, but – crucially – neither stifle nor reify difference *within* anthropology.

By this, we are not rehashing the familiar liberal argument that anthropologists need to make more room in existing spaces for a plurality of voices to proliferate, important though that ambition is. Rather, our central point is that we need to shake up and transform *those very spaces*, partly by laying bare the ways in which they frame, extol, include or exclude different kinds of voices, and partly by reaching *beyond* those spaces in order to enter, connect with and co-create other spaces of thought, practice and possibility. In other words, it is by interrogating the relationship between the hegemonic anthropological 'we' and its spaces of scholarly and political production that we can begin the vital task of destabilizing and reimagining not only who 'we' are but also what anthropology is and could be.

Such an agenda could not be more timely. Recent years have seen renewed movements towards 'decolonizing anthropology' (Harrison 1991; see McGranahan and Rizvi 2016), the emergence of experimental online spaces, such as Allegra Lab (which 'explores creative ways to fill the "dead space" that exists between traditional modes of academic publication and ongoing scholarly and societal debates'; http://allegralaboratory.net/) and #xcol ('an open anthropological infrastructure for the research of novel modes of ethnographic fieldwork'; http://xcol.org/), as well as the formulation of alternative modes of engagement and discussion, such as the European Association of Social Anthropologist's popular series of conference-based Laboratories (2014–present). Such initiatives both flag the urgent need for disciplinary overhaul and offer distinctive ways of enacting it. Our project, then, can be seen as one further intervention in this contemporary moment, in which the parameters of anthropological thought, practice, inclusion and connection are being reworked. And as we shall attempt to show in this volume, it is by reaching out rather than by merely drawing (others) in that the anthropological 'we' can open itself to transformation, not as a taken-for-granted, exclusionary collective, but as an open-ended question that embodies anthropology's own status as an 'unfinished project' (Pina-Cabral). Such a move is inherently risky and discomfiting, but – as we hope this collection will reveal – also much-needed and potentially transformative.

Liana Chua is Senior Lecturer in Anthropology at Brunel University London. She has worked on Christianity, conversion, ethnic politics, development and resettlement in Malaysian Borneo, and is currently leading a large research project on the social, political, cultural and affective dimensions of the global nexus of orangutan conservation in the so-called 'age of the Anthropocene'. Her other research and teaching research interests include materiality, museology and anthropological knowledge practices. She is the author of *The Christianity of Culture: Conversion, Ethnic Citizenship, and the Matter of Religion in Malaysian Borneo* (Palgrave Macmillan, 2012), and co-editor of volumes on anthropological evidence, power in Southeast Asia, and Alfred Gell's 'anthropological theory of art'.

Nayanika Mathur is Associate Professor in the Anthropology of South Asia and Fellow of Wolfson College at the University of Oxford. She is the author of *Paper Tiger: Law, Bureaucracy and the Developmental State in Himalayan India* (Cambridge University Press, 2016) and co-editor of 'The New Public Good: For an Anthropology of Bureaucracy' (*Cambridge Journal of Anthropology*, 2015). She is currently writing a book tentatively entitled *Crooked Cats: Human-Big Cat Entanglements in the Anthropocene*. Rooted in South Asia, *Crooked Cats* describes how humans share space with big cats that might – but also might not – be predatory. Additionally, Nayanika is developing a second project that explores the effects of new technologies in the everyday working of government in India.

Notes

1. We would like to thank Amiria Salmond, whose contributions to our workshop and conversations with Liana Chua have helped us think through and articulate the idea of reaching across spaces.
2. See Holbraad and Pedersen 2017 and Salmond 2014 for discussions of various programmes of ontologically inflected anthropology, some of which do treat ontologies as objective entities that exist in the world.
3. Anthropologists have, of course, turned critical ethnographic lenses onto the institutional cultures and structures of higher education (e.g. Bourdieu 1988; Gell 1999; Strathern 2000). Most of these, however, have not grappled with the often unmarked gendered and racial inequalities often entrenched in these systems.
4. This does not suggest that such anthropologies are geographically or nationally bounded; rather, we highlight their 'metropolitan' (Hannerz 2008: 219) character as centres of anthropological training and knowledge production whose influence pervades the global terrain of anthropology.
5. Indeed, we are acutely aware of our complicity in this system by publishing in this particular format with a well-known international publisher. We are also conscious that many of the contributors to this volume are based in the hegemonic anthropological centres that we critique (although the original workshop had a much larger and more diverse geopolitical spread). What we are trying to enact is a critique from *within* these centres that, like Navarro, Williams and Ahmad's (2013) critique, seeks to draw mainstream attention to this volume's concerns.
6. Our experience of trying to publish an earlier incarnation of this collection in a top-ranking international anthropology journal is instructive. Strikingly, the pieces that attracted the strongest critiques during peer review were those that deviated structurally, conceptually and linguistically from the standard template of 'good' anthropology articles. Not uncoincidentally, perhaps, these were mainly written by scholars outside the anglophone mainstream or whose politics and methods may have appeared somehow tangential to the 'pure' scholarship that is usually prized by such journals.
7. Other notable international bodies include the International Union of Anthropological and Ethnological Sciences (IUAES), which will soon combine with the WCAA to form a single bicameral association called the World Anthropological Union (WAU), the American Anthropological Association's Commission on World Anthropologies (CWA), and the more loosely organized World Anthropology Network (WAN).

References

Ahmed, S. 2012. *On Being Included: Racism and Diversity in Institutional Life*. Durham, NC: Duke University Press.
Ahmed, S. 2017. *Living a Feminist Life*. Durham, NC: Duke University Press.
Asad, T. (ed.). 1973. *Anthropology and the Colonial Encounter*. London: Prometheus Books.
Ben-Ari, E. 1999. 'Colonialism, Anthropology and the Politics of Professionalisation', in J. van Bremen and A. Shimizu (eds), *Anthropology and Colonialism in Asia and Oceania*. Hong Kong: Curzon, pp. 382–409.
Benedict, R. 1946. *The Chrysanthemum and the Sword: Patterns of Japanese Culture*. Boston, MA: Houghton Mifflin.
Boellstorff, T. 2016. 'For Whom the Ontology Turns: Theorizing the Digital Real', *Current Anthropology* 57(4): 387–407.
Bošković, A. (ed.). 2008. *Other People's Anthropologies: Ethnographic Practice on the Margins*. New York: Berghahn Books.
Bošković, A., and T.H. Eriksen. 2008. Introduction to A. Bošković (ed.), *Other People's Anthropologies: Ethnographic Practice on the Margins*. New York: Berghahn Books, pp. 1–19.
Bourdieu, P. 1988. *Homo Academicus*, trans. P. Collier. Stanford, CA: Stanford University Press.
Brenneis, D. 2004. 'A Partial View of Contemporary Anthropology', *American Anthropologist* 106: 580–88.
Brodkin, K., S. Morgen, and J. Hutchinson. 2011. 'Anthropology as White Public Space?' *American Anthropologist* 113: 545–56.
Buchowski, M. 2012. 'Intricate Relations between Western Anthropologists and Eastern Ethnologists', *Focaal* 63: 20–38.
Cardoso de Oliveira, R. 1999. 'Peripheral Anthropologies 'versus' Central Anthropologies', *Journal of Latin American Anthropology* 4: 10–31.
Chakrabarty, Dipesh. 2007. *Provincialising Europe: Postcolonial Thought and Historical Difference*. Princeton, NJ: Princeton University Press.
Chua, L. 2015. 'Troubled Landscapes, Troubling Anthropology: Co-presence, Necessity, and the Making of Ethnographic Knowledge', *Journal of the Royal Anthropological Institute* 21: 641–59.
Clifford, J., and G. Marcus (eds). 1986. *Writing Culture: The Poetics and Politics of Ethnography*. Berkeley, CA: University of California Press.
Da Col, G., and D. Graeber. 2011. 'Foreword: The Return of Ethnographic Theory', *HAU: Journal of Ethnographic Theory* 1: vi–xxxv.
Douglas, M. [1966] 2002. *Purity and Danger: An Analysis of Concepts of Pollution and Taboo*. London: Routledge.
Evans-Pritchard, E.E. [1937] 1976. *Witchcraft, Oracles and Magic among the Azande*, abridged by E. Gillies. Oxford: Clarendon Press.
Fahim, H. (ed.). 1982. *Indigenous Anthropology in Non-Western Countries*. Durham, NC: Carolina Academic Press.

Geertz, C. 1973. 'Thick Description: Toward an Interpretive Theory of Culture', in *The Interpretation of Cultures: Selected Essays*. New York: Basic Books, pp. 3–30.

Gell, A. 1999. 'Introduction: Notes on Seminar Culture and Some Other Influences', in E. Hirsch (ed.), *The Art of Anthropology: Essays and Diagrams*. London: Berg, pp. 1–28.

Gerholm, T., and U. Hannerz. 1982. 'Introduction: The Shaping of National Anthropologies', *Ethnos* 47: 5–35.

Gusterson, H. 2017. 'Homework: Toward a Critical Ethnography of the University. AES Presidential Address, 2017', *American Ethnologist* 44(3): 435–50.

Gutiérrez y Muhs, G., et al. (eds). 2012. *Presumed Incompetent: The Intersections of Race and Class for Women in Academia*. Logan, UT: Utah State University Press.

Hannerz, U. 2008. 'Anthropology's Global Ecumene', in A. Bošković (ed.), *Other People's Anthropologies: Ethnographic Practice on the Margins*. New York: Berghahn Books, pp. 215–30.

Harrison, F.V. (ed.). 1991. *Decolonizing Anthropology: Moving Further Toward an Anthropology for Liberation*. Washington, DC: American Anthropological Association.

Henare, A., M. Holbraad, and S. Wastell. 2007. 'Introduction', in *Thinking through Things: Theorizing Artefacts Ethnographically*. London: Routledge, pp. 1–31.

Holbraad, M. 2012. *Truth in Motion: The Recursive Anthropology of Cuban Divination*. Chicago, IL: University of Chicago Press.

Holbraad, M., and M.A. Pedersen. 2017. *The Ontological Turn: An Anthropological Exposition*. Cambridge: Cambridge University Press.

Kawa, N., C. McCarty, and J. Clark. 2016. 'The Social Network of US Academic Anthropology', paper presented at the American Anthropological Association Annual Meeting, November.

Krotz, E. 1997. 'Anthropologies of the South: Their Rise, Their Silencing, Their Characteristics', *Critique of Anthropology* 17: 237–51.

Kuwayama, T. 2004. *Native Anthropology*. Melbourne: Trans Pacific Press.

Malinowski, B. 1922. *Argonauts of the Western Pacific*. London: Routledge and Kegan Paul.

Malinowski, B. 1967. *A Diary in the Strict Sense of the Term*. New York: Harcourt, Brace and World.

Mathews, G. 2010. 'On the Referee System as a Barrier to Global Anthropology', *The Asia-Pacific Journal of Anthropology* 11: 52–63.

Mathews, G. 2015. 'East Asian Anthropology in the World', *American Anthropologist* 117: 364–72.

McGranahan, C., and U.Z. Risvi (eds). 2016. 'Decolonizing Anthropology Series', *Savage Minds*, http://savageminds.org/series/decolonizing-anthropology/.

Mutman, M. 2006. 'Writing Culture: Postmodernism and Ethnography', *Anthropological Theory* 6: 153–78.
Narayan, K. 1993. 'How Native is a "Native" Anthropologist?' *American Anthropologist* 95(3): 671–686.
Navarro, T., B. Williams, and A. Ahmad. 2013. 'Sitting at the Kitchen Table: Fieldnotes from Women of Color in Anthropology', *Cultural Anthropology* 28: 443–63.
Ntarangwi, M. 2010. *Reversed Gaze: An African Ethnography of American Anthropology*. Urbana, IL: University of Illinois Press.
Nyamnjoh, F. 2011. 'Cameroonian Bushfalling: Negotiations of Identity and Belonging in Fiction and Ethnography', *American Ethnologist* 38: 701–13.
Ohnuki-Tierney, E. 1984. '"Native" Anthropologists', *American Ethnologist* 11: 584–86.
Pobłocki, K. 2009. 'Whither Anthropology without Nation-State? Interdisciplinarity, World Anthropologies and Commoditization of Knowledge', *Critique of Anthropology* 29: 225–52.
Restrepo, E., and A. Escobar. 2005. 'Other Anthropologies and Anthropology Otherwise: Steps to a World Anthropologies Framework', *Critique of Anthropology* 25: 99–129.
Ribeiro, G.L., and A. Escobar. 2006. Introduction to G.L. Ribeiro and A. Escobar (eds), *World Anthropologies: Disciplinary Transformations within Systems of Power*. Oxford: Berg, pp. 1–25.
Said, E. 1979. *Orientalism*. London: Vintage Books.
Salmond, A. 2014. 'Transforming Translations (Part II): Addressing Ontological Alterity', *HAU: Journal of Ethnographic Theory* 4: 155–87.
Savonick, D., and C.N. Davidson. 2017. 'Gender Bias in Academe: An Annotated Bibliography of Important Recent Studies', LSE Impact Blog, http://blogs.lse.ac.uk/impactofsocialsciences/2016/03/08/gender-bias-in-academe-an-annotated-bibliography/.
Social Anthropology Forum. 2015. 'Rethinking Euro-Anthropology', *Social Anthropology* 23: 330–64.
Spivak, G. 1988. 'Can the Subaltern Speak?', in C. Nelson and L. Grossberg (eds), *Marxism and the Interpretation of Culture*. Urbana, IL: University of Illinois Press, pp. 271–313.
Stocking, G.W. 1992. *The Ethnographer's Magic and Other Essays in the History of Anthropology*. Madison, WI: University of Wisconsin Press.
Stoller, P. 1997. *Sensuous Scholarship*. Philadelphia, PA: University of Pennsylvania Press.
Strathern, M. 1988. *The Gender of the Gift: Problems with Women and Problems with Society in Melanesia*. Berkeley, CA: University of California Press.
Strathern, M. 2000. *Audit Cultures: Anthropological Studies in Accountability, Ethics, and the Academy*. London: Routledge.

Tengan, T.K.P., T.O. Ka'ili, and R. Fonoti (eds). 2010. *Genealogies: Articulating Indigenous Anthropology in/of Oceania*. Special issue of *Pacific Studies* 33: 2/3.

Uberoi, J.P.S. 1968. 'Science and Swaraj', *Contributions to Indian Sociology* 2(1): 119–24.

Uberoi, P., N. Sundar, and S. Deshpande (eds). 2007. *Anthropology in the East: Founders of Indian Sociology and Anthropology*. Chicago, IL: University of Chicago Press.

Vasavi, A.R. 2011. 'Pluralising the Sociology of India', *Contributions to Indian Sociology* 45(3): 399–426.

Vermeulen, H.F., and A.A. Roldán (eds). 1995. *Fieldwork and Footnotes: Studies in the History of European Anthropology*. London: Routledge.

Vigh, H., and D. Sausdal. 2014. 'From Essence Back to Existence: Anthropology beyond the Ontological Turn', *Anthropological Theory* 14(1): 49–73.

Viveiros de Castro, E. 1998. 'Cosmological Deixis and Amerindian Perspectivism', *Journal of the Royal Anthropological Institute* (N.S.) 4: 469–88.

Wellman, C., and A. Piper. 2017. 'Publication, Power, and Patronage: On Inequality and Academic Publishing', *Critical Inquiry*, http://criticalinquiry.uchicago.edu/publication_power_and_patronage_on_inequality_and_academic_publishing/.

Yamashita, S., J. Bosco, and J.S. Eades. 2004. 'Asian Anthropologies: Foreign, Native and Indigenous', introduction to *The Making of Anthropology in East and Southeast Asia*. New York: Berghahn Books, pp. 1–34.

PART I

Revisiting the Anthropological 'We'

Chapter 1

ANTHROPOLOGY AT THE DAWN OF APARTHEID

RADCLIFFE-BROWN AND MALINOWSKI'S SOUTH AFRICAN ENGAGEMENTS, 1919–34

Isak Niehaus

In this chapter I ask who we as anthropologists imagine ourselves to be, by considering how we position ourselves in relation to governments and corporations that facilitate and fund our work. In recent years, following significant changes in the institutional landscape of intellectual work in Britain, how anthropologists should relate to these powerful social actors has become a topic of intense concern. Until recently, the government funded university departments through a system of 'block grants'. Now we, as anthropologists, depend upon student fees and upon grants based on impact assessments for salaries, and upon the priorities of private corporations and public bodies, such as the Economic and Social Research Council (ESRC), for research funds (Gutherson 2011; Fardon 2011).

These changes threaten to disrupt the delicate balance we as anthropologists negotiate in our ethical obligations towards governments, funding bodies, research participants, disciplinary colleagues and the broader public (Association of Social Anthropologists of the UK and the Commonwealth [ASA] 2013). There is an ever-present danger that the interests and concerns of governments and funding corporations, which do not align with those of research participants and broader publics, might exert a dominant impact on our work, and stifle intellectual creativity. Gutherson (2011) warns that for a discipline that has 'reconstructed itself around critical theory', the effects could be 'intellectually deadly'. He argues that few classical texts would have been of any interest to funders such as BAE Systems or Bristol-Myers Squibb (ibid.: 2). What is at stake is not simply a matter of ethics, it is how we define the anthropological we. Our disciplinary identity is a relational one, constructed through strategically negotiating with, and navigation between, the interests of different stakeholders.

In this chapter, I contemplate how experiences during the early 1900s can inform present-day dilemmas. At that time, as Kuklick (1991) shows, anthropology lacked any clear institutional base, and demonstrations of the discipline's utility assumed over-riding importance. I focus specifically on Alfred Radcliffe-Brown's and Bronislaw Malinowski's engagements with South Africa from 1919 until 1934.[1] These are insightful because of the pre-eminent status of these anthropologists, and because of the high stakes involved. As Gluckman (1975) points out, arguments about human difference possess special salience in a country where the government has pursued harsh racial and ethnic discrimination.

During this time, the 'native question' assumed cardinal importance in the country. The Union of South Africa was constituted in 1910, following colonial conquest and the South African war. Very few Africans held voting rights, and land alienation was extreme. By 1919, Africans were legally prohibited from acquiring land outside Native Reserves, which comprised only 8 per cent of the country's total land surface. Yet more than a million African labour tenants resided on white-owned farms, and over 200,000 African men worked in the Witwatersrand mines, which produced 40 per cent of the world's gold (Beinhart 1994: 98). Even larger numbers of African factory workers resided in the rapidly growing urban slum-yards and locations. Popular discontent over land and labour issues often culminated in violence. In 1921, police killed two hundred members of a religious sect who refused to pay taxes and vacate state land at Bulhoek (Edgar 1988). The following year, 230 people died during violent confrontations between white miners and the government over the employment of cheaper African labourers. During the national elections of 1924, J.B.M. Hertzog's National Party defeated Jan Smuts' South African Party. Hertzog entrenched the 'colour bar' and ensured favourable employment for whites in all state-run enterprises. He also sought to counter urbanization by retribalizing Africans, bolstering chieftaincy and developing the reserves. In 1933, during the great depression, Hertzog and Smuts' parties merged to form a 'fusion' government. This government removed Africans from the voters roll and still pursued segregationist policies. Elements within government were, nonetheless, receptive to liberal opinion.

I look beyond the theories for which Radcliffe-Brown and Malinowski are best remembered, towards the complex political and institutional engagement of their work. As cosmopolitan European intellectuals, they were united in their rejection of diffusionist dogma. Yet they differed vastly in their political commitments, understandings of the South African landscape and in how they engaged with government. During his tenure at the University of Cape Town, from 1921 to 1925, Radcliffe-Brown sought to promote scientific, sympathetic understanding of cultural difference within an integrated society. From a position of analytical independence, Radcliffe-Brown sought to popularize anthropological knowledge and speak truth to power. From 1929, Malinowski mentored several South African anthropologists, and in 1934 he visited the country to address an important educational conference. Malinowski's utilitarian vision of science led him to collaborate more closely with colonial authorities in policy formation, and his romantic, holistic vision of different cultures led him to propagate segregationist policies.

From the privileged vantage point of history, it is possible to ascertain the different long-term impacts of these strategies. I suggest that Malinowski's strategy of collaborative engagement offered greater immediate advantages than Radcliffe-Brown's strategy of analytical independence, but it also bore long-term costs. In retrospect, it is apparent that Radcliffe-Brown's work informed liberal activism against racial segregation, whereas Malinowski's arguments provided intellectual legitimacy to the discriminatory systems of Bantu Education and, ultimately, to apartheid.

Alfred Radcliffe-Brown, 1920–26

Radcliffe-Brown's intellectual biography provides evidence of a critical, independent mindset. Born in Birmingham in 1881, his upbringing was far from privileged. After his father's death in 1886, his maternal grandparents took care of him, while his mother worked as a companion (Kuper 1983: 37). As a young man, Radcliffe-Brown was influenced by the social reformer Havelock Ellis, and by the Russian anarchist thinker Pyotr Kropotkin. He met Kropotkin in Kent to discuss the ills of England. Kropotkin reportedly advised him first to try to understand social life before attempting to change it, and to begin by studying 'primitive' societies, before investigating more complex ones, such as England (Langham 1981: 371).

Radcliffe-Brown proceeded to read Moral and Mental Sciences at Cambridge, and then completed a postgraduate diploma in anthropology under Alfred Haddon and W.H.R. Rivers (Stocking 1995: 307). As a student, he earned the nickname 'Anarchy Brown'. His fieldwork in the Andaman Islands (1906–8) and in Western Australia (1910–11) was modelled on the approaches that his mentors had devised during the Torres Straits expedition. He aimed to reconstruct pre-colonial ways of life, and relied greatly on the memories of his informants (Kuper 1983: 44). His conduct in Australia, nonetheless, sparked controversy. While his party collected information on marriage systems near Sandstone, Radcliffe-Brown hid two Aboriginal men, fleeing from a police posse, in his tent (ibid.: 45).

In his subsequent lectures at Cambridge, Birmingham and at the London School of Economics (LSE), and in his writings, Radcliffe-Brown broke away from the concerns of his mentors. He explicitly rejected the doctrine that certain customs were survivals from earlier times, without contemporary significance. The doctrine, he argued, prejudges the utility of customs and does not explain people's conservativism (Radcliffe-Brown 1913a). Drawing on philosophies of the enlightenment (Barnard 1992), and on Durkheim's sociology, Radcliffe-Brown developed an alternative approach, focused on the synchronic analysis of social structure. This is apparent in his attempt to correlate totemic beliefs with different marriage systems (Radcliffe-Brown 1913b).

In 1914, Radcliffe-Brown and Malinowski both attended a meeting of the British Association for the Advancement of Science in Australia, where they seemed to form an alliance against historical diffusionist theories. The outbreak of the First World War prevented their return to Europe. For the next five years, Radcliffe-Brown taught English at a prestigious Sydney grammar school, and became Director of Education in the Kingdom of Tonga. In 1918 he also served as a volunteer in Fiji, where British ships had introduced a ravaging influenza epidemic. These experiences reinforced his critical views of colonial authorities (Campbell 2014: 98, 124).

Radcliffe-Brown contracted tuberculosis in the Pacific, and on medical advice decided to join his brother, Herbert, in South Africa, where the latter worked as a mining engineer (Stocking 1995: 305). Here Radcliffe-Brown taught English and psychology at different colleges in Johannesburg, and worked as curator at the Transvaal Museum in Pretoria. On his request, Haddon wrote to South Africa's then Prime Minister, Jan Smuts, to plead for the establishment of an ethnological bureau, and to draw his attention to Radcliffe-Brown's presence in the country.² Smuts informed Radcliffe-Brown that the government had established a School of African Life and Languages at the University of Cape Town. Following rigorous selection procedures, Radcliffe-Brown was appointed as professor at the school (Schapera 1990). The school was created to study the languages and customs of the largest section of the country's population, and to assist administrators in overcoming barriers to linguistic and cultural understanding (Phillips 1993: 22). But there was much opposition to the school in parliament, and the government cut its annual grant from £3,000 to £1,500 in 1921 (Gordon 1990: 40).

As Professor of Social Anthropology, Radcliffe-Brown sought to promote rigorous scientific understanding of the lives of indigenous people, but maintain critical distance from the government.³ In his inaugural lecture, he said it was now possible to study 'the South African native' scientifically. Social anthropology, he argued, concerns 'the characteristics of man in society' and investigates the languages, economic systems, moral laws and beliefs that people owe to their social environments. Through systematic comparisons, it seeks to discover laws of coordination between elements of social systems. Radcliffe-Brown warned his audience that segregation was impossible in South Africa. The country was profoundly integrated; contact with Europeans had modified 'lower types', and the existence of a 'vast body of cheap labour' had changed 'the European type'. In such a context, anthropology was vital to future guidance. 'We cannot trust government', he said, to 'people who . . . had but the slightest knowledge of the knowledge which regulated the growth and change of the human spirit'. Natives did not obey government laws because they appealed to their consciousness; 'they obeyed the laws simply because they feared the power of the white man'. The solution, he argued, was the careful, 'long, strenuous and difficult scientific study' of changes in human life.⁴

Radcliffe-Brown's tenure was highly productive. In Cape Town, he published *The Andaman Islanders*, several essays on Australia, and articles in which he spelt out his vision for the discipline.⁵ He felt that he could do more for research by teaching students about scientific theory than by doing fieldwork himself. In a letter to his colleague, William Norton, Radcliffe-Brown asked, 'what sorts of fieldwork in geology can a man carry out who had no special interest as a geologist?'⁶ He also collaborated with Winifred Hoernlé, lecturer in ethnology at the University of the Witwatersrand, to establish a joint framework for social anthropological studies.

In 'The Methods of Ethnology and Social Anthropology' (1923), he argues that a historical approach, called ethnology, has thus far dominated the study of culture. Ethnology aims to explain institutions, such as government, by tracing their stages of development from the earliest times to the present. 'Whenever we have adequate historical data, we may study culture this way' (ibid.: 4). But in the case of 'uncivilized people', where such data are absent, scholars rely on hypothetical reconstructions of the past. Ethnologists are prone to make unsubstantiated conjectures about the origins of institutions. For example, James Fraser postulated that totemism arose from the mistaken belief that women were impregnated by the food they ate. However, such claims cannot explain its continued existence. Social anthropology, by contrast, seeks to formulate general laws underlying culture, based on well-authenticated facts. Unlike ethnological hypotheses, we can verify social anthropological observations. Radcliffe-Brown's own theory, that animal species significant in the social lives of hunters become objects of totemic observation, can be confirmed, rejected or modified by further observations, and by comparisons with material from elsewhere. For progress to be made, fieldwork should be conducted by trained persons, able to test a hypothesis in the field.

He demonstrates this approach by means of an analysis of classificatory kinship systems (1922b) and the status of the mother's brother (1924a). Among the Tsonga, who are patrilineal, a close relation exists between the mother's brother and sister's son. Boys were permitted special liberties: they ate food prepared for him, and claimed some of his property as inheritance. Junod (1917) had postulated that these relations were a survival from an earlier matrilineal stage, but Radcliffe-Brown saw them as part of a wider system. He observes that relations with the mother's brother contrast sharply to those with the father's sister, whom boys treated with reverence and respect. For Radcliffe-Brown, these relations exemplify the principles of 'equivalence of siblings' and an 'extension of sentiments'. Boys extended sentiments from the mother onto her brother, and threated him as a sort of 'male mother' – with tenderness, love and indulgence. By contrast, they perceived the father's sister as an authoritative 'female father'.[7] Because greater familiarity existed in relations between persons of the same sex, boys treated the mother's brother with greater closeness than would be possible towards their own mother. This contrasted with the situation in matrilineal societies, where the mother's brother was far more authoritative.

Radcliffe-Brown supervised Hoernlé's fieldwork on the Nama in urban locations of Windhoek, South West Africa (now Namibia). Based on this research, she wrote a report to the government, which told a tragic story of dispossession and poverty and bemoaned the imposition of prohibitive taxes and the withdrawal of state rations (Bank 2016: 23). She also used his concepts of 'social value', the 'sib' and 'joking relationships' to analyse the material she collected on ritual, social organization and marriage (Hoernlé 1923, 1925a, 1925b). With her, he was elected to the editorial board of *Bantu* (later *African*) *Studies*. Radcliffe-Brown also served as external examiner of her students – Eileen and Jack Krige, Max Gluckman, Ellen Hellmann and Hilda Kuper (nee Beemer) – who subsequently made an important mark on the discipline.

Former students recalled that Radcliffe-Brown's lectures at the University of Cape Town were both lively and stimulating. Isaac Schapera, who switched from law to anthropology, described him as 'a bloody good undergraduate teacher'. 'He never lectured from notes, but he was so lucid you wrote everything down.' But 'with graduate studies he did not know what to talk about. He said it all already'.[8] Student enrolment in anthropology grew from eleven students in 1922 to forty-five students in 1925 (Phillips 1993: 27). Schapera, the only student to proceed to graduate studies, later produced an enormous corpus of work on the Tswana. However, William Norton's courses in Bantu philology seldom attracted more than a single student. This frequently brought him into conflict with Radcliffe-Brown (ibid.: 22).

Radcliffe-Brown did not use science as a cloak to avoid engagement with an increasingly repressive South African regime. In correspondence with Norton, he emphasized the school's insecure financial situation, and wrote: 'The trouble is that we have to make a show. Once we have succeeded we shall be more free to choose our own work without reference to outside considerations'.[9] He nonetheless questioned the direct utility of anthropology in policy formation. In his opinion, science should be separated from policy and the anthropologist 'must avoid prejudice and bias', and keep himself 'free from concern with the practical applications of the laws that it is his business to discover' (Radcliffe-Brown 1922b: 12). But anthropology did offer comprehension of 'a different set of human beings, who acted and thought in a different way' (ibid.: 15). A sympathetic understanding of social laws and customs could 'assist efforts to deal with the maladies of civilization' and help avoid friction arising from the 'government of native races'. Future welfare, he argued,

> depends upon finding some way in which two different races, with very different forms of civilisation, *may live together in one society*, politically, morally and socially in close contact, without the loss to the white

race of things in its civilisation that are of greatest value, and without increasing unrest and disturbance. (Ibid.: 15; my italics)

Radcliffe-Brown deployed various means to promote anthropological knowledge to a broader audience. He gave public lectures on topics such as 'How Natives Should be Treated',[10] 'Art and Civilization',[11] 'The Functions of Universities',[12] 'The Mind of the Savage' (A Critique of Levy Bruhl)[13] and 'The Ascent of Man'.[14] Radcliffe-Brown also established an ethnological museum at the university, to which Hoernlé donated thirty-two objects, purchased from the Nama (Bank 2016: 17). (The collection was later transferred to the South African Museum.)

Under his direction, the school organized vacation courses for missionaries and civil servants. The Native Affairs Department did not grant employees special leave for attending the courses, but paid those who gained the school's diploma a bonus of £50 per annum (Phillips 1993: 26). Radcliffe-Brown did not shy away from criticism. In a lecture offered to the vacation school, he criticized officials for the harm they were causing. He argued that during the Bambata rebellion, Zulu people objected not only to taxes but also to the form they took. By levelling poll tax on young men, the government undermined the authority of their fathers, who administered household property. Radcliffe-Brown urged missionaries, who 'take it upon themselves to change a civilization of a people',[15] to make a sincere attempt to understand the functions and meanings of native customs. For example, should missionaries succeed in abolishing sacrifices to the ancestors, they would most likely weaken native families. Before officials could eliminate the belief in witchcraft, they had to understand the forces that sustained it. Conversion to Christianity, Radcliffe-Brown argued, would not suppress these beliefs. The church itself had conducted witch trials, and teachings of miracles reinforced the belief in magic. Other means of explaining misfortune and of relieving unrest – such as blaming the government and voting for the opposition in the next election – were more likely to have the desired effect.

Insecure officials might well have felt threatened by his pronouncements, but Africans and white liberals were often complementary. J.D. Jabavu, South Africa's leading black intellectual, commented: 'The acquisition of his [Radcliffe-Brown's] services by the university' 'is nothing less than a piece of good fortune'. He praised Radcliffe-Brown's 'unbiased racial outlook', and he urged the government to 'provide more liberal support for this cause'.[16] Radcliffe-Brown found a constituency among more liberal magistrates in the Transkei, whom he twice addressed on aspects of native law. In a letter to Radcliffe-Brown, M. Welsch, Transkei's chief magistrate, who was an anti-segregationist, wrote: 'Hearing you . . . opened up new avenues of thought' and stimulated 'more intelligent interest in the problems which so frequently confront us in our work'.[17]

Radcliffe-Brown's support for the aspirations of South Africa's majority was also apparent in his work as vice-chairman of the Cape Peninsula Native Welfare Society. In this capacity, he told journalists of the plight of the seven thousand natives living in Cape Town who were charged with vagrancy, upon being found outside the city's locations.[18] The society supported a popular request to name a new settlement 'Langa', after chief Langalibalele, who was banished to Robben Island for leading a rebellion by the Hlubi in 1873. It had no reservations about 'honouring a rebel', and argued that outsiders might mispronounce the alternative name, Nqubele ('success' in Xhosa) (Coetzer 2009: 7).

In 1925, Radcliffe-Brown testified to the national Economic and Wage Commission. In the wake of the 1922 revolt, Hertzog advocated a 'civilized labour policy' that would serve the interests of white workers, and established the commission to investigate the feasibility of different policies. The commissioners failed to reach unanimity, and issued two separate reports. Mills et al. found that skilled (white) labourers earned far higher wages than their international counterparts, but that unskilled (black) labourers were underpaid (Union of South Africa 1926). Andrews et al. were more supportive of Hertzog. They found that the wages of white workers, who were more skilled than their British counterparts, had not risen in relation to national income. 'To maintain a white civilization in South Africa', they argued, 'white workers had to receive a civilized wage' (Union of South Africa 1926: 255). Industries should hire white workers instead of Africans.

Radcliffe-Brown opposed segregation and retribalization. He stated that it was neither possible nor desirable to exclude 'the native' from European areas 'and leave him to develop an economy of his own'. He said that European-owned industries depended upon native labourers, and that 300,000 natives lived in urban areas, with no connections to the reserves. He also cautioned: 'Anything you say about the native individually could not apply generally'. 'Some had changed materially and they approximate to the European both in mode of life, economic occupations, and their outlook on life generally and in their individualism' (Union of South Africa 1926: 356). 'This process', he argued, 'cannot be reversed and must be controlled in the interests of the native' (ibid.: 357). 'No limit can be placed on the development of native capacity' and 'the range of occupations available to natives should be widened' (ibid.: 357). He also pleaded for more land to safeguard against exploitation, and criticized the 1913 Natives Land Act for undermining the native economy, and for weakening the family system on which life was organized. Moreover, Radcliffe-Brown condemned the criminal prosecution of African workers who broke service contracts. He argued that European lawyers had devised this provision 'with a singular lack of logic'. Africans treat debt seriously, but 'no such thing as contract exists in native law'. 'The native looks at the contract as a mysterious device on the part of the white man for getting the best out of him.' 'The native has the highest respect for his own law', but 'attracts no stigma for undergoing a term of imprisonment for breach of contract' (ibid.: 329).

In 1926, Radcliffe-Brown resigned to take up a Chair in Social Anthropology in Sydney. In a letter to Haddon,[19] he explained that he had successfully advertised anthropology, and that the discipline was by now well-established in South Africa. Sydney provided a more suitable base from which to pursue his interests in Australia and Asia. There were also better prospects for attracting funding to build up a department and to support field research.

Bronislaw Malinowski, 1909–34

Bronislaw Malinowski came of age in a context coloured by romantic nationalist sentiments. Born in Cracow, Poland, in 1884, he was the son of Lujan Malinowski, a Slavic philologist and folklorist at Jagiellonian University. Lujan descended from the *szlachta* nobility, who had lost their status as a governing class under Russian rule. Many *szlachta*, like Lujan, abandoned the countryside and joined the urban intelligentsia, where they took it upon themselves to carry 'the torch of learning' and to preserve Polish culture (Young 2004: 9, 11).

In 1902, four years after his father's death, Malinowski entered the same university to study physics, mathematics and philosophy. In his thesis, Malinowski defended the principle of an 'economy' of thought. Ideas, he argued, formulated what people instinctively knew, were refined through the process of trial and error, and ultimately aimed at self-preservation of individual and species (Malinowski 1908). This theory informed his subsequent utilitarian vision of culture, and commitment to the direct application of scientific knowledge. From Poland, Malinowski moved to Leipzig to study philosophy and psychology. Here Wilhelm Wundt's argument for interdependence of 'mental expressions' – such as language, myth and religion – lay the groundwork for a holistic conception of culture (Kuper 1983: 11).

Malinowski's infatuation with Annie Brunton, a South African pianist, brought him to London, where he enrolled to study anthropology at the LSE. It is through Brunton, he claimed, that he developed a fascination with England, where, he believed, 'culture had reached its highest standards' (Young 2004: 129). In 1912, Brunton left London to take up a position as music teacher in Cape Town, but Malinowski remained to complete a library-based PhD on the family among Australian aborigines.

In 1914, he accompanied Radcliffe-Brown to a meeting of the British Association for the Advancement of Science in Australia. Malinowski too did not return to Europe after the outbreak of the First World War, but instead arranged to do fieldwork in the Mailu and Trobriand Islands. He quickly attained fluency in the vernacular and collected extremely detailed ethnographic information on different layers of social life (Kuper 1983: 16). His field diary, nonetheless, shows outbursts of anger at the Trobrianders (Malinowski 1967). Malinowski developed far greater antipathy towards missionaries, who he wrote 'destroy the native's joy in life', than towards the paternalistic administrators of the islands (Young 2004: 341, 382–90).

At the LSE, where he took up a teaching position in 1922, he built a reputation as a renowned scholar, largely based on his famous Trobriand monographs. In these monographs, he sought to demonstrate that, when viewed in an appropriate context, the beliefs and customs of 'primitives' appeared entirely rational. Malinowski also distinguished himself as an exceptionally skilled politician of the academe, who constructed a large cosmopolitan network of students, and successfully advertised anthropology to the university management and broader colonial establishment (Goody 1995: 26–41, 68–78).

He maintained far closer relations with the government than Radcliffe-Brown might have advised, and vocally supported Lord Frederick Lugard's policy of 'indirect rule', in which Britain sought to control natives through their own institutions. Malinowski (1929: 23) wrote that 'direct rule incorrectly assumed that we can transform Africans into semi-civilized pseudo-European citizens within a few years'. Undoing the 'old system of traditions', he warned, might result in 'black bolshevism' (ibid.: 25). Gellner (1988: 558) suggests that Malinowski might well have associated indirect rule with the situation of Poland under the Habsburg Empire, for which he had 'undistinguished admiration'. The empire kept central European nations from fighting each other, protected them from the Russians, and ensured the preservation of indigenous cultures, which gave richness to life.

In 1929, Malinowski helped the International Africa Institute (IAI) secure a five-year grant for ethnological research from the Rockefeller Foundation. The grant was used to launch the journal *Africa*, and to fund the work of research fellows. The fellows were to receive a year's training in research methods at the LSE, before doing fieldwork in different African locations. In this capacity, he came to mentor several South African graduate students, some as IAI fellows, others as independent scholars. They included Meyer Fortes, Isaac Schapera, Eileen Krige, Jack Krige, Ellen Hellmann, Max Gluckman and Hilda Kuper (students of Radcliffe-Brown and Hoernlé); P.J. Schoeman (from Stellenbosch); Monica Wilson and Zacharias Matthews (from the Eastern Cape); Jack Simons (a specialist in native law); Tim Mtimkulu (a church leader); and O.E. Emanuelson (an inspector of schools from Natal).

While these fellows did research, Malinowski made the case for practically relevant anthropology. For him, contra Radcliffe-Brown, anthropology offered more than a simple 'habit of mind'. The discipline could and should contribute directly to solving problems of governance (Malinowski 1929, 1930a). He argued that ethnographic knowledge was vital for supervising any system of indirect rule, and that anthropologists were better equipped than District Officers to study 'the actual way in which tribal practice and tribal laws work' (Malinowski 1929: 28). Only in-depth studies of actual land use by natives can reveal the 'indispensable minimum that must be reserved for them' (ibid.: 33). Knowledge of incentives that drive men 'to strenuous, prolonged and often unpleasant effort' was essential to keeping natives satisfied while working for white men (ibid.: 36).

Malinowski was outspoken on South African issues. Unlike Radcliffe-Brown, he did not see integration as inevitable. In a talk on the BBC, he argued that Britain would 'yield to competitive political pressures' if it does not fully exploit the colonies (Malinowski 1930b: 4). But Britain should also defend the long-term interests of natives, on whose labour colonial developments depend. Malinowski deplored the fact that natives currently work under conditions resembling slavery. The imposition of taxes induced men to leave the reserves, and adverse conditions in the compounds seriously impinged upon their liberty. These measures were not a corrective to 'native laziness'. Natives objected to forced labour, but worked energetically in their own reserves.

The real evil [is that] we force the native to labour on products which he does not wish to produce so that he must satisfy needs which he does not need to satisfy. The money he is being paid is useless to him. (Malinowski 1930b: 13)

Malinowski (1930b) criticizes Smuts for opening Africa for more investment and white settlement. This, he warns, would lead to the formation of a rigid caste-like system. 'The existence of two racial stocks, side by side is inevitably a source of serious dangers, and the starting point of a long series of troubles' (ibid.: 28). The 'steam-roller of universal western culture' would also provoke fierce resistance. It was preferable to slow down the pace of development, limit European settlement and African labour migration, and maintain large tribal reserves where natives can be 'developed along indigenous lines' (ibid.: 29).

In a polemical essay, Malinowski accuses proponents of racial equality of hypocrisy. 'To profess that racial differences do not exist and that black and white should be equally treated, may well be enough for a personal pious wish, but every honest European knows that he never acts up to such protestations' (1931: 999). Racial differences and prejudices were real. 'Members of non-European races feel race prejudice as strongly as we do' and 'would welcome a colour bar protecting them from Europeans' (ibid.). 'Half-castes', he continues, 'are a burden to their parents as a rule and a cause of serious maladjustment in every community' (ibid.: 1000). Instead, we should 'allow either race to lead its own life, free from interference'. In South Africa, he writes, 'a strong case has been made by the natives themselves and by their real friends for complete segregation' and for 'territorial, cultural and economic autonomy for either race' (ibid.). Malinowski advocates that whites should be deported from East Africa, to 'give the coloured races elbow room', and continues to suggest that it was possible 'to preserve a country for its own race' (ibid.: 1001).

Malinowski's arguments for cultural autonomy placed him at odds with his more liberal South African students, who were committed to improving the lot of black people within the framework of a common society. They appreciated his focus on current affairs, and seminar-based teaching, but complained about aspects of his personality, his functionalism and political views. Schapera twice resigned as Malinowski's research assistant;[20] Fortes felt insulted in seminars and refused to submit field reports from Ghana for more than six months;[21] Matthews (1981: 104) described his functionalist arguments as 'overdone'; Wilson was irked by his dismissal of history (Morrow and Saunders 2013: 291); and Hilda Kuper recalled that he disapproved of her interests in Marxism (Kuper 1984: 196). More conservative students, such as Eileen and Jack Krige, and the Afrikaner nationalist P.J. Schoeman, were more accepting of his approach. To Malinowski's credit, he remained fiercely loyal to all students.

During July and August 1934, the Rockefeller Foundation sponsored Malinowski to visit South Africa to tour the country, meet students in the field, and address conferences of the New Education Fellowship. In Johannesburg, Malinowski stayed with Winifred and Alfred Hoernlé, who arranged for him to visit mining compounds, locations and townships.[22] He accompanied Hilda Kuper to Swaziland, where she was starting to do fieldwork. Here King Sobhuza II, the Swazi monarch whom Malinowski described as 'keen on keeping up with old institutions',[23] hosted them. Malinowski also spent a day with General Smuts, at his home outside Pretoria.

The three papers that Malinowski presented to the New Education Fellowship conferences – convened by the South African government to discuss trends towards the secularization of knowledge (Krige 1997) – were exceptionally well attended. To his wife, Elsie Masson, Malinowski wrote, 'I am taking matters as seriously as possible, for the Native question is a rather tragic thing here'.[24] On 9 July, his paper 'Sex and Modern Life' provoked much interest: scores of listeners could 'only find seats on the floor'.[25] Malinowski suggested that changing conditions, such as the emergence of economically independent women, brought about new opportunities to practise sex in undesirable ways. Contraception, he observed, made love-making easy and afforded a means to regulate parenthood wisely. 'I do not sympathize with repressive policeman methods. I do not approve of pushing the woman back into the kitchen. If I had to choose between contraception and Hitler, I would always punt for contraception.' Under these conditions, sex education was essential. Pupils needed to be taught the beauty of sex in relationships between two partners, and that its fullest expression is to be found in parenthood (Malherbe 1937: 193–98). Malinowski criticized the law by which a woman teacher should relinquish her position upon marriage.[26] 'If we expect women teachers to give sex and sociological instruction, is it sound that we leave it to spinsters without experience of love and motherhood?'[27]

In his second talk, Malinowski underlined the significance of the family as agent in the transmission of culture. Contra notions of 'primitive promiscuity', he argued, monogamous marriages existed in all primitive societies. Only with a wife can a man set up a household and cultivate fields, and only as a father can he attain adult status. In the past, the family has overcome disintegrating forces such as extortions by chiefs, slavery and compulsory labour. But in contemporary times, it faced new challenges. The family has ceased to be a unit of production and consumption, and contraception as well as nurseries threaten its continued viability. Malinowski urged the government to ensure real advantages to those who enter into marriage and produce families. Cold scientific planning can never supersede maternal love, the attachments between spouses, and the father's interests in his wife's offspring (Malherbe 1937: 346–51).

In Johannesburg, nearly two thousand listeners attended Malinowski's third talk, which was chaired by Jan Smuts, then Minister of Justice. Malinowski made a passionate plea for native autonomy. He argued that under the present system natives were compelled to make themselves useful to Europeans, and even to fight the white men's battles. 'Just as the Afrikaans-speaking Afrikaner wanted his own, so the native too would ask for home-rule, political and economic independence, and the right to self-determination.' As a white man, Malinowski said, he considered the white man's interests to be paramount, but did not object to 'natives claiming the right to develop along their own lines'.[28]

Turning to education, Malinowski deplored the imposition of European-style schooling 'upon people in simple tribal conditions of Africa' (Malinowski 1936: 482). Africans do possess the mental capacity for European-style education, but such schooling estranged them from 'traditions still controlling the tribe' (ibid.: 494). Mission schools in particular, taught children contempt for the ways of their parents, and raised dangerous political ambitions. The white community, he observed, is 'not prepared to grant a native, however educated and intelligent, that place to which he is entitled by training'. But rather than blame the government for limiting native opportunities, he argues:

> It [schooling] ought also to give him a clear idea from the outset of his artificially imposed disabilities, so as not to develop in him the hope that through education he can become the white man's 'brother' and his economic and political equal. (ibid.: 505)

African children 'must acquire some elements of the invading culture' that are useful for the capacities in which they are employed by Europeans. These should include the languages of government, arithmetic, technical subjects, natural history and an 'inverted anthropology' of European laws and customs to counter 'malicious gossip' about whites. Children should be taught by fellow tribesmen, in a manner congruent with traditional pedagogy, and their schooling should be harmonized with the education they receive at home. 'The vast majority of Africans still live in an African world from which they have to emerge, but partially and occasionally' (Malinowski 1936: 506). But education alone does not guarantee progress. 'They need more land than we have left them, more economic opportunities than we have opened up for them, and greater political autonomy' (ibid.: 515).

None of the other anthropologists who spoke at the conference questioned the value of European schooling for Africans. Winifred Hoernlé (1936) argued that the 'old tribal system' could not be maintained in its original state. Rather than stimulate the development of a race consciousness, she suggested, 'our aim should, surely, be a sound and healthy spirit of South African citizenship, which can animate both blacks and whites' (1936: 79). She also bemoaned the fact that Africans were not taught the universal principles of science, which could benefit them no less than their white masters (1936: 86). Alfred Hoernlé argued that Africans did not ask 'for development along their own lines', and that advocates of this policy had failed 'to tell us what those lines are' (Malherbe 1937: 417). There was also criticism from other sources. A black listener asked Malinowski whether native education should be 'based on bread-and-butter lines, instead of purely African or European lines'.[29]

Malinowski's talks on sex education might well have upset the prudish and patriarchal proclivities of Afrikaner nationalists, but his position on education accorded with Hertzog's emphasis on segregation and the retribalization of Africans. It also resonated with the recommendations of the Native Economic Commission of 1932 that social education focused on developing the reserves should replace mission schooling. It is telling that the rectors of all Afrikaans-medium universities invited Malinowski to address their students, who were beset by fears of racial integration.[30] Malinowski declined, owing to a demanding schedule, but he did tell a reporter of the Afrikaans newspaper *Die Volksblad* that he had sided with Afrikaners during the South African war, and that as a Pole, who had also experienced oppression, he empathized with their situation in South Africa.

> I understand that your traditional encounter with the native generated racial hatred. As an anthropologist, I know that this is unavoidable in any society where two races live next to each other. I do not blame Afrikaner people where they refuse to acknowledge the native as absolute equal – the native is possibly very different. [My translation][31]

Serious debate followed Malinowski's departure from South Africa. Proponents of segregated education urged the government to transfer

African education to the Native Affairs Department. Following the electoral victory by D.F. Malan's National Party in 1948, a segregated system of Bantu Education became a hallmark of the South African apartheid policies.

Conclusions

The historical material presented here shows stark differences in the ways in which key anthropologists perceived the nature of their work, and of their obligations, with regard to governments and other potential funders. In many respects these differences defy notions of a collective anthropological we. Through their South African engagements, Radcliffe-Brown and Malinowski both sought to secure a more visible presence for the emerging anthropological discipline. They nonetheless understood the South African situation very differently, and advocated widely divergent strategies. Radcliffe-Brown saw the anthropological task as seeking to comprehend cultural differences within the context of a single, integrated and rapidly changing social system. He used diverse means – including museum exhibits, vacation courses and public lectures – to 'popularize' anthropology (Erickson 2006) and to promote the sympathetic, scientific understanding of indigenous people. Yet even though Radcliffe-Brown testified to official commissions, and sought to promote the interests of the disenfranchised, he maintained a position of analytical independence. In London, Malinowski advocated direct collaboration with the colonial establishment. Malinowski's interventions transcended advocating a scientific outlook, and often took the form of specific contributions to problems of governance. These ranged from recommendations about the greater fairness in the maintenance of a colour bar, to the creation of Native Reserves and school curricula. His broader ideological commitment to protecting autonomous cultures put him in league with powerful political actors, including proponents of indirect rule such as Lord Lugard, African traditionalists such as King Sobhuza II, and emerging Afrikaner nationalist thinkers such as P.J. Schoeman.

Their engagements with South Africa show the complexities of anthropological engagements. Although Radcliffe-Brown's scholarly interventions did help secure a fragile institutional base for anthropological pursuits in a fairly hostile environment, Malinowski's strategy of collaborative engagement was eminently more successful in negotiating the intricacies of funding regimes. In helping to secure research funds from the Rockefeller Foundation, Malinowski paved the way for the emergence of an 'expansive moment' in Africanist anthropology (Goody 1995). My reading of archival and documentary sources suggests that Malinowski's strategic engagements did not simply amount to opportunistic salesmanship, but were based on deeply rooted and sincerely held views.

However, the long-term implications of their different modes of engagement are evident in the South African legacies of their work. The arguments that Radcliffe-Brown, Hoernlé and their students advanced lay the foundations for an anthropological critique of apartheid. They rejected the kind of analysis proposed in Malinowski's posthumously published work, *The Dynamics of Culture Change* (1945). Here he argues that Africa comprises three orders of cultural reality – the African, Western and transitional – that were related yet subject to their own determinisms. Radcliffe-Brown and Hoernlé's students preferred to see southern Africa as an integral part of the modern world, comprising a single, socially interdependent field of interaction (Gluckman 1940, 1947). They advocated for the advancement of African interests within the framework of this complex social structure (Hoernlé 1936). Malinowski's commitment to the preservation of cultures aligned him with later-day apologists for apartheid (Gordon 2007), and provided a language to legitimate the exclusion of Africans from centres of wealth and power. In South Africa, separation was never equal. By the mid 1970s, Africans still owned no more than 13 per cent of the country's land, and the government spent only R71 per capita on the schooling of an African child, but R724 on a white child (South African Institute of Race Relations [SAIRR] 1980: 450).

Radcliffe-Brown and Malinowski's engagement with South Africa might well bear important lessons for those imagining anthropology's disciplinary identity today. It cautions against considering only the immediate strategic gains of collaborative engagements with government and potential funders, without considering their long-term costs. The space of the 'threshold' – occupied by Radcliffe-Brown in his relations with South African authorities (Hastrup 2013) – seems to offer more sustained analytical, ethical and political possibilities.

Acknowledgements

I thank Andrew Bank, Florence Bernault, Rob Gordon, Jonathan Parry, Michael Young and the late Patrick Harries for their kind assistance. I also acknowledge the help of staff members at the manuscript sections of the Cambridge University, London School of Economics, and University of Cape Town libraries. An earlier, slightly different, version of this chapter was published under the same title in the journal *Focaal* 74(3), 2016.

Isak Niehaus teaches social anthropology at Brunel University London. He has done extensive research in rural South Africa, on topics such as population removals, witchcraft beliefs and accusations, masculinity and HIV/AIDS. His most recent monograph is entitled *In the Shadow of Biomedicine: Inside South Africa's AIDS Pandemic* (forthcoming, Zed Books). Isak is also interested in the history of anthropology, and is currently engaged in writing a biography of Alfred Radcliffe-Brown.

Notes

1. In 1920 Alfred Brown added his mother's surname and changed to Radcliffe-Brown (Schapera 1989). I use the latter surname throughout this chapter to avoid confusion.
2. Letter, A.C. Haddon to Jan Smuts, 16 April 1920, Haddon Papers, Cambridge University Manuscripts Library, envelope 8.
3. *The Cape Times*, 25 August 1921, reprinted in Gordon (1990: 40).
4. *The Cape Times*, 25 August 1921, reprinted in Gordon (1990: 47).
5. Radcliffe-Brown (1922a, 1922b, 1923a, 1923b, 1924a, 1924b and 1926)
6. Letter, A. Radcliffe-Brown to W. Norton, 4 May 1922, Norton Papers, African Studies Collection, Jagger Library, University of Cape Town.
7. *Malume*, the indigenous term for mother's brother, is based on the stem *ma* (mother), whereas *rarana*, the term for father's sister, is based on the stem *ra* (father).
8. Schapera in Kuper (2001: 4).
9. Letter, A. Radcliffe-Brown to W. Norton, 4 May 1922.
10. *Rand Daily Mail*, 2 October 1920.
11. *The Cape Times*, 5 June 1921.
12. *The Cape Times*, 16 March 1922; *The Argus*, 14 March 1922.
13. *The Cape Times*, 17 April 1924.
14. *The Cape Times*, 11 February 1925, 12 February 1925 and 17 February 1925.
15. *The Cape Times*, 24 March 1924.
16. *The Cape Times*, 24 March 1924.
17. Letter, M. Welsch, Umtata, to A. Radcliffe-Brown, Fortes Papers, Cambridge University Manuscripts Library, Ms.Add 8405/1/54/1-24.
18. *Cape Times*, 22 December 1922.

19. Letter, A. Radcliffe-Brown to A. Haddon, 23 October 1923, Haddon Papers, Cambridge University Manuscripts Library, envelope 8.
20. Schapera in Kuper (2001: 7).
21. Letter, B. Malinowski to M. Fortes, 11 March 1936, Fortes Papers, Cambridge University Manuscripts Library, Ms.Add 8405/1/45/6.
22. Letter, B. Malinowski to E. Masson, 17 July 1934 (Wayne 1995: 194).
23. Letter, B. Malinowski to E. Masson, 2 August 1934 (Wayne 1995: 196).
24. Letter, B. Malinowski to E. Masson, 24 July 1934 (Wayne 1995: 193).
25. *Rand Daily Mail*, 10 July 1934.
26. *Cape Argus*, 9 July 1934; *Die Burger*, 10 July 1934.
27. *Rand Daily Mail*, 25 July 1935.
28. *Rand Daily Mail*, 26 July 1934.
29. *Rand Daily Mail*, 26 July 1934.
30. Letter, E.G. Malherbe to B. Malinowski, 3 August 1934, Malinowski Papers, LSE Manuscripts Library.
31. *Die Volksblad*, 25 July 1934.

References

Association of Social Anthropologists of the UK and the Commonwealth (ASA). 2013. *Ethical Guidelines for Good Research Practice*. www.theasa.org/downloads/ASA%20ethics%20guidelines%202011.pdf (retrieved 10 November 2015).

Bank, A. 2016. *Pioneers of the Field: South Africa's Women Anthropologists*. New York: Cambridge University Press.

Barnard, A. 1992. 'Through Radcliffe-Brown's Spectacles: Reflections on the History of Anthropology', *History of the Human Sciences* 5: 1–20.

Beinhart, W. 1994. *Twentieth-Century South Africa*. Oxford: Oxford University Press.

Campbell, I. 2014. 'Radcliffe-Brown and "Applied Anthropology" in Cape Town and in Sydney', in R. Darnell and F. Gleach (eds), *Anthropologists and Their Traditions across National Borders*. Lincoln, NE: University of Nebraska Press, pp. 111–40.

Coetzer, N. 2009. 'Langa Township in the 1920s: An (Extra)ordinary Garden Suburb', *SAJAH* 24: 1–19.

Edgar, R. 1988. *Because They Chose the Path of God: The Story of the Bulhoek Massacre*. Johannesburg: Ravan Press.

Erickson, T. 2006. *Engaging Anthropology: The Case for a Public Presence*. Oxford: Berg.

Fardon, R. 2011. 'Feigning the Market: Funding Anthropology in England', *Anthropology Today* 27(1): 2–5.

Gellner, E. 1988. 'The Political Thought of Bronislaw Malinowski', *Current Anthropology* 28: 557–59.

Gluckman, M. 1940. 'Analysis of a Social Situation in Modern Zululand', *Bantu Studies* 14: 1–30.
Gluckman, M. 1947. 'Malinowski's "Functional" Analysis of Social Change', *Africa* 17: 103–21.
Gluckman, M. 1975. 'Anthropology and Apartheid: The Work of South African Anthropologists', in M. Fortes and S. Patterson (eds), *Studies in African Social Anthropology*. New York: Academic Press, pp. 21–40.
Goody, J. 1995. *The Expansive Moment: The Rise of Social Anthropology in Britain and Africa, 1918–1970*. Cambridge: Cambridge University Press.
Gordon, R. 1990. 'Early Social Anthropology in South Africa', *African Studies* 49: 15–48.
Gordon, R. 2007. 'Tracks Which Cannot Be Covered: P.J. Schoeman as Public Intellectual in Southern Africa', *Historica* 51: 98–126.
Gutherson, H. 2011. 'Lowering British Higher Education', *Anthropology Today* 27(1): 1–2.
Hastrup, K. 2013. 'Andaman Islanders and Polar Eskimos: Emergent Ethnographic Subjects c. 1900', *Journal of the British Academy* 1: 3–30.
Hoernlé, A. 1923. 'The Expression of the Social Value of Water among the Naman of South-West Africa', *South African Journal of Science* 20: 5–72.
Hoernlé, A. 1925a. 'The Importance of the Sib in the Marriage Ceremonies of the South-Eastern Bantus', *South African Journal of Science* 22: 481–92.
Hoernlé, A. 1925b. 'The Social Organisation of the Nama Hottentots of Southwest Africa', *American Anthropologist* 27: 1–24.
Hoernlé, A. 1936 (2015). 'The Indigenous System of Social Relations' (with an introduction by I. Niehaus), *Anthropology Southern Africa* 38(1/2): 75–87.
Junod, H. 1917 (1966). *Life of a South African Tribe*. New York: New Hyde Park.
Krige, S. 1997. 'Segregation, Science and Commissions of Enquiry: The Contestation over Native Education Policy in South Africa, 1930–1936', *Journal of Southern African Studies* 23: 491–506.
Kuklick, H. 1991. *The Savage Within: The Social History of British Anthropology, 1885–1945*. Cambridge: Cambridge University Press.
Kuper, A. 1983. *Anthropology and Anthropologists: The Modern British School*. London: Routledge and Kegan Paul.
Kuper, A. 2001. 'Isaac Schapera – A Conversation (Part 1: South African Beginnings)', *Anthropology Today* 17: 3–9.
Kuper, H. 1984. 'Function, History, Biography: Reflections on Fifty Years in the British Anthropological Tradition', in G. Stocking (ed.), *Functionalism Historicized: Essays on British Social Anthropology*. Madison, WI: University of Wisconsin Press, pp. 192–213.
Langham, I. 1981. *The Building of British Social Anthropology: W.H.R. Rivers and His Cambridge Disciples in the Development of Kinship Studies, 1898–1931*. Dordrecht: D. Reidel.

Malherbe, E. (ed.). 1937. *Educational Adaptation in a Changing Society*. Cape Town: JUTA.

Malinowski, B. 1908 (1993). 'On the Principal of the Economy of Thought', in R. Thornton and P. Skalnik (eds), *The Early Fieldwork Writings of Bronislaw Malinowski*. Cambridge: Cambridge University Press, pp. 89–116.

Malinowski, B. 1929. 'Practical Anthropology', *Africa* 2: 22–38.

Malinowski, B. 1930a. 'The Rationalisation of Anthropology and Administration', *Africa* 3: 405–30.

Malinowski, B. 1930b. 'Race and Labour', *The Listener* 4 (supplement 8), 1–32.

Malinowski, B. 1931. 'A Plea for an Effective Colour Bar', *Spectator* 146: 999–1001.

Malinowski, B. 1936. 'Native Education and Culture Contact', *International Review of Missions* 25: 480–515.

Malinowski, B. 1945. *The Dynamics of Cultural Change: An Enquiry into Race Relations in Africa*. New Haven, CT: Yale University Press.

Malinowski, B. 1967. *A Diary in the Strict Sense of the Term*. New York: Harcourt, Bruce & World.

Matthews, Z.K. 1981. *Freedom for My People*. London and Cape Town: Collings.

Meskell, L., and P. Pels. 2005. 'Introduction', in *Embedding* Ethics: Shifting Boundaries of the Anthropological Profession. Oxford: Berg Publishers, pp. 1–28.

Morrow, S., and C. Saunders. 2013. '"Part of One Whole": Anthropology and History in the Work of Monica Wilson', in A. Bank and L. Bank (eds), *Inside African Anthropology: Monica Wilson and Her Interpreters*. New York: Cambridge University Press, pp. 283–307.

Phillips, H. 1993. *The University of Cape Town, 1918–1948: The Formative Years*. Cape Town: UCT Press.

Radcliffe-Brown, A. 1913a (1976). 'The Study of Social Institutions', *Cambridge Anthropology* 3: 32–48.

Radcliffe-Brown, A. 1913b. 'Three Tribes of Western Australia', *Journal of the Royal Anthropological Institute* 43: 143–49.

Radcliffe-Brown, A. 1922a. *The Andaman Islanders*. Cambridge: Cambridge University Press.

Radcliffe-Brown, A. 1922b. 'Some Problems of Bantu Sociology', *Bantu Studies* 1: 1–18.

Radcliffe-Brown, A. 1923a. 'Notes on the Social Organisation of Australian Tribes. Part 2', *Journal of the Royal Anthropological Institute* 53: 1–35.

Radcliffe-Brown, A. 1923b (1958). 'The Methods of Ethnology and Social Anthropology', in M. Srinivas (ed.), *Method in Social Anthropology: Selected Essays by A.R. Radcliffe-Brown*. Chicago, IL: University of Chicago Press, pp. 1–28.

Radcliffe-Brown, A. 1924a (1958). 'The Mother's Brother in South Africa', in *Structure and Function in Primitive Society*. London: Cohen and West, pp. 542–55.

Radcliffe-Brown, A. 1924b (1986). 'Science and Native Problems: How to Understand the Bantu', *Anthropology Today* 2: 17–21.

Radcliffe-Brown, A. 1926. 'The Rainbow Serpent Myth of Australia', *Journal of the Royal Anthropological Institute* 56: 19–25.

Schapera, I. 1989. 'A.R. Brown to Radcliffe-Brown', *Anthropology Today* 5: 10–11.

Schapera, I. 1990. 'The Appointment of Radcliffe Brown to the Chair of Social Anthropology at the University of Cape Town', *African Studies* 49: 1–13.

South African Institute of Race Relations (SAIRR). 1980. *Annual Survey of Race Relations, 1978*. Braamfontein: SAIRR.

Stocking, G. 1995. *After Tylor: British Social Anthropology 1888–1951*. Madison, WI: University of Wisconsin Press.

Union of South Africa. 1926. *Report of the Economic and Wage Commission*. Cape Town: Government Printer.

Wayne, H. (ed.). 1995. *The Story of a Marriage: Volume II. The Letters of Bronislaw Malinowski and Elsie Masson*. London: Routledge.

Young, M. 2004. *Malinowski: Odyssey of an Anthropologist, 1884–1920*. New Haven, CT: Yale University Press.

Chapter 2

THE SAVAGE NOBLE

ALTERITY AND ARISTOCRACY IN ANTHROPOLOGY

David Sneath

Us and Them: Zombie Theory of Social Evolution

Ulrich Beck (2005) uses the term 'zombie-categories' for concepts that he sees as sociologically alive but empirically dead. I adapt his terminology to discuss social theories that, although technically dead, refuse to go away and remain active in our analytic strategies, despite formal refutation.

One of the most influential of these constructs is the evolutionist theory of primitive society. As Pina-Cabral notes (this volume), anthropology was founded upon the study of a certain type of Other; it emerged in the era of colonial evolutionist social theory that assumed fundamental difference between 'our' civilized and 'their' primitive social forms. By the mid twentieth century, the widely accepted view was that pre-state societies formed tribes, organized 'from below' by kinship relations, rather than 'from above' by the administrative structures characteristic of states.

Rooted in nineteenth- and early twentieth-century classical social theory, this evolutionist vision proposed that societies progressed through different stages of development from stateless hunter-gatherers to industrialized and centralized nation-states. The simplest pre-state societies formed *bands*, and the more complex formed *tribes*, rather than kingdoms or nations, organized by kinship relations. Anthropologists specialized in the study of such tribal societies and their different kinship structures. Different theoretical schools – structural-functionalist, structuralist and Marxist – constructed their own models for the workings of tribal societies, but all of them were concerned with variants of 'kinship society'.

The kinship core of the tribal concept was elaborated into a particular model of segmentary descent groups, inspired by the work of L.H. Morgan, and popularized by Fortes and Evans-Pritchard in their seminal 1940 work *African Political Systems*. Here the model used by Evans-Pritchard to describe the Nuer was proposed as a general model for the structure of non-state societies in which the branching segments of a patrilineal genealogy formed political and territorial units, composed of the descendants of common ancestors. These grouped together on the basis of their genealogical distance to create successively larger political units. This model of kinship society was generalized, so that in his textbook *Tribesmen*, Sahlins (1968: 15) presents it as the social organization of 'the tribe'.

By the end of the twentieth century, most of this theory had been critiqued and abandoned. Evolutionism, particularly unilineal evolutionism, had been rejected as a triumphalist colonial narrative that was both empirically inadequate and ideologically suspect (Fried 1975; Wolf [1982] 1997: 76). Archaeology had challenged the old teleological periodization of the human past in terms of technical development (Hodder 2001). Critics had pointed out the ahistorical nature of the models of social structure produced by this classical anthropology, and the way in which they tended to obscure the colonial context of its production (Asad 1973). In the wake of Said's 1978 critique of Orientalism, the discipline became increasingly aware of the dangers of reproducing Western tropes and selectively exoticizing and normalizing aspects of the 'societies' it represented. The realization that ethnography was bound to offer a partial, personal account of the object of its study displaced the claims that anthropological analyses offered objective and scientific truths.

Critiques of the term 'tribal' (Fried 1975; Southall 1996; Sharp 1996) showed the analytic category and models of its structure to be unviable. In particular, the central notion of kinship structure collapsed in the face of analytical and ethnographic critique. The work of David Schneider (1984) showed that kinship had been treated as a privileged analytical category, creating the appearance of a 'structure' by classifying all sorts of relations or groupings in terms of kinship rather than other categories; if a classically trained anthropologist encountered a group of people who could trace relations of descent and marriage, he or she was inclined to describe them as a kinship group. In Schneider's study of society on the Pacific island of Yap, he had originally treated the landholding institution known as the *tabinau* ('house') as such a kinship unit – a patrilineage. He later realized that he had been quite wrong (Schneider 1984: 21). Membership of the institution was defined by working on the land for the head of the *tabinau*, not by 'kinship' (however that term be defined). It made no more sense to think of the *tabinau* as a patrilineage than it would to conceive of a European family farm as one; the farmer's children might commonly work on the farm and inheritance might usually follow the male line, but that did not mean the farm was essentially a unit of kinship, since it was actually all about farming and landholding. This critique emerged from Schneider's work on American kinship in which he included himself as an informant (Schneider 1968: 13). The attempt to apply contemporary anthropological kinship theory to the 'we' category led to profound doubts over the exoticizing effect of classical analysis.

Feminist scholarship pointed to the naturalizing and normalizing assumptions of classical treatments of kinship bonds that might be better regarded as relations of power (Collier, Rosaldo and Yanagisako 1982). Adam Kuper's 1988 work *The Invention of Primitive Society* provided a retrospective on the rise and fall of evolutionist models in anthropology, and dismantled what was left of theories of kinship structure. As he later puts it:

> the lineage model, its predecessors and its analogs, have no value for anthropological analysis . . . First, the model does not represent folk models which actors anywhere have of their own societies. Secondly, there do not appear to be any societies in which vital political or economic activities are organized by a repetitive series of descent groups. (Kuper 2004: 93)

Similarly, the concept of the tribe had been thoroughly critiqued by the late twentieth century. Critiques such as Fried's 1975 *The Notion of Tribe*, and revisionist works such as Vail's 1989 *The Creation of Tribalism in Southern Africa*, helped to establish the view that 'tribalism' was a product of colonial classification and administration. Aidan Southall, for example, in his 1996 entry 'Tribe' in the *Encyclopedia of Cultural Anthropology*, wrote: 'Tribe is a self-fulfilling Orientalist prophesy in which vague notions of outsiders are essentialized' (Southall 1996: 1331). Tribe has become a term of largely historical interest for the discipline. Its effect, as Sharp (1996) noted, was to assume the distinction between the Western 'us' and the tribal 'them'.

> Early ethnographers ... speculated that ... tribes were ascriptive groups based solely on kinship. This was patently untrue, but it allowed people in the west to believe that primitive and civilized worlds were fundamentally different. (Sharp 1996: 883)

But although they may be formally dead, the old theories of evolutionist anthropology remain remarkably present, indeed active, particularly in the teaching of the subject. So, although the term 'tribe' has been widely dropped as an analytical term by most anthropologists (but by no means all; see Bodley 2011: 1), the shape and style of analysis created by these redundant concepts has remained remarkably durable. The term 'simple' or 'small-scale' societies has largely replaced the term 'tribal' society, but the analysis of the internal workings of such societies has remained surprisingly similar to the classical and structural-functionalist models. The concept of the 'chiefdom', for example, changed very little since the characterization proposed by Marshall Sahlins (1968: 24) in which its hierarchy is built upon the structure of the 'conical clan' (see Eriksen 2001: 104). Along with other structural-functionalist schemes for kinship structure, the conical clan model itself had been thoroughly critiqued (Kuper 2004: 91), but anthropology lacked anything to replace the clan-shaped gap in the wider evolutionist-derived analytical perspective. So, although Eriksen notes that the conical clan must be seen as an anthropological concept, not an emic one, he has little choice but to reproduce it.

This persistence reflects the continued use of evolutionist concepts such as 'chief' and 'chiefdom'. Anthropology inherited the term 'chief' from a colonial order in which civilizations were governed by monarchs and aristocrats, and more primitive tribal societies were ruled by chiefs and paramount chiefs. The colonial usage was later rationalized by structural-functionalist modelling of many African political systems as smaller in scale, less centralized, and territorially looser than 'the state'. But as the true grounds for the term had always been to distinguish civilized from more primitive societies, this terminology did not correspond to descriptions of any European forms of leadership since the Dark Ages. Europe, the assumption was, had 'passed that stage', it had entered 'historical time', whereas polities in much of the rest of the world were viewed as examples of earlier stages, particularly in areas without systematic written histories to contradict the models projected onto them by the theorist (e.g. Service 1975: 82). The effect was to reproduce the conceptual apartheid by which the colonized were subject to the primitivist language of tribe and chief, while the colonizers only used such terms for the most distant eras of their own historical narratives.

Evolutionary Distance and the Naturalization of Power Relations

Anthropology emerged as a discipline dedicated to the study of 'primitive peoples', an alterity that assumed the 'we' of anthropological enquiry to be modern men and women of the educated classes. The space between 'us' and 'them' was, in this sense, an evolutionary distance. As a necessarily interested form of knowledge, anthropology was centrally concerned with finding out what we moderns could learn from more primitive societies, in terms of both human fundamentals and the evolution of social institutions.

Early twentieth-century evolutionist social science saw descent groups as the elementary units into which humans organized themselves. There was variation – indeed, there was evolution – in the cultural understanding of human descent and its social implications. But, however constituted, the bonds of kinship were seen as in some senses essential.

One effect of the model of tribal society was to cast internal power relations in terms of tradition and public consent. In pre-state society, the theory went, kinship relations would prevent exploitative relations. Furthermore, leaders frequently lack instruments of coercion and must rely upon a mixture of traditional authority and persuasion to get things done.

In the Morganian vision, primitive political units *were* kinship units, forming themselves, as it were, from the ground up. He proposed a general scheme for pre-state society in which members of *gens* (clans) were united by common descent. These clans came together to form tribes, and these grouped themselves together to form 'confederations' (Morgan [1877] 1964: 66). These structures were ahistorical, appearing as a sort of collective cultural product. Morgan ([1877] 1964) based his work on liberal politician George Grote's 1846–56 theory of ancient Greek state formation, and described the confederated League of the Iroquois in these terms, providing an early model for anthropological accounts of 'primitive' societies. Morgan's commitment to the articles of faith of populist democratic politics led him to conclude that the most ancient form of society – kinship society organized into *gens* (clans) – must embody the principles of liberty, equality and fraternity.

It is worth noting in passing that subsequent scholarship has shown that there is no reason to believe that Morgan's scheme was correct, even for ancient Greece. Firstly, the 'clan' does not seem to predate the state at all, but probably appeared after it, and like the later Roman *gens* ('clan'), seems to be primarily an institution of the elite. Secondly, the *phyle* ('tribe') does not seem to have been a kinship unit, but an administrative one, in which people were registered for the purposes of local civil and military government (Starr 1961: 125, 134). In the Roman case too, the *gens* was not the pre-state social building block that the nineteenth-century social theory assumed, but appears to have been produced by it (Cornell 1995: 85).

In the nineteenth and early twentieth century, however, Morgan's model was highly convincing. It was part of a wider body of social theory that imagined rural, and by implication pre-civilized, society in terms of *Gemeinschaft* communality (Tönnies 1887), something that 'we' moderns had largely lost. Just as for Marx pre-state society was something approaching primitive communism, for Durkheim pre-modern society was dominated by forms of collectivity manifest in types of solidarity. In his model of 'segmental organization', clans formed social and political units bound together by the mechanical solidarity of likeness and a sort of group mentality. Power here is attached to the group as a whole, not to some dominant individual or clique. Clans become social agents in their own right, and this vision of society composed of groups rather than individuals remained influential in anthropology so that kinship units seem to combine or split with others almost as if they were themselves social persons.[1]

The other major theory of power used by structural-functionalist anthropology was Weberian. For Weber, social domination was the product of two different phenomena – *Macht*, generally translated as 'power', and *Herrschaft*, usually translated as 'authority'. For Weber, 'power' was associated with coercion, indicating the chance of an actor getting their way despite resistance. 'Authority' was simply the probability that a command would be obeyed. For Weber, such authority came in three forms: charismatic, traditional and legal-rational. Structural-functionalist anthropology was able to describe various relations in terms of 'traditional authority' rather than power. Evans-Pritchard (1938: 77), for example, describes the authority of the 'native chief' in positive terms as derived from 'tradition and the moral backing of his people'.

Since that time, however, the influence of Foucauldian notions of power, or more precisely 'power-knowledge' (*pouvoir-savoir*), has effectively collapsed distinctions between a sort of positive, customary, non-coercive sense of legitimate leadership and the more stark and critical notion of power that can coerce if need be. Written, as it was, in the shadow of colonial domination, Evans-Pritchard's account is understandable enough, since it cast the local ruler as more legitimate than a foreign state. But a description of, say, a hereditary European ruler in the same terms would raise a number of questions for contemporary scholarship. Most political anthropologists would now wish to include 'tradition' in any exploration of the manifold relations of power that constitute the social body (Foucault [1976] 1980: 93).

Similarly, since Evans-Pritchard's time, treatments of power have come to reflect the influence of Gramscian notions of hegemony – that is, the 'structuring of consent' by which dominant groups maintain their position (e.g. Hansen and Stepputat 2001). Treatments of power that are informed by readings of Foucault and Gramsci have largely displaced Weberian ones, and yet readings of the older ethnography tend to retain the original theoretical frame, letting the notion of 'traditional authority' speak for itself. One effect of leaving the material in its original analytical housing has been to give the defunct approaches an afterlife as 'zombie' forms of the original theory.

Indeed, the wider theoretical frame of evolutionist-era anthropology has remained so influential that it continues to eclipse and obscure many of the most important features described in the original ethnography. For example, the evolutionist vision of the acephalous tribal organization, the model of segmentary kinship society, so outshone the details of the society that was supposed to typify the type (Evans-Pritchard's account of the Nuer) that it was the model that has become enshrined in teaching texts, rather than the ethnography. Take, for example, a textbook description of Nuer segmentary opposition:

> In a segmentary political system, the compass of the political community depends on the scope of the conflict. If the Nuer had aristocratic lineages or even a king, the situation would naturally have been different. A necessary condition for segmentation is the equality, or equivalence, of the segments at each level. . . . (Eriksen 2001: 163–64)

The Nuer have no 'aristocratic lineages' in this account (see also Lewellen 2003: 30) because they have come to stand for the egalitarian, pre-state, segmentary lineage society of evolutionist social science in which there are 'no sharp divisions of rank, status or wealth' (Fortes and Evans-Pritchard 1940: 5–10). In fact, the Nuer did have aristocratic lineages, and this point goes to the heart of the wider argument I seek to develop here.

Rather than dismissing such classical texts as too flawed to be of interest, is there room to re-examine the original ethnographies with current perspectives in mind, attempting to reinterpret these accounts in the light of subsequent theoretical and ethnographic work? This would entail suspending intellectual commitment to evolutionist social theory, such as the notion of a society structured by kinship – or indeed any sort of society – formed through bottom-up processes and assumed solidarities, and instead looking to see how relations of power constituted the social body.

This is what I have attempted do for a number of classic texts in a forthcoming monograph advancing an argument similar to the one I summarize here. In this chapter, I touch upon just two examples – Evans-Pritchard's work on the Nuer and Malinowski's ethnography of the Trobriand Islands. There are good reasons, I think, to attempt this sort of re-framing. Firstly, it offers an opportunity to dispense with the intellectual apartheid of applying different theoretical frameworks to the analysis of the colonizers and the colonized. Secondly, whereas the classical scholarship identified the state with centralization, and the 'arts of government' with the state, there has been a movement in political anthropology since that time, influenced by the later Foucault, to detach governance from the state. Government, in this sense, is 'to structure the possible field of action of others' (Foucault 1983: 221) and need no longer be seen as the preserve of the centralized bureaucratic state.

What then appears when one does re-examine these ethnographies, not as accounts of kinship society but as descriptions of polity? The most striking feature of all the ethnographies I examined is the importance of *aristocracy* – the rule of a hereditary elite. I do not want to make any claims as to the universality of this sort of political form, and in this chapter I make no attempt to engage with any of the generalizations of elite theory. The point I make here is that the attempts of early ethnographers to find and document varieties of kinship society, coupled with the evolutionist notions of primitive society as 'pre-class', combined to divert anthropological attention from aristocratic relations and ideologies. But with re-reading, these features re-emerge.

Nuer Aristocracy

Surprisingly perhaps, given the impression created in the subsequent literature, Evans-Pritchard explicitly writes of Nuer aristocrats in his 1930s publications,[2] throughout his 1940 monograph, and in other books of his Nuer trilogy.[3] Each 'tribe' had a set of related aristocratic families. 'The descendants of Jok-Kir form the aristocratic nucleus of the Gaajok tribe; the descendants of Thiang-Kir and Kun-Kir form the aristocratic nucleus of the Gaajak tribe; and the descendants of Gwang-Jok and Nyang-Thiang together form the aristocratic nucleus of the Gaagwang tribe' (Evans-Pritchard 1940: 207).

The Nuer term for the nobility was *diel*, a word also used for the aristocracy in the neighbouring kingdom of Shilluk. Evans-Pritchard (1940: 220) explains: 'The *diel* are an aristocratic clan, numerically swamped in the tribe by strangers and Dinka, but providing a lineage structure on which the tribal organization is built up'. Members of these families traced descent from the nobles who originally conquered and claimed the territory in which they lived. As such, they were the hereditary landowners of a region and the political leaders of all those living there.

> If you are a *dil* [singular of *diel*] of the tribe in which you live you are more than a simple tribesman. You are one of the owners of the country, its village sites, its pastures, its fishing pools and wells. Other people live there in virtue of marriage into your clan, adoption into your lineage, or of some other social tie. You are a leader of the tribe . . . Wherever there is a *dil* in a village, the village clusters around him as a herd of cattle clusters around its bull. (Evans-Pritchard 1940: 215).

Evans-Pritchard more commonly uses the term 'dominant lineage' to describe the Nuer noble houses. The phrase can be mistaken for a numerical description, as if the dominant lineage was the majority lineage of a given settlement. But exactly the opposite was the case. Evans-Pritchard gives no figures, but it is clear that the aristocrats are small in number. He describes them twice as 'numerically swamped' (1940: 220, 226), as 'a small minority' (ibid.: 214) and 'a small proportion' (ibid.: 203). Yet this small minority was politically dominant. The genealogies that Evans-Pritchard describes, the many generations of ancestors that Nuer could recite, were those of the aristocratic families, not those of the majority of the people of Nuerland. It was these genealogies that were politically significant and, in his model, provided the political structure of the wider Nuer polity.

> Every Nuer village is associated with a lineage, and, though the members of it often constitute only a small proportion of the village population, the village community is identified with them in such a way that we may speak of it as an aggregate of persons clustered around an agnatic nucleus by the common designation of the village community by the name of the lineage. (Evans-Pritchard 1940: 203)

The vast majority of Nuer 'society' was made up of the descendants of conquered Dinka (*Jaang-Nath*) and non-aristocrats called *rul*, a term translated by Evans-Pritchard (1940: 214) as 'strangers' rather than 'commoners'.⁴ These were the families who clustered about their aristocratic 'bull' (*tut*) and who supplied the bulk of the manpower to wage the small-scale wars that broke out over territory, cattle or aristocratic honour.

Evans-Pritchard describes the ways in which non-aristocrats were attached to noble lineages in terms of marriage, adoption and association, so that it almost seems as if everyone in the village was a member of the dominant aristocratic lineage. But a close reading shows that this was not the case. The exclusivity of aristocratic status had to be preserved. 'Strangers [persons of *rul* status] have to be incorporated into the community of the dominant lineage and excluded from its agnatic structure' (Evans-Pritchard 1940: 234). This 'community', then, was a decidedly unequal one. Persons of lower *rul* and *Jaang-Nath* status were permitted residence only because of their ties to the noble lineage who formally owned the village and gave their name to it. They did not become members of the 'agnatic' noble lineage.

The lives of these commoners were quite literally worth less than those of the aristocrats. Although Evans-Pritchard emphasizes the fluidity and variability of rates of compensation for different classes of persons, there is no doubt that *at best* the death of a commoner might be assessed as worth the forty-odd cows commonly quoted as the blood-price of an aristocrat, and it was usually worth considerably less, as little as ten (Evans-Pritchard 1940: 217–18). The persons worth least in this system were those captured or incorporated through Nuer expansion into Dinka territory. Indeed, such people could be killed with impunity by their masters. 'Thus if a man kills an unadopted Dinka of his own household, who was not born in Nuerland, there is no redress...' (Evans-Pritchard 1940: 219).

The system of knowledge that Evans-Pritchard describes reflects the values of this nobility. The non-aristocratic families of a village who had marriage links with the aristocrats were *gaat nyiet*, meaning 'children of girls' (Evans-Pritchard 1940: 227). This is a description from the point of view of the aristocrat – these people are related to him or her through women, even though they were undoubtedly also 'children of boys or men' in a technical sense. Similarly, the translation that Evans-Pritchard gives of the term *rul* as 'stranger' for the non-aristocratic Nuer (*Nath*) seems to reflect the values of the aristocratic minority who thought of themselves as the original owners of the land. But *rul* people were clearly not strangers in any literal sense, since they were permanent residents of their home villages just as the nobility was.

To contemporary readers, the nature of this minority dominance is, I think, at least as fascinating as the political relations ordering the larger sections that were modelled by the structural-functionalists in terms of segmentary opposition. But Evans-Pritchard was not primarily interested in the processes by which the aristocracy retained its dominance. By the time he came to write up his Nuer ethnography, he had fastened upon the model of segmentary lineage society, and was keen to emphasize the lack of hierarchy and institutions of centralized power in Nuer society. In some passages, however, he acknowledges that it was the institutions of aristocracy that constituted Nuer political relations.

> How can it be explained that among people so democratic in sentiment and so ready to express it in violence a clan is given superior status in each tribe? We believe that the facts we have recorded provide an answer in terms of tribal structure ... As there are no tribal chiefs and councils, or any other form of tribal government, we have to seek elsewhere for the organizing principle within the structure which gives it conceptual consistency and a certain measure of actual cohesion, and we find it in aristocratic status. (Evans-Pritchard 1940: 235–36)

How is it, then, that the standard readings of Evans-Pritchard's ethnography of the Nuer are of the sort presented by Eriksen, a society *without* kings and aristocrats? The problem was, I think, that the ethnography was read, even perhaps by its author, as an example not of aristocracy but of a society structured by kinship and agnatic descent.[5] The comparative frame was not to be other more or less centralized aristocracies found in Europe and various 'civilized' parts of the world, but other primitive societies, living closer to nature. And true to this vision of primitive society, Evans-Pritchard stressed the lack of class and hierarchy. He writes (1940: 215): 'the *diel* have prestige rather than rank and influence rather than power'. Elsewhere he adds: 'The Nuer cannot be said to be stratified into classes' (ibid.: 7). It is clear that the extent of aristocratic privilege varied in Nuer territories, which were diverse and in some cases recently expanded, incorporating many people described as Dinka (*Jaang*), and Evans-Pritchard stressed the more egalitarian features whenever he could, in part, I think, because he was struck by the contrast with the more centralized and hierarchical neighbouring Zande empire and the kingdom of Shilluk.[6]

This emphasis on egalitarianism extended most famously to the 'Leopard-Skin Chief' who Evans-Pritchard insisted was a mediator and ritual specialist, rather than a power-holder. His analysis was challenged by a number of later anthropologists, including Howell

(1954), Newcomer (1972), Haight (1972), Gough (1971) and Greuel (1971), and later by Johnson (1981, 1994). Here I will only note that the evidence suggests that Evans-Pritchard was wrong on this point and that these nobles held a position of political power, albeit one that had been powerfully undermined by historical processes since the late nineteenth century. But it is important to recognize the context in which Evans-Pritchard's encounter with his informants took place. The British colonial administration was still in the process of subjugating and pacifying Nuerland by force, and faced armed resistance often led by prophets (*guk kuoth*). The colonial administrators had largely failed, to their evident frustration, to find compliant local rulers ('chiefs') through whom they could achieve their aims, notably tax-gathering, road-building and the delivery of homicide suspects for trial. The position of Government Chief – that is, a local ruler recognized by the colonial administration and a node in the system of indirect rule – was an unpopular one. It is understandable, then, that Evans-Pritchard who, as Hutchinson (1996: 36) noted, identified with the Nuer aristocracy, should stress the *lack* of power the local nobility had to control other Nuer in the ways the colonial government desired. Their role was largely ritual, he argued; they could only persuade, not compel other Nuer to do as they were told. But the fact of aristocracy remained clear in Evans-Pritchard's account, even if it was presented in as egalitarian a light as possible.

Should the Nuer be regarded as an aristocracy rather than a society? I think there are a number of reasons that they should. Evans-Pritchard (1940: 221) noted that 'persons of Dinka descent form probably at least half the population', and many of the ethnographers who succeeded Evans-Pritchard have stressed the dynamic nature of what had been called 'Nuer society' and drawn attention to the historical process by which Nuer conquests were continually incorporating Dinka people and territory. Southall (1976) and Johnson (1994) both stressed the similarity and interconnection between the Nuer and the Dinka, and Newcomer (1972) argued that the two groups were essentially the same people. What, in the end, seems to have differentiated a Nuer from a Dinka was allegiance to either Nuer or Dinka aristocratic lineages. In Evans-Pritchard's account, the only sort of kinship that defines political groups is that of 'agnatic' aristocratic descent. Villages (which Evans-Pritchard described as 'communities') were created by power relations – by processes of capture or conquest. For most people, there was no bottom-up process by which kinship relations generated political units; extended kinship links were politically insignificant for the majority and were subordinated to those of the local aristocracy. Relations of power constituted the social body, forming subject positions and structuring people's fields of action. There is no need, then, to suppose some 'social' or 'cultural' entity that distinguishes 'The Nuer' or 'The Dinka' independent of the power relations of aristocracy.

Malinowski and the Trobriand Aristocracy

Malinowski's ethnography of the Trobriand Islands provided a foundational set of texts for the relatively young discipline of anthropology, and his work has been continuously taught, examined and critiqued. The Trobriands are known in anthropology for many striking features, including matrilineality, elaborate yam exchanges and the celebrated kula circulation of shell valuables. But Trobriand society is rather less well known as an aristocracy, although in Malinowski's time it undoubtedly was one.

Although Malinowski explicitly and famously rejected evolutionism in his later writings, advocating scientific functionalism, he retained a series of analytical terms and interests that dated from the previous century, most notably the notions of kinship society, totemism and magic. He described the Trobriand society as tribal, ruled by chiefs headed by a paramount chief, following the conventions of both colonial administration and the evolutionist/primitivist theories of the time. He generally used the term 'rank' rather than 'class' to describe the different social strata, and evolutionist scholarship continued to make use of the notion of rank to distinguish primitive political forms from the more advanced 'class societies' (Sahlins 1968).

However, the parallels between Trobriand society and European aristocracy were so strong that Malinowski and other observers could not help but describe the one in the terms of the other. The term 'commoner' for the lower strata is routinely used by Malinowski and later authors. Although he only occasionally used the term 'noble' for the upper strata, generally sticking to the term 'chiefly', he routinely describes noble matrilineages (*dala*) and their villages as 'aristocratic', and makes wide use of the terms 'vassal' and 'tribute'.[7]

In structural-functionalist anthropology, the Trobriands became a matrilineal example of kinship society, self-organized into descent groups, each of which operated by the same general principles of kinship (Keesing 1975: 69–71). This representation remains highly influential (Robbins 2001: 145; Eriksen 2001: 102) and reflects Malinowski's presentation of society in terms of totemic kinship.

Malinowski introduced the term 'sub-clan' for the *dala* matrilineages that Seligman (1919: 693) had termed 'families', for example, implying that these were sub-sections of the larger kinship categories.[8] He distinguishes these descent groups from households, which are generally virilocal, but stressed their importance in units of residence that he describes as 'villages' and 'village clusters'.

Some villagers enjoyed superior rights to other residents. Malinowski uses the notion of citizenship to explain this difference.

> It is only the members of the sub-clan who can use the title *toli* (owner of) with regard to the village garden lands ... [that] have the right of citizenship, that is, the absolute and unquestionable right of residence. They can also deny residence to any of the people who live in the village in virtue of one or other of the derived rights of residence or the customary indulgences. The citizens also have the ultimate right to cultivate as many plots of the common soil as is necessary for any one of them. (Malinowski [1935] 1965: 344)

Malinowski writes at somewhat rambling length about land tenure. Although he describes the 'ownership' of land, he downplays its economic significance, viewing it as 'rather a ceremonial prerogative than the exclusive right of economic use' ([1935] 1965: 330). Trobriand land tenure was so complex and interwoven with other aspects of life, Malinowski argued, that it would be misleading to try and specify a set of rules. Rather than confusion and discord, Malinowski concludes, this complexity reveals a unifying web of relations in which each person has a place.[9] 'The far-reaching order and harmony which underlies the multiplicity of claims can be definitely assumed in the light of our previous knowledge', he adds (ibid.). This picture of the dense social fabric in a rural idyll is reminiscent of Tönniesian notions of *Gemeinschaft*, and reflects what Niehaus (this volume) describes as Malinowski's 'romantic, holistic vision'. Faced with the ethnographic complexity that Malinowski presents, the reader is firmly steered towards the conclusion that this rich web of rights creates a sort of roughly equitable entitlement within these village kin-republics. A clearer but rather different picture emerges from the work of Leo Austen, who served as Resident Magistrate in the Trobriands for five years from 1931 and wrote a number of publications on island society.

> ... land is held by chiefs and village headmen, who may own large areas, but commoners also own small plots of land by inheritance or lease-purchase ... In the olden days ... commoners as a rule held no title to land except through a person of rank, and then the title was one of usufruct only. (Austen 1945: 48–49)

The idea that before colonial administration most of the people working on the land only held usufruct rights to land through a member of the aristocracy fills in many of the blank spaces left by Malinowski's picture of village republics. The importance of what he calls 'rank', the expectation of wealth among the 'chiefly' aristocracy and the routine demonstrations of deference by commoners towards members of the nobility (*guya'u*) become clearer when seen as the privileges of what in other contexts would be described as the land-owning class. The aristocratic monopoly on rights to land had, by all accounts, suffered encroachment under colonial administration. But the political order that Malinowski described was still one in which ultimate rights to most of the productive land belonged to a relatively small number of noble lineages. It was the members of these landowning lineages that were the 'citizens' of Malinowski's village republics, and most of the information he recorded concerns them.

Information about the 'non-citizens' of Malinowski's Trobriands is rather scattered in his ethnography. They are clearly dependent upon the nobility, but this is passed over with little or no comment. Malinowski gives no information as to the relative numbers of these different sets of people, but the style of description creates the impression that most residents somehow belong to the large matrilineage that owned the village and its lands.

In 1950, anthropologist Harry Powell made a survey of the village of Omarakana, the seat of the 'Paramount Chief' and Malinowski's base for fieldwork. Powell found thirty-nine different named *dala* matrilineages among the 325 people living in Omarakana, each *dala* having 'an average of less than ten members'. These resident 'sub-clans', then, did not contain many more members than, say, rural families in many parts of the world. Only two of the thirty-nine *dalas* were noble, according to Powell (1960: 124), the rest counted as commoners (*tokay*). This dissolves the vision of residential units composed of ideally one, but sometimes several, kinship groups. The village had dozens, and even a tiny hamlet several. They were not, then, anything like a kinship unit in residential form. Furthermore, 75 per cent of the residents recorded in his survey were not members of the *dala* that had rights to the hamlet's land.[10]

The observation that most inhabitants were not members of the landholding lineage transforms our understanding of Malinowski's description of the social order. Rather than an inclusive term, his notion of 'citizenship' turns out to be a privilege enjoyed by a relative few. This is not, however, as strange as it might seem. A form of citizenship linked to noble birth and restricted to a minority was a familiar concept for Malinowski, whose own family counted as Polish nobility. Until the partition of the Polish-Lithuanian Commonwealth in 1795, the key political distinction in this enormous 'republic of nobles' was that between citizens and subjects. Only nobles were full citizens of the commonwealth, entitled to a wide range of rights and able to vote and stand for election to political office. But some 90 per cent of the inhabitants were non-citizens, most of them serfs tied to the landed estates of the *szlachta* nobility (Fedorowicz 1982).

But the impression Malinowski gives of general Trobriander entitlement to land appears misleading even with respect to the rights of the landowning lineage. Annette Weiner, who began fieldwork in 1971, used the term 'manager' rather than the colonial-era 'headman' to describe the men in charge of villages and hamlets. She notes: 'No one has automatic rights to live on *dala* land, even her or his own *dala* land, without contracting an exchange relationship with the hamlet manager' (Weiner 1976: 43). This 'exchange relationship' turns out to be similar to paying rent; it entailed cultivating yams for the land 'manager'. 'Land is lent out for others to use. The primary return for land use and residence is yam production . . . Because the system of land control only admits a few men, most men find themselves using other *dala* land' (ibid.: 167).

Written in terms of aristocracy rather than tribal society, the picture that emerges is this: before the colonial era, land was owned by the nobility, and titles to the various hamlet and village estates were inherited matrilineally by local lords who apportioned lands and received agricultural produce from their tenants, who generally included members of their own matrilineages. Some estates were managed by commoners, described as 'headmen' by the colonial administration, but much of the land seems to have ultimately belonged to one or other noble family. During the twentieth century, some commoner families gained title to some of the land, but much of this was in effect on long-term lease from the original landowners.

Malinowski saw the hierarchical stratification of the Trobriands as one of the region's most striking features. But he placed the political relations of noble power into the analytical frames of kinship and totemism. He wrote: 'Chieftainship in the Trobriands is the combination of two institutions: first, that of headmanship, or village authority; secondly, that of totemic clanship, that is the division of the community into classes or castes, each with a certain more or less definite rank' (Malinowski 1922: 62). For him, clanship was about hierarchy, not equality, but this somehow fell away in later readings. In general, he speaks of 'rank' rather than class, and 'people of rank' to mean aristocrats – that is, *guya'u*, persons of royal or 'chiefly' rank, and *gumguya'u*, people of non-royal but noble birth. Those of lower rank are the *tokay*, or commoners, and he also mentions a lower class of 'pariahs' living in certain villages. The central and most important distinction, however, was between noble (*guya'u*) and common (*tokay*) birth.

Malinowski found the Trobriand nobility to be more refined and dignified than their commoners. The 'chiefs and persons of rank', he notes, are 'very frequently of the finer looking type' and 'behave in a quite different way towards strangers'. Whereas the commoners behave with 'jocular familiarity', the nobles 'show excellent manners, in the full meaning of the word' (Malinowski 1922: 52). When describing the 'friendly familiarity' of native women, he adds: 'Naturally, here also, the manners of women of rank are quite different from those of low class commoners' (ibid.: 53).

The most senior nobles were members of the Tabalu matrilineage, who occupied senior court positions and most of the subordinate positions of 'chief' (ruling noble) throughout the island. Other noble lineages, such as the Mwauri, Mulobwaima and Tudava, were ranked lower than the Tabalu (Malinowski 1948: 121).

> Rank also entails a definite ceremonial, the main principle of which is that elevation must be commensurate to rank. The chief's head must not be overtopped by anybody. When commoners are moving about, he must be seated on a high platform; if he stands they must bend ... I myself have witnessed all the people present in the village of Bwoytalu dropping from various elevations to the ground, as if mown down by a hurricane, at the sound of the long drawn *O guya'u!* announcing the arrival of one of my Omarakana friends who came to visit me in that village of low rank. In Omarakana also I have frequently seen people of low rank approaching the chief in a crouching position, dragging their hunting-spears behind them as was due and proper. (Malinowski 1922: 33–34)

These public displays were the privileges of the noble class, not just individual office holders – thus, 'A woman of rank has to a large extent the same privileges as a man of rank, and will be treated with a similar show of deference by men who are commoners' (Malinowski 1922: 34–35). As with many nobilities, the Trobriand aristocracy demonstrated their superior status through consumption as well as dress and deportment. Certain foods were not eaten by the nobility, although these varied from place to place.

Before colonial administration, the ruling *guya'u* nobility had the power of life and death over their subjects (Malinowski 1922: 64–65; Seligman 1919: 696). They also enjoyed a series of other privileges and monopolies. Commoners were not allowed to own coconuts, betel nuts or pigs, all of which belonged to the ruling noble of a district or village. Rulers clearly took these monopolies seriously, but under colonial rule they found their privileges challenged and undermined by government administrators (Connelly 2007: 136). Contrary to the well-known narrative of British colonial administration propping up or amplifying the power of local rulers, colonial officials progressively undermined aristocratic and royal power, much to Malinowski's horror.

Malinowski condemned the decline in noble power and wealth, complaining:

> Nowadays, when the power of the chiefs is broken, when they have much less wealth than formerly to back up their position, and cannot use even the little force they ever did and when the general breaking up of custom has undermined the traditional deference and loyalty of their subjects, the production of canoes and other forms of wealth by the specialist for the chief is only a vestige of what it once was. (Malinowski 1922: 162)

Malinowski's feelings reflect, perhaps, his family's history. Much of the Polish *szlachta* nobility had been ruined by the emancipation of the peasantry, and Malinowski's paternal grandfather was among those forced to leave their country estates and find work in the towns (Young 2004: 8). The more one studies Malinowski's work, the more important his positioning at the top of Trobriand society, and the more evident his identification with the aristocracy becomes. Most of Malinowski's informants, particularly those he considered to be good informants, were nobles or their sons. As Young (2004: 392) notes, 'With his aristocratic pretentions, Malinowski felt a natural affinity for the chiefly sub-clan of the Tabalu, the highest-ranking Trobrianders and "owners of the soil"...'. One of the best-known photographs of Malinowski shows him seated on an elevated platform alongside Trobriand nobles. The object he is holding turns out to be a marker of aristocratic rank – a lime pot made from a large gourd (Weiner 1988: 98). In effect, then, Malinowski is pictured as a Trobriand lord.

In Malinowski's account, Trobriand social organization is produced by the logic of kinship, in this case matrilineal descent. He writes (1922: 36): 'we have the curious fact that a man at maturity has to change residence from his father's village to that of his mother's brother'. Elsewhere he describes this as a 'tribal law' and this fitted so well with classical theories of kinship and descent theory that it became a standard feature of Trobriand social structure described in textbooks (e.g. Keesing 1975: 69).

It turns out, however, that this 'tribal law' only applied to the landholding elite. Weiner (1976: 42) writes: 'The Trobriands are usually presented as a classic example illustrating the "rules" of avunculocal residence. In actuality, most men live in their fathers' hamlets. Avunculocal residence applies only to the few men in each generation who are heirs to the status of manager. Most men never have the opportunity to manage their own *dala* land and do not reside on it'.

What, then, of the famous kula, the enormous circuit of shell valuable exchange that became one of the most celebrated subjects of anthropology? It is clear from Malinowski's account that kula was to some degree exclusive (Malinowski 1922: 81). Nevertheless, it is described as a general social practice. It turns out that the kula was originally an exclusive and aristocratic activity. Powell (1951: 14) remarked that 'the *Kula* was traditionally forbidden to the commoners'. Weiner explains that, '. . . until early this century, Kiriwina kula was restricted to chiefs, their brothers, sisters' sons, and their own sons' (1992: 138).

Malinowski's ethnography took place at a time when noble control of the kula was breaking down.[11] European pearl-traders were paying commoners using new forms of wealth, including shell valuables (Austen 1945: 21). Access to powered boats also broke the monopolies of the past by which kula trips only took place in the canoes owned by nobles or village estate owners (Malinowski 1922: 118–19). Careful as he was to cast the Trobriand order in the best light, Malinowski wrote as if the recently widened access to all sorts of wealth were the timeless, essential features of a traditional tribal society. But commoner participation in the kula was clearly a recent development.

Malinowski's analysis of kula allowed him to make powerful critiques of the assumptions regarding primitive economics and helped to establish 'exchange' as a central category for twentieth-century anthropology. But in her later work, Annette Weiner is critical of both the wider theory and his analysis of kula in particular. 'After five hundred pages of describing the intricacies of kula exchanges, Malinowski could discover no reasonable native justification for these events other than that Trobrianders' desire to "give for the sake of giving"' (Weiner 1992: 33). Later she explains:

> In the 1920s, few readers were well informed about 'primitive' economics so that Argonauts of the Western Pacific imaginatively drew parallels between Trobriand kula players and ancient Greek heroes. Had Malinowski pursued these links beyond the title he might not have

been so perplexed about why Trobrianders were dedicated to kula ...
In the Homeric case, eminence depended upon one's social identity as
an aristocrat and one's ability to compete successfully among equals
in what Beidelman calls 'agonistic exchange' that was the only means
through which one could elevate one's authority over others. Being
equal demanded the appropriate background – a legacy of ancestors,
correct marriages, and particular allies and only among aristocrats
could the jockeying for a reputation that made the person totally
autonomous take place. (Weiner 1992: 33)

Malinowski's harmonious vision of the Trobriands reflected the *guya'u* nobility's perspective – a picture of contented subjects bound by custom and respect, in which almost all the important relationships were between landowning families, both noble and commoner. In retrospect, Malinowski's mistake, if it can be called that, was to extrapolate down and out from the centre to create a general model of a society that operated by the principles of kinship and exchange that were central concerns of the anthropology of his time.

Looking again at Malinowski's model of tribal society, it seems that almost every element applied only to the elite. Villages were not composed of one or two sub-clans; it is just that only one or two families were landowning. Members of an owning *dala* matrilineage did not have joint rights to the land; use-rights were in the gift of the owners or managers. Most men did not work on the land of their *dala* matrilineage; they worked on land granted to them by a landowner or manager in return for yams. Most men did not go to live with their maternal kin; only those inheriting matrilineal estates did, the rest stayed with their fathers and inherited their use-rights to land along with the obligation to supply yams.

Why Aristocracy?

Many anthropologists have made use of the term 'aristocracy', particularly in the colonial era. In Africa, for example, aristocracies were readily recognized in the larger and more powerful indigenous states (e.g. Nadel 1935, 1942; Kuper 1947; Gluckman 1965: 158; Mair 1974: 9). But the term attracted far less analytical interest than notions of kinship structure. Fortes and Evans-Pritchard (1940: 13) mention aristocracy only in passing in *African Political Systems*, and other applications of the term tended to use it within the scheme of Marxist evolutionary stages to indicate 'feudal' class relations (e.g. Terray 1975; Azarya 1978). And although Boas (1906) wrote of noble and commoner classes among the societies of the North Pacific Coast, later scholarship tended to look to the evolutionist terminology of rank to describe social stratification (Codere 1957). Boasian anthropologists continued to write of aristocracy in societies such as the Kwakiutl (e.g. Benedict 1934: 220), but within an evolutionist frame;[12] Irving Goldman, who made the widest comparative use of the term 'primitive aristocracies', was concerned with 'exploring the role of religious thought in the course of development of the aristocratic system . . .' (Goldman 1975: 5). It was in this frame that Sahlins presented the notion of the 'chiefdom' in which 'tribal culture anticipates statehood in its complexities . . . political regimes organised under powerful chiefs and primitive nobilities' (1968: 20).

Outside this evolutionist genre, anthropological discussion of inequality centred on grander and more general terms such as 'hierarchy'. In his magnum opus *Homo Hierarchicus*, for example, Dumont examined what he termed 'hierarchical society' whose core values could be thought of as holism, in contradistinction to the possessive individualism of the *nouveau régime*, which he treats as synonymous with 'egalitarianism'. The 'we' in Dumont's work is quite explicitly the modern, egalitarian man, and he looks to Alexis de Tocqueville to 'give us some insight into hierarchical society' (Dumont 1970: 17), quoting from him extensively.

Tocqueville, however, does not use the term 'hierarchy' as a counterpoint to egalitarianism.[13] The term he uses throughout *Democracy in America* is 'aristocracy'. Dumont took one term to stand for the other, but they are different in important ways. The Greek roots of 'hierarchy' are religious – the rule of the high priest – and the term appeared in European languages to describe pyramidal systems of celestial and ecclesiastical ranking. Aristocracy, however, was a civic, political term: the rule of the 'excellent' (*aristos*).[14]

While the term hierarchy implies a bounded and neatly ordered structure of superior ranks beneath a single head, aristocracies have often been ramified, attenuated and far from centralized. So hierarchy serves Dumont's purposes well because it allows him to identify it with holism and, since hierarchies tend to be thought of as ordered unities, it made the idea of a single supreme value more convincing. But this bundling together of hierarchy, holism and – the other key term Dumont uses – traditional society, so that they are all made to stand for one another, has created, I think, a number of problems. Not least, of course, the presentation of Brahmanical ideological projects as a sort of totalizing and timeless ontology (Appadurai 1988; Gupta 2005; Dirks 2001).

With his Fustelian view as to the primacy of the religious and cosmological, it is understandable that Dumont saw hierarchy as the essential feature of stratified political forms in which status is inherited. On reflection, however, this is not generally true. Aristocracies are stratified, of course, but this is not the product of a single pyramidic whole. Historically, they have frequently been decentralized and truncated. The different strata do not depend on the apex position of the overlord or even the political or cosmological whole that might include them. Rather, aristocrats come together to create a large political entity, and their own positions are frequently independent of it, as encapsulated in Weber's notion of patrimonialism. So, for example, the *Res Publica* of ancient Rome was the joint project of the aristocracy, as represented by the senate (Lintott 1999: 17, 65);[15] and in the 'republic of nobles' of the sixteenth–eighteenth-century Polish-Lithuanian Commonwealth the monarch was elected by the nobility and held almost no power over them (Fedorowicz 1982).

Just as they need not depend upon a centralized state, aristocracies do not require religious unity. Islamic Ottoman aristocrats ruled Christian and Jewish subjects; indeed, a majority of Ottoman subjects were Christian until the late fifteenth century (Braude 2014: 13). Aristocratic rulers generally enjoy religious legitimation, but their position need not depend upon a particular religious or cosmological schema. Christian conversion in Scandinavia was driven by the conversion of monarchs and their courts, so that nominally Christian nobilities ruled over pagan subjects whom they then converted (Staecker 2003). Furthermore, although centralizing states and religious institutions may seek to form boundaries around them, aristocracies frequently form networks that extend beyond political and religious boundaries.

While the origins of the term hierarchy are celestial, the basis of aristocracy is, for Tocqueville, more terrestrial: 'Land is the basis of an aristocracy, which clings to the soil that supports it; for it is not by privileges alone, nor by birth, but by landed property handed down from generation to generation, that an aristocracy is constituted. A nation may present immense fortunes and extreme wretchedness, but unless those fortunes are territorial there is no aristocracy, but simply the class of the rich and that of the poor' (Tocqueville 1841: 29). This is something shared by the Nuer *diel* and the Trobriand *guya'u*, both of whom were the 'owners of the land'.

In her 1992 monograph *Inalienable Possessions: The Paradox of Keeping-While Giving*, Annette Weiner describes a category of wealth of central importance to many historically known societies which has been largely overlooked in anthropology. She terms this 'inalienable wealth', the archetypal form of which is the landed estate – the 'immovable property' of Romano-Germanic law. Her central critique of Malinowski is that he did not recognize Trobriand activities such as kula to be about the inalienable wealth of elite status in which 'prized shells are like the famous trophies for which Greek aristocrats vied' (Weiner 1992: 133). This sense of pride and distinction was rooted in the prestige of the 'chiefly' lines, and the inalienable historical privileges they held.

Alongside this proprietorial relationship to land can be added superiority, descent and privilege as central features of aristocracies. Nobles were not simply different in some way; they were superior and entitled to respect. Their status was inherited down one or both lines of descent, and entitled them to privileges of various kinds, including, as Weber (1947) noted, the right to use particular symbols. The superiority of aristocrats was generally self-evident. As Bourdieu (1977: 164) notes, 'Every established order tends to produce ... the naturalization of its own arbitrariness'. The concept of nobility entailed ethical as well as status connotations, and in most historically stable systems of dominant power-knowledge, virtue was distributed among different segments of society in roughly the same proportions as wealth and power.

But why use the term *aristocracy* for the comparative study of landed hereditary elites and the social formations that they rule? Is it not a Eurocentric term, carrying too much geographically and historically particular baggage to be applied cross-culturally?

Firstly, it is clear that the terminology of *chiefly* and *kinship society* that the discipline has inherited is far more deeply entangled in ethnocentric colonial-era ideologies than is the word *aristocracy*. It was only to societies thought in the colonial era to be primitive that the language of tribe and chief was applied. Aristocracy was, and continues to be, used to describe the hereditary elites all over the world when deemed sufficiently civilized. Anthropologists and historians of Japan and China routinely use the term (e.g. Lebra 1993; Robertson 2005; Heng 1999; Tackett 2014), knowing full well that there will be differences as well as resemblances with the hereditary elites of Europe. Writers describe ancient Greek, Roman, Incan and Mesopotamian aristocracies without imagining them in the image of the *aristo*s of the French Revolution. Geographic, cultural and historical distance, then, need not prevent the application of the term since, after all, some translation is required for any comparative historical or anthropological vision.

Secondly, it is difficult to find a better alternative term. An obvious candidate is the phrase 'hereditary elite', but unless the content of a set of implicated terms can somehow be remade, specialized terms of this sort will tend to perpetuate the original conceptual framework. Until the clumsy term 'hereditary elite' was used for all aristocracies, the expression would run the risk of becoming a sort of euphemism for 'chiefly rank'. The choice of terminology, then, is bound to reflect the nature of the writing project. To really leave behind the zombie models of evolutionist social science and make a comparative study of hereditary ruling elites, it makes sense, I think, to choose the term most widely used for other hereditary elites – particularly the European ones of the colonizing powers.

Anthropology is often described in terms of cultural translation, but as Clifford (1997: 182) pointed out, this necessarily distorts and recasts the understandings that anthropologists seek to render in another language. This is necessarily an interested process. As Bassnett and Lefevere (1995: vii) note, 'All rewritings, whatever their intention reflect a certain ideology and poetics'. Since anthropology requires translation, arguably even when the ethnographic language is the same as the analytic one, there seems little alternative but to try to be as conscious and reflexive as possible about the process.

In rewriting meanings, then, understandings do not adhere to the particular signs, but to the place they occupy in the wider semiotic system of language. A writer might reproduce a particular word in the source language, but the reader's understanding would depend upon the position that term took in their own interpretive framework. So, for example, one could avoid translating the Kiriwinan term *guya'u* or the Nuer word *dil* at all. But if the reader thinks of the term as meaning 'chief', then this is hardly an improvement on using the English word instead. So although for some sorts of writing projects it would be better to use the words the various hereditary elites used for themselves, for the purposes of this project I suggest approximate translations ('noble', 'aristocratic') as alternatives to the older etic terms applied to them ('chief', 'chiefly').

Having developed and mastered their own specialized comparative analytical terminology, anthropologists have been loath to abandon it. Why would one want to use terms used for Euro-American history or society when the anthropological ones were less ethnocentric, more general, better adapted to application beyond 'the west'? But the problem was, they were not. By effectively marking 'primitive' societies with special terms and theories, this evolutionist terminology (tribe, clan, lineage etc.) was in effect more Eurocentric, not less.

Conclusion: Ethnography and Politgraphy

Why has so much zombie kinship society theory been retained in anthropology, so that the power relations of aristocracy continued to be read as evidence for types of kinship society?

> The original sin of anthropology was to divide the world into civilized and savage. The social systems of all those other peoples supposedly rested upon a foundation of blood relationships. Anthropologists therefore became at once the experts on the primitive and on kinship. In the 1970s Western kinship systems began to undergo radical change. Simultaneously, the old orthodoxies about kinship crumbled in anthropology. Young ethnographers generally lost interest in the topic. Kinship systems have nevertheless not gone away, out there in the world. But to understand them we must first abandon the opposition between the modern and the traditional, the West and the Rest. (Kuper 2008: 717)

Alterity, then, was a key component of anthropological analytical strategies from the outset. The discipline emerged from the nineteenth-century study of exotica, and found its place in the Euro-American academy as a specialist form of knowledge about more primitive social forms. Rather than using the same analytical terms applied to the study of European polities, anthropologists developed their own based upon what are now seen to be largely fallacious theories of social evolution. Difference and otherness, then, was what made these 'societies' interesting.

On the other hand, certain senses of affinity were also of central importance. The discipline as a whole pictured a sort of general humanity as its object of study, probing for illusive human universals as well as clues as to how some evolutionary or developmental process transformed 'them' into 'us'. Within this frame, personal affinity played a key role. Malinowski's ready sympathy for the Trobriand aristocracy – based on a real, if limited, identification – helped propel him towards a form of deeply conservative holism that cast aristocratic (but not administrative) relations of power in the most positive terms possible. Similarly, for Sharon Hutchinson, Evans-Pritchard identified with the Nuer aristocrats:

> The wry, dry, unflappable narrator of Evans-Pritchard's writings identifies, as I soon discovered, not simply with Nuer men as a group but, more specifically, with senior members of 'aristocratic' lines. Evans-Pritchard's vision of Nuer social life appears at times so unified as to preclude the possibility of ideological struggle among groups within it. (Hutchinson 1996: 31)

Another feature of the anthropological tradition has tended to prevent thorough-going re-evaluations of the earlier accounts that presented 'tribal' societies in classless, non-coercive terms. This was a sort of shadow of the Noble Savage and was pioneered, as with so much else, by Malinowski. The anthropologist should demonstrate their lack of ethnocentrism by avoiding negative evaluations of their studied society, and championing the 'native' view. One of the problems, however, was *which* native's view this should be. In a differentiated, unequal polity, the view of the noble is likely to be very different from that of the commoner.

Approaching the subjects of ethnography as political orders, rather than holistic social systems, offers the prospect of destabilizing classical notions of society. Sociological theory emerged from an intellectual tradition steeped in the ideology of national populism, as well as modernist evolutionism. Having challenged and displaced monarchical and aristocratic representations of history, the young social sciences sought to universalize analytical frames developed in descriptions of the origins of the nation-state polities in which the authors lived. Durkheimian sociology can be seen to have developed from Renan's theory of the nation and elaborated it for universal application (Sneath 2007: 157–61). In this thought, solidarity (which could be viewed as the successful 'orchestration of consensus') is naturally produced by social units pictured as tiny versions of the idealized nation. As Laclau (2005: 154) notes, national populist political thought requires 'the people', and 'the construction of the "people" is the political act *par excellence*'. Peoples needed to exist in their own rights, since claims regarding the popular will became the source of political legitimacy. So 'peoples' became objects of knowledge – the *ethnos* was subject to the study of ethnologists and ethnographers.

A revisionist anthropology might look again at its commitment to ethnography as a description of a primarily social and cultural entity, and consider the possibility that what these accounts have left to us are, on reflection, forms of politgraphy – the study of social bodies constituted by power relations.

David Sneath is Reader in the Division of Social Anthropology and Director of the Mongolia and Inner Asia Studies Unit (MIASU) at the University of Cambridge. He is the author of *The Headless State: Aristocratic Orders, Kinship Society, and Misrepresentations of Nomadic Inner Asia* (Columbia University Press, 2007) and *Changing Inner Mongolia: Pastoral Mongolian Society and the Chinese State* (Oxford

University Press, 2000). His recent research explores the representations of steppe societies in social and historical studies, and the political economy and ecology of Mongolia and Inner Asia.

Notes

This chapter presents arguments contained in a forthcoming monograph provisionally entitled *The Savage Noble: The Anthropology of Aristocracy and Revisionist Readings of Power*.

1. Eriksen, for example, reflects this trend when he writes: 'In many societies, including the Trobriand Islands and Swat valley, several lineages considered to be related occasionally form alliances and so appear as clans – as kin groupings at a higher systemic level' (2001: 104).
2. See, for example, Evans-Pritchard 1933: 8, 1934, 1935.
3. See Evans-Pritchard 1951: 9, 18, 27. See also 1956: 120 for *dil* as 'aristocratic' spirits.
4. Dinka author Francis Deng uses the term 'commoner', however, to translate the word for non-aristocrats (*kic*) among the neighbouring Dinka (see Deng 1972: 22).
5. As McKinnon (2000: 49) notes, 'Evans-Pritchard discounts the political significance of the hierarchical differentiation between dominant and attached lineages, aristocrats and strangers/Dinka because this differentiation is constructed along affinal and matrilateral lines, which, for Evans-Pritchard, belong not to the political domain but, rather, to the domestic domain'.
6. Evans-Pritchard (1937, 1948) described aristocracy among the Azande on the basis of his own fieldwork, and the Shilluk on the basis of the fieldwork of Pumphrey (1941) and Howell (1941).
7. For example, Malinowski [1935] 1965: 15, 33, 40, 84, 232, 342, 385.
8. Weiner (1976: 51) notes that 'Malinowski and Powell glossed *kumila* as "clan", confusing the issue by assuming that a *dala* was a smaller replica of a *kumila* . . . [but] Trobriand *kumila* are not descent lines'.
9. See also Malinowski 1921: 8.
10. In a later paper (1969: 190), Powell presents his figures in a different format, suggesting that 78 per cent of residents were not members of *dalas* that had rights to land.
11. Aristocratic power may have decayed in other parts of Melanesia as well. The Oceanian anthropologist and writer Epeli Hau'ofa, whose work is examined by Tengan (this volume), argued that equality and elective leadership had been overemphasized in anthropological representations of the region. He noted: 'It is probable . . . that Melanesian societies with hereditary authority structures are more common than we have realised' (Hau'ofa 1981: 293). See also May 2001: 203–36.

12. Ruth Benedict (1934: 174–88) uses the term nobility for the hereditary Kwakiutl elite and even the term aristocracy (ibid.: 220) to describe their political order. However, this is fitted into a version of the standard evolutionist narrative. In her synthetic analysis/chapter, she writes: 'Primitive society is integrated in geographical units. Western civilization, however, is stratified, and different social groups of the same time and place live by quite different standards and are actuated by different motivations' (ibid.: 230).
13. Tocqueville uses the term 'hierarchy' only once in *Democracy in America* (1841) when referring to a 'despotic' classing of subjects.
14. For Aristotle, aristocracy meant the rule of the virtuous few (Arnheim 1977), but when the term was revived in the renaissance it was used to mean states ruled by noblemen, as opposed to monarchies. For Hobbes, aristocracy was a wide category for any state ruled by a sovereign assembly of part of the public (Hobbes [1651] 1996: 123–25), and in his eighteenth-century political typology Montesquieu makes aristocracy one species of republic, alongside democracies, to be distinguished from monarchies and despotisms. Only later, with the Dutch Patriot conflict and the French Revolution, was the term 'aristocrat' applied to nobles, and the idea that monarchies could include aristocracies emerged (Doyle 2010: 6).
15. As Lintott (1999: 86) put it, 'the senate was both the political form taken by the Roman aristocracy and also an important means of social self-expression by that class, in so far as it constituted a form of club. . .'.

References

Appadurai, A. 1988. 'Putting Hierarchy in Its Place', *Cultural Anthropology* 3(1): 36–49.
Arnheim, M. 1977. *Aristocracy in Greek Society*. London: Thames & Hudson.
Asad, T. 1973. *Anthropology and the Colonial Encounter*. London: Ithaca Press.
Austen, L. 1945. 'Cultural Changes in Kiriwina', *Oceania* 16: 15–60.
Azarya, V. 1978. *Aristocrats Facing Change: The Fulbe in Guinea, Nigeria and Cameroon*. Chicago, IL: University of Chicago Press.
Bassnett, S., and A. Lefevere. 1995. 'General Editors' Preface', in L. Venuti, *The Translator's Invisibility: A History of Translation*. London: Routledge, pp. vii–viii.
Beck, U. 2005. 'The Cosmopolitan State: Redefining Power in the Global Age', *International Journal of Politics, Culture, and Society* 18: 143–59.
Benedict, R. 1934. *Patterns of Culture*. Boston, MA: Houghton Mifflin.
Boas, F. 1906. 'The Tribes of the North Pacific Coast', in *Annual Archaeological Report, 1905*. Toronto: Minister of Education, Ont., pp. 235–49.
Bodley, J. 2011. *Cultural Anthropology: Tribes, States, and the Global System*. Lanham, MD: Rowman & Littlefield.

Bourdieu, P. 1977. *Outline of a Theory of Practice*. Cambridge: Cambridge University Press.
Braude, B. 2014. 'Introduction', in *Christians and Jews in the Ottoman Empire: The Abridged Edition*. Boulder, CO: Lynne Rienner, pp. 1–50.
Clifford, J. 1997. *Routes: Travel and Translation in the Late Twentieth Century*. Cambridge, MA: Harvard University Press.
Codere, H. 1957. 'Kwakiutl Society: Rank without Class', *American Anthropologist* 59(3): 473–486.
Collier, J., M. Rosaldo, and S. Yanagisako. 1982. 'Is There a Family? New Anthropological Views', in B. Thorne and M. Yalom (eds), *Rethinking the Family: Some Feminist Questions*. New York: Longman, pp. 25–39.
Connelly, A. 2007. 'Counting Coconuts: Patrol Reports from the Trobriand Islands Part I: 1907–1934', MA thesis. Long Beach CA: California State University.
Cornell, T. 1995. *The Beginnings of Rome: Italy and Rome from the Bronze Age to the Punic Wars (1000–246 BC)*. London: Routledge.
Deng, F. 1972. *The Dinka of the Sudan*. New York: Holt, Rinehart & Winston.
Dirks, N. 2001. *Castes of Mind: Colonialism and the Making of Modern India*. Princeton, NJ: Princeton University Press.
Doyle, W. 2010. *Aristocracy: A Very Short Introduction*. Oxford: Oxford University Press.
Dumont, L. 1970. *Homo Hierarchicus: The Caste System and Its Implications*. Chicago, IL: University of Chicago Press.
Eriksen, T. 2001. *Small Places, Large Issues: An Introduction to Social and Cultural Anthropology*, 2nd edn. London: Pluto Press.
Evans-Pritchard, E. 1933. 'The Nuer Tribe and Clan (I)', *Sudan Notes and Records* XVI(I): 1–53.
Evans-Pritchard, E. 1934. 'The Nuer Tribe and Clan (II)', *Sudan Notes and Records* XVII(I): 1–57
Evans-Pritchard, E. 1935. 'The Nuer Tribe and Clan (III)', *Sudan Notes and Records* XVIII(I): 37–87.
Evans-Pritchard, E. 1937. *Witchcraft, Oracles and Magic Among the Azande*. Oxford: Clarendon Press.
Evans-Pritchard, E. 1938. 'Some Administrative Problems of the Southern Sudan', in *Oxford Summer School of Colonial Administration*. Oxford: Oxford University Press, pp. 75–77.
Evans-Pritchard, E. 1940. *The Nuer: A Description of the Modes of Livelihood and Political Institutions of a Nilotic People*. Oxford: Clarendon Press.
Evans-Pritchard, E. 1948. *The Divine Kingship of the Shilluk of the Nilotic Sudan*. Cambridge: Cambridge University Press.
Evans-Pritchard, E. 1951. *Kinship and Marriage Among the Nuer*, Oxford: Oxford University Press.
Evans-Pritchard, E. 1956. *Nuer Religion*. Oxford: Clarendon Press.
Fedorowicz, J. (ed. and trans.). 1982. *A Republic of Nobles: Studies in Polish History to 1864*. Cambridge: Cambridge University Press.

Fortes, M., and E. Evans-Pritchard (eds). 1940. *African Political Systems*. Oxford: Oxford University Press.
Foucault, M. [1976] 1980. 'Two Lectures', in C. Gordon (ed.), *Power/Knowledge: Selected Interviews and Other Writings, 1972–1977*. Brighton: Harvester, pp. 78–108.
Foucault, M. 1983. 'The Subject and Power', in H. Dreyfus and P. Rabinow (eds), *Michel Foucault: Beyond Structuralism and Hermeneutics*. Chicago, IL: University of Chicago Press, pp. 208–26.
Fried, M. 1975. *The Notion of Tribe*. Menlo Park, CA: Cummings.
Gluckman, Max. 1965. *Politics, Law and Ritual in Tribal Society*. Oxford: Blackwell.
Goldman, I. 1955. 'Status Rivalry and Cultural Evolution in Polynesia', *American Anthropologist*, New Series 57(4): 680–97.
Goldman, I. 1970. *Ancient Polynesian Society*. Chicago, IL: University of Chicago Press.
Goldman, I. 1975. *The Mouth of Heaven: An introduction to Kwakiutl Religious Thought*. New York: John Wiley and Sons.
Gough, K. 1971. 'Nuer Kinship: A Reexamination' in T. Beidelman (ed), *The Translation of Culture: Essays to E.E. Evans-Pritchard*, London: Tavistock, pp. 1–38.
Greuel, P. 1971. 'The Leopard-Skin Chief: An Examination of Political Power Among the Nuer', *American Anthropologist* 73(5): 1115–1120.
Gupta, D. 2005. 'Caste and Politics: Identity over System', *Annual Review of Anthropology* 34: 409–27.
Haight, B. 1972. 'A Note on the Leopard-Skin Chief', *American Anthropologist* 74(5): 1313–1318.
Hansen, T., and F. Stepputat. 2001. 'Introduction: States of Imagination', in *States of Imagination: Ethnographic Explorations of the Postcolonial State*. Durham, NC: Duke University Press, pp. 1–38.
Hauʻofa, E. 1981. *Mekeo: Inequality and Ambivalence in a Village Society*. Canberra: Australian National University Press.
Heng, C. 1999. *Cities of Aristocrats and Bureaucrats: The Development of Medieval Chinese Cityscapes*. Honolulu, HI: University of Hawai'i Press.
Hobbes, T. [1651] 1996. *Leviathan*. Oxford: Oxford University Press.
Hodder, I. (ed.). 2001. *Archaeological Theory Today*. Cambridge: Polity Press.
Howell, P. 1941. 'The Shilluk Settlement', *Sudan Notes and Records* XXIV(I): 47–68.
Howell, P. 1954. *A Manual of Nuer Law*. London: Oxford University Press.
Hutchinson, S. 1996. *Nuer Dilemmas. Coping with Money, War, and the State*. Oakland, CA: University of California Press.
Johnson, D. 1981. 'The Fighting Nuer: Primary Sources and the Origins of a Stereotype', *Africa: Journal of the International African Institute* 51: 508–27.
Johnson, D. 1994. *Nuer Prophets: A History of Prophecy from the Upper Nile in the Nineteenth and Twentieth Centuries*. Oxford: Clarendon Press.

Keesing, R. 1975. *Kin Groups and Social Structure*, Orlando, FL: Harcourt Brace Jovanovich College Publishers.

Kuper, A. 1988. *The Invention of Primitive Society: Transformations of an Illusion*. London: Routledge.

Kuper, A. 2004. 'Lineage Theory: A Critical Retrospect', in R. Parkin and L. Stone (eds), *Kinship and Family: An Anthropological Reader*. Oxford: Blackwell, pp. 79–96.

Kuper, A. 2008. 'Changing the Subject: About Cousin Marriage, among Other Things', *The Journal of the Royal Anthropological Institute* (N.S.) 14: 717–35.

Kuper, H. 1947. *An African Aristocracy: Rank among the Swazi*. Oxford: Oxford University Press.

Laclau, E. 2005. *On Populist Reason*. London: Verso.

Lebra, T. 1993. *Above the Clouds: Status Culture of the Modern Japanese Nobility*. Berkeley, CA: University of California Press.

Lewellen, T. 2003. *Political Anthropology: An Introduction*. Westport, CT: Praeger.

Lintott, A. 1999. *The Constitution of the Roman Republic*. Oxford: Oxford University Press.

Mair, L. 1974. *African Societies*. Cambridge: Cambridge University Press.

Malinowski, B. 1921. 'The Primitive Economics of the Trobriand Islanders', *The Economic Journal* 31: 1–16.

Malinowski, B. 1922. *Argonauts of the Western Pacific: An Account of Native Enterprise and Adventure in the Archipelagoes of Melanesian New Guinea*. London: George Routledge & Sons.

Malinowski, B. [1935] 1965. *Coral Gardens and Their Magic*. Vol. 1. Bloomington, IN: Indiana University Press.

Malinowski, B. 1948. *Magic, Science and Religion and Other Essays*. Glencoe, IL: The Free Press.

May, R. 2001. *State and Society in Papua New Guinea: The First Twenty-Five Years*. Canberra: Australian National University Press.

McKinnon, S. 2000. 'Domestic Exceptions: Evans-Pritchard and the Creation of Nuer Patrilineality and Equality', *Cultural Anthropology* 15(1): 35–83.

Morgan, L. [1877] 1964. *Ancient Society: Researches in the Lines of Human Progress from Savagery through Barbarism to Civilisation*. New York: Holt.

Newcomer, P. 1972. 'The Nuer Are Dinka: An Essay on Origins and Environmental Determinism', *Man* (N.S.) 7: 5–11.

Nadel, S. 1935. 'Nupe State and Community', *Africa: Journal of the International African Institute* 8(3): 257–303.

Nadel, S. 1942. *A Black Byzantium*. Oxford: Oxford University Press.

Powell, H. 1951. Fourth Fieldwork Report. Kiriwina, Trobriand Islands, January 1st–March 31st, 1951, unpublished paper, http://trobriandsindepth.com/PDFs/POWELL%204.pdf.

Powell, H. 1960. 'Competitive Leadership in Trobriand Political Organization', *Journal of the Royal Anthropological Institute* 90: 118–45.

Powell, H. 1969. 'Genealogy, Residence and Kinship in Kiriwina', *Man* (N.S.) 4: 177–202.
Pumphrey, M. 1941. 'The Shilluk Tribe', *Sudan Notes and Records* XXIV(I): 1–46.
Robbins, R. 2001. *Cultural Anthropology: A Problem-based Approach.* Itasca, IL: Peacock Publishers.
Robertson, J. (ed.). 2005. *A Companion to the Anthropology of Japan.* Malden, MA: Blackwell.
Sahlins, M. 1968. *Tribesmen.* Englewood Cliffs, NJ: Prentice-Hall.
Said, E. 1979. *Orientalism.* London: Vintage Books.
Schneider, D. 1968. *American Kinship: A Cultural Account.* Chicago, IL: University of Chicago Press.
Schneider, D. 1984. *A Critique of the Study of Kinship.* Ann Arbor, MI: University of Michigan Press.
Seligman, G. 1919. *The Melanesians of British New Guinea.* London: Cambridge University Press.
Service, E. 1975. *Origins of the State and Civilization: The Process of Cultural Evolution.* New York: Norton & Co.
Sharp, J. 1996. 'Tribe', in A. Kuper and J. Kuper (eds), *The Social Sciences Encyclopedia*, 2nd edn. London: Routledge, pp. 883–84.
Sneath, D. 2007. *The Headless State: Aristocratic Orders, Kinship Society, and Misrepresentations of Nomadic Inner Asia.* New York: Columbia University Press.
Southall, A. 1976. 'Nuer and Dinka Are People: Ecology, Ethnicity and Logical Possibility', *Man* (N.S.) 11: 463–91.
Southall, A. 1996. 'Tribe', in D. Levinson and M. Ember (eds), *Encyclopedia of Cultural Anthropology.* New York: Henry Holt, pp. 1329–36.
Staecker, J. 2003. 'The Cross Goes North: Christian Symbols and Scandinavian Women', in M. Carver (ed.), *The Cross Goes North: Processes of Conversion in Northern Europe, AD 300–1300.* Woodbridge: Boydell Press, pp. 463–82.
Starr, C. 1961. *The Origins of Greek Civilisation 1100–650 BC.* London: Jonathan Cape.
Tackett, N. 2014. *The Destruction of the Medieval Chinese Aristocracy.* Cambridge, MA: Harvard University Press.
Terray, E. 1975. 'Classes and Class Consciousness in the Abron Kingdom of Gyaman', in M. Bloch (ed.), *Marxist Analyses and Social Anthropology.* London: Malaby Press, pp. 85–136.
Tocqueville, A. 1841. *Democracy in America. Volume 1.* New York: J & H.G. Langley.
Tönnies, F. 1887. *Gemeinschaft und Gesellschaft.* Leipzig: Fues's Verlag; 2nd edn 1912, 8th edn 1935. Leipzig: Buske; reprint 2005. Darmstadt: Wissenschaftliche Buchgesellschaft.
Vail, L. (ed.). 1989. *The Creation of Tribalism in Southern Africa.* London: James Currey.

Weber, M. 1947. *The Theory of Social and Economic Organization*. New York: Oxford University Press.

Weiner, A. 1976. *Women of Value, Men of Renown: New Perspectives in Trobriand Exchange*. Austin, TX: University of Texas Press.

Weiner, A. 1988. *The Trobrianders of Papua New Guinea*. Orlando, FL: Harcourt Brace Jovanovich.

Weiner, A. 1992. *Inalienable Possessions: The Paradox of Keeping-While Giving*. Berkeley, CA: University of California Press.

Wolf, E. [1982] 1997. *Europe and the People without History*. Berkeley, CA: University of California Press.

Young, M. 2004. *Malinowski: Odyssey of an Anthropologist, 1884–1920*. New Haven, CT: Yale University Press.

PART II

Alterity and Affinity in Anthropology's Global Landscape

Chapter 3

THE ANTHROPOLOGICAL IMAGINARIUM

CRAFTING ALTERITY, THE SELF AND AN ETHNOGRAPHIC FILM IN SOUTHWEST CHINA

Katherine Swancutt

Anthropology, the study of humankind, is often considered to be the study of the self, the other and sometimes the 'exotic' (Kapferer 2013a). As a discipline, it brings into focus the shared experiences of anthropologists and their interlocutors, while tossing up questions about who is studying whom, what counts as strange or familiar, and how anthropology comes to be produced through ethnographic fieldwork. Yet the question of who the anthropologist happens to be is rarely explored, as anthropologists tend to occlude themselves from the ethnographic portraits they produce. The near invisibility of anthropologists in their own works is traceable to more than just their efforts at showcasing the peoples of study. Perhaps somewhat paradoxically, the 'hidden' presence of anthropologists is often itself a product of the classic self-other distinction in anthropology.

Typically, both anthropologists and their interlocutors are thought to occupy two sides of the proverbial coin. One side of that coin evokes radical difference and otherness, glossed as 'alterity' in anthropological circles. The other side encompasses similarity, commonality, or what anthropologists call 'affinity'. Alterity and affinity are, then, terms that evoke the qualities of relationships or exchanges between anthropologists and their interlocutors. Yet like most coins, anthropology is not only built on exchanges, but is prone to unsettling the values and notions it conveys. It is therefore not uncommon for anthropologists and their interlocutors to occupy a middle ground, in which they imagine each other as being both radically other and radically similar at once.

Anthropologists have routinely discussed how they and their interlocutors blur the relationships of alterity and affinity between them (see, for example, Balzer 2011; Bamo, Harrell and Ma 2007; Goulet and Miller 2007; Holmes and Marcus 2008; Rappaport 2008; Vitebsky 2008; Willerslev 2012; and the contributions to this volume). Liana Chua, for example, observes that 'anthropological knowledge is continually co-produced in discursive, social, material, and other ways, with its implications and effects often exceeding the ethnographer's competence and control' (2015: 646). Similarly, Piers Vitebsky suggests that anthropologists build up a shared history and 'cultural repertoire' with their interlocutors through return fieldwork visits, which may exceed the control of everyone in fieldwork, sometimes through unexpected and emotional dialogues (2008: 251). I have discussed elsewhere how anthropologists and their interlocutors may draw upon a shared corpus of ethnographic, and sometimes anthropological, knowledge that enables them to engage in 'hyper-reflexive' dialogues – particularly in cases where the interlocutor doubles as another anthropologist or ethnologist (Swancutt and Mazard 2016; Swancutt 2016a, 2016b). Fieldwork thus offers ample opportunities, although by no means the only ones, where anthropologists and their interlocutors may profoundly shape each other's biographies, professions and ways of conceptualizing their histories, knowledge and practices (see the chapters by Isak Niehaus and David Sneath in this volume).

In this chapter, I discuss how the anthropological self is imaginatively assembled through ethnographic filmmaking. To this end, I make an argument that runs parallel to Caroline Humphrey's (2008) discussion of how persons come to be 'assembled' through their involvement in specific 'decision-events'. But rather than focusing on how events shape persons, I consider how anthropologists and their interlocutors assemble each other through creative acts of alterity-making and affinity-making. More specifically, I discuss how ethnographic filmmaking enables anthropologists and their interlocutors to co-produce unique imaginaries that potentially shape their worlds and those of their audiences.

My argument is built on an ethnographic filmmaking project that I carried out during summer 2016 in Southwest China, in which I inadvertently became a featured character flanked by the team of ethnologists with whom I created it. The filmmaking arose out of fieldwork that I have conducted for a decade among the Nuosu, a

Tibeto-Burman ethnic group known also by their Chinese ethnonym of Yi. Both my previous research on the Nuosu and the filmmaking took place in the Liangshan (Cool Mountains) region of the Ninglang Yi Autonomous County in Yunnan Province, China. The film was the first project of a research unit that I had launched on return from my summer 2015 field trip to Ninglang, at the suggestion of the Nuosu ethnologist I call Bahmat, who boldly suggested that doing this would facilitate our exchanges in the future (Swancutt 2016b: 61–62). On return to Britain, and while still in dialogue with Bahmat, I laid the institutional groundwork for a 'twinned unit', with one branch at my university and another to be run by Jiarimuji, a Nuosu anthropologist at a Chinese university in Yunnan's capital of Kunming. I then prepared for my next trip to Ninglang, where I would produce an ethnographic film with Jiarimuji, as the first project of our twinned units.

Local Imaginings of Foreign (Anglophone) Scholarship

When I returned to Ninglang in late July 2016 for the filmmaking, I found notable continuities with my fieldwork from the previous summer. Things picked up much as they had left off when the ethnologist I call Mitsu recruited me to judge a singing competition at the annual Torch Festival pageantries in Ninglang County, as he had done during my 2015 trip (Swancutt 2016b: 59–60, see also 62). Amid this second year of judging, I shared with Mitsu, Bahmat and other local ethnologists the news that the research unit we had envisioned a year earlier had become a reality. Jiarimuji had already alerted Mitsu to our plan for producing an ethnographic film, and I explained that one key reason for making the film was that it could represent the scholarly exchanges between China and Britain envisioned for the research unit. The film would be both ethnographic and ethno-historical, as it would follow in the footsteps of the British journalist Alan Winnington, who had been invited by the Chinese Communist Party to document the dismantling of slavery among the Nuosu in Ninglang during the Democratic Reforms (Ch. *minzhu gaige* 民主改革) of 1956–57. Winnington, who was born in London in 1910 and died in Berlin in 1983, was a card-carrying member of the Communist Party who had lived his life in exile after travelling to China, where his British passport expired during the Cold War and was not renewed because of his political leanings. Yet Winnington published *The Slaves of the Cool Mountains* in 1959, while he was based in Beijing, through an independent radical publishing house in Britain (see Figure 3.1). His book is filled with numerous black and white photos taken during his year's stay among the Nuosu.

Mitsu was particularly impressed with Winnington's book and wondered how I came up with the idea for an ethnographic film on it. I explained that the idea arose in discussion with Jiarimuji in Kunming, during the final days of my summer 2015 fieldwork. Jiarimuji had discovered Winnington's book when researching the Democratic Reforms, whereas I had purchased a copy of it several years earlier. Neither of us had done much with the book, other than considering it a journalist's record of Ninglang's past. But as we discussed our visions of new research units, Jiarimuji suggested doing a joint project on Winnington's travels in Ninglang, which could represent the Nuosu-British exchanges enabled through our research. Originally, we had envisioned a two-phase project, where I would travel to Ninglang to interview Nuosu persons who knew Winnington, or perhaps their descendants. Jiarimuji would then travel to Europe, where he wished to interview the descendants of Winnington. We thus built role-reversals into the project, although we had not initially considered it to be a filmmaking initiative. In April 2016, though, when funds became available for modest video equipment, we decided to do the fieldwork and filming in Ninglang.

It was not just Mitsu, Bahmat and the other ethnologists who were excited by Winnington's book. Almost everyone to whom we showed the volume took great interest in poring over its photographs while praising it as a work on recent Nuosu history. To my surprise, Winnington's work was received as a complete novelty in Ninglang, although knowledge of foreign research across the wider Liangshan mountain region, and Southwest China more generally, is a well-known phenomenon. The Austrian-American explorer Joseph Rock (1884–1962), who famously studied the Naxi of nearby Lijiang, was familiar at least in name to some – including to a Nuosu nobleman who appeared in our film. Winnington, though, was so unknown that Mitsu wanted to photocopy his 'rare' book almost immediately. He envisioned plans whereby Jiarimuji and myself would translate Winnington's volume into Chinese, after which he would translate it again into Nuosu, and the three of us would go on to publish and sell numerous copies of this trilingual version across the Liangshan mountains, where it would become a celebrated work.

One standout feature of Winnington's book, then, was that it revealed that the Nuosu of Ninglang were of special interest to foreign scholars of the past. Across Southwest China, foreign scholarship on ethnic minority groups carries considerable cachet, particularly where it can be linked up to Chinese ethnological research. Emily Chao has shown how influential Joseph Rock's field studies (between the 1920s and 1940s) were to the 'invention of *dongba* culture' and the founding in 1981 of the Dongba Cultural Research Institute in Lijiang city, which is devoted to ethnological research on Naxi (Chao 2012: 56, see also 53). Lijiang is in fact a prefecture-level city, with an administrative reach that includes the Ninglang Yi Autonomous County, which means that it is also the source of state funding for the ethnological institute in Ninglang (founded in the late 1990s) where the other Nuosu ethnologists whom I know work.

Without wishing to overstate the parallels to the Naxi case, many of the Nuosu to whom I showed Winnington's book were intrigued that he was a British communist who had arrived in Ninglang to document the dismantling of Nuosu slavery (see Figure 3.2). As they saw it, Winnington had come to inform the British of the important role that the Nuosu held in China's modern history. They were not concerned that Winnington would have shared the Chinese view that their forebears had been members of a 'slave society', following the Marxian-Morganian criteria in vogue among Chinese ethnologists at the time. They rather expected that Chinese and other communist scholars of the 1950s would have taken the ethno-political stance of openly praising the efforts of the People's Liberation Army (PLA) to disband Nuosu slavery, while dismissing Nuosu animistic religion as 'superstition' (Winnington 1959: 118). Mitsu even magnanimously forgave any ethnographic mistakes that Winnington had made, noting that a foreigner who visited Ninglang in his day would have found it difficult to communicate with full fluency. Some youth pined over the rapid loss of older generations who, as Winnington's photos showed, had weathered the Democratic Reforms. Although Winnington's book was largely (and often entirely) unreadable to them in English, these Nuosu felt it stirred memories and made them crave opportunities to discover more about their history. It was especially important that Winnington appeared to have spread their fame far and wide. Several Nuosu whose relatives were mentioned in Winnington's book even drew the conclusion that it was a best-seller in England, where their elders had become household names. Why else would I make a film that documented their life histories?

Images of Ethno-history and Ethno-politics

Tellingly, Winnington's photos evoked memories of past generations that resonated with conceptualizations of what Nuosu 'culture' is today. There is an increasing circulation of Nuosu images in Ninglang via television, popular films and karaoke-friendly music videos in DVD or VCD form, billboards promoting tourism in the county centre, and publications, calendars, posters or even beer labels produced in Ninglang or across the border in Sichuan Province. Nuosu websites nowadays double as platforms for imagining the many forms that Nuosu culture may take within and beyond China (Kraef 2013a, 2013b, 2014). Images, music, videos and articles from these websites are downloaded to mobile telephones that travel between the Ninglang County centre and its rural villages. While electricity may be intermittent in the villages, where computers are (except in some schools) still a rarity, popular Nuosu images are nonetheless prolific in almost every Nuosu home.

During my 2015 trip, I learned that the local Ninglang television station had, within the space of just a few years, started producing programmes on local cultural events. This was brought to my attention in a charming (although somewhat disarming) fashion, when a dignitary of Ninglang invited me to lunch with Mitsu because he had seen us judging the Torch Festival competitions on television the night before. I had not yet seen the programme or known that it had aired. When I returned to Ninglang in 2016, I got to know the television station employees much better, and they regaled me with clips of the programmes they were currently editing or had recently completed. These programmes featured interviews with former cadres and knowledgeable persons who work closely with the local ethnological institute and sometimes publish in their in-house journal. It was clear that ethno-historical documentaries, produced for a popular local audience, were on the rise in Ninglang.

Revealingly, for its programmes on local history, the Ninglang television station made moving film clips of photographs originally taken in the mid 1950s, which are displayed in the permanent collections of the county's Old Museum and New Museum. Some of these photographs have dark themes, such as portraits of exhausted or abused former slaves, the items used for delegating corporeal punishment to them (e.g. stocks, shackles, manacles and whips), and guerrilla warfare between Nuosu and the PLA. Other photos offer what are meant to be uplifting themes, such as panoramic snapshots of the

PLA marching into Ninglang to dismantle slavery and serf-holding, rally speeches by former slaves and the gifting of provisions to locals during the formation of the Ninglang Yi Autonomous County, or the introduction of 'cultural' gifts, such as travelling circus performances in Ninglang by troupes of the Han nationality (the ethnic majority of China). While most locals in Ninglang are unaware that these photos are displayed in their museums, they are familiar with the history of slavery across the Liangshan mountains and the images that often accompany it. That history is circulated, in various official and unofficial versions, through stories from the generation who witnessed the Democratic Reforms, state education, China's policies on minority ethnic groups, popular television, state-funded ethnological work, and Nuosu or foreign anthropologists. Photographic and filmic understandings of the Democratic Reforms in Ninglang – which held its sixtieth anniversary celebrations during my 2016 visit – thus routinely inform local imaginings of Nuosu life, and often in sensational ways.

As Emily Chao observes, Chinese-made films and television series typically reflect the official and popular views that there are 'biopolitical' differences between the Han and ethnic minorities, as well as between urban and rural persons – differences that even 'fifth-generation filmmakers' have continued to propagate (2012: 76). Ethnologists in China, such as the Naxi scholars with whom Chao has worked, often perpetuate essentialistic thinking because, 'as intellectuals educated in Chinese universities, they themselves had long ago internalized Han constructions of prestige which were informed by imperial prejudices toward minority ethnic groups . . . despite the contemporary Chinese state's valorization of ethnic difference' (ibid.: 76). Due to their educational background, the Nuosu scholars I know entertained similar imaginings of Nuosu alterity and Han affinity, which they occasionally harnessed when engaging with a foreign anthropologist, such as myself.

Yet my Nuosu interlocutors, whether they were scholars or rural persons, never appeared to have exclusively internalized the Han aesthetics of prestige. Instead, they tended to shuttle between valorizing the chiefly Nuosu, but also Han, conceptualizations of a good, full life. Some ethno-historians in Ninglang, such as Mitsu, worked closely with local cadres to promote Nuosu interests by co-authoring publications, judging Torch Festival competitions (as a cultural and civic duty) and discussing how to improve life for everyone in the county. These scholars explicitly propagated what I have elsewhere called the Nuosu 'mode of building esteem', but were savvy at doing this in dialogue with Han sensibilities (Swancutt 2016c). When navigating local and official conceptualizations of ethno-politics, these ethnic minority scholars thus entered the social space that Koen Wellens calls:

> the grey zone [which] is an area of overlap where grass-root minority cadres and local minority intellectuals such as schoolteachers are involved in a mediation process between the local presence of the party-state and minority culture. They are part of both the party-state apparatus and minority society and as such they both 'translate' central policies into local implementation while at the same time claiming space within the administrative system for certain aspects of local minority culture. (2009: 445)

Not surprisingly, this careful politicking affected how our filmmaking team imagined and ultimately produced relationships of alterity and affinity, both on and off screen. Our team could not help but notice that ethno-politics underpinned the sixtieth anniversary celebrations of Ninglang, which became an autonomous county in the People's Republic of China at the onset of the Democratic Reforms in 1956. We observed that, throughout summer 2016, the Ninglang television station was completely booked up with filming events for this celebration. Mitsu therefore regaled the station, and anyone helping us on the film, with visions of its scholarly and ethno-political benefits, which he added would spread Ninglang's name in its sixtieth anniversary year. While he could not convince any of the station's already overstretched workers to join our team in shooting or editing the film, he did gain permission for us to use the station's editing machines when they were not in use. Through Mitsu's ethno-politicking, the generosity of the Ninglang television station, and the Nuosu who took part in our project, we completed and screened our 68-minute film within the span of two months. Before showing, though, how we shot, edited and screened our film, I wish to briefly discuss our use of 'filmic imaginaries' and what I call the 'anthropological imaginarium'.

Anthropological Imaginaries of the Invisible

Earlier I mentioned that alterity evokes difference, whereas affinity evokes similarity or commonality. These terms describe the qualities of relationships between persons. But anthropologists also use these terms as heuristic tools, or imaginaries, through which they conceptualize and experience the world. Neither the 'imagination' nor 'imaginaries' are equated in recent anthropology with the unreal or make-believe 'fantasy' (Mittermaier 2011: 18–20; see also Poirier 2005: 7–11 and Stewart 2012: 13–21). Instead, the term 'imaginary' evokes phenomena that unfold in people's minds and wider worlds, taking on pretty much any form of reflection or imagination, which might gain wider currency through scholarly reflections, film plots, religious visions, prophetic dreams and so on. Imaginaries that become formative, ontologically speaking, to how people conceptualize or experience the world may acquire dramatic 'world-making' effects, in the sense given to the term by Abramson and Holbraad (2014). Famous examples of world-making imaginaries include Paul's vision at Damascus that led to his conversion and became a formative moment for Christianity, or apparitions of the Virgin Mary at Fátima, which led to a host of sightings and her canonical coronation in the Catholic Church. The invention of film – which unleashed unprecedented imaginaries – was yet another world-making event.

Probably many anthropologists and their interlocutors have been influenced by the techniques of filmmaking, which 'originated at the same time as ethnographic fieldwork became established as a key method of anthropology around the 1900s' (Otto 2013: 195). The influence of film on anthropological imaginaries should therefore not be underestimated. Despite this, it is still not a conventional choice to focus the camera on relationships between anthropologists and their interlocutors. This technique was, however, harnessed by Christian Suhr, Ton Otto and Steffen Dalsgaard in their film titled *Ngat Is Dead – Studying Mortuary Traditions* (2009). Otto explains in a companion article to the film that he chose to become a featured character on screen, together with his adoptive fieldwork family among the Balua of Papua New Guinea, so that he could fulfil Ngat's final request (Otto 2013: 200). In line with Ngat's wishes, Otto participated in his mortuary rites, arranged for them to be filmed, and held a local screening of the film when the initial editing was completed. As Otto explains, this plan enabled local Baluan reflections on the film to arise in dialogue with the views of Suhr, Otto and Dalsgaard. Each of these views was then collectively incorporated into the final production work. Looking back at the film retrospectively, from a position of hindsight, Otto observes:

> The film created a reflexive space both for the filmmakers and for the people involved, who welcomed it as a recording of their traditional practices. The method of feedback enhanced and focused this reflexive space and through our recordings of it we were able to integrate this with the recording of the film. (Ibid.: 201)

One key contribution of Suhr, Otto and Dalsgaard's film, then, is that it reveals the relationships of alterity and affinity between the (foreign) anthropological filmmaking team and their Baluan interlocutors. It is, of course, not necessarily easy to capture moments of 'relating' on film with a compelling anthropological imaginary. This is the case even though Otto, drawing on David MacDougall (1998) and Jennifer Deger (2006), rightly suggests that images facilitate dialogues between anyone involved in filmmaking because 'people can easily relate to images even though they do it in their own culturally specific ways' (2013: 197). Filmmakers who want relationships of affinity or alterity to surface on screen often must use imaginative techniques that make them visible to audiences. Or, as Christian Suhr and Rane Willerslev suggest, filmmakers who wish to evoke the often-invisible qualities of social life must harness techniques that can 'break the visual "skin" of the world' (2013: 4).

In a provocative article titled 'Can Film Show the Invisible?', Suhr and Willerslev propose that ethnographic films created with 'the right balance between realism and constructivism, simplicity and complexity, resonance and dissonance . . . can push us beyond the frontiers of the visible world into the uncharted regions of the invisible' (2012: 294). Their idea is not that film can reveal what is ordinarily invisible to the human eye, such as spirits, other people's dreams, dark matter or the integrated forces of global capitalism. But they propose that film can '*evoke*' imaginaries that lie outside the field of human vision, which enable audiences to experience on screen a close approximation of the total ethnographic experience that unfolds in the field (ibid.: 282, see also 290–91). They build their argument on Maurice Merleau-Ponty's concept of 'the view from everywhere', in which vision comes in layers, starting from the omnipresent God's-eye view of the world that enables a transparent perception of it from all angles at once. Suhr and Willerslev argue, though, that filmmakers must cater to the more limited field of human vision, which encompasses only one or several perspectives, while also detecting the '*absence*' of hidden angles just beyond the line of sight (ibid.: 286). It is thus possible for film audiences to detect the subtler elements of ethnographic experience on film, even if they do not see them unfold in their totality. To fully capitalize on the visual capacities of their audiences, filmmakers must therefore evoke the typically invisible elements of ethnography (see Figure 3.3). This would appear, on the surface of things, to be a tall order.

Suhr and Willerslev, though, propose that the invisible can be evoked through the classic (albeit simple) film technique of montage, which can illuminate the ethnography, as much as possible, in the round (2012: 284). They suggest that montage is effective because it enables more than the juxtaposition of frames in the editing stages of a film. Montage surfaces in cases where the filmmaker avoids cutting frames, so that an extensive 'long take – the hallmark of observational cinema – is transformed into the most disruptive and disconcerting of montage effects' that forces the viewer to penetrate layers of depth and detail in the image and come closer to obtaining the omnipresent God's-eye view of it (ibid.: 291). Depending on how filmmakers unleash their imaginaries through editing techniques, they argue, 'the montage of ethnographic films provides us with a complementary and resourceful means of making us imagine other people's worlds' (ibid.: 293). Film can thus go a step further than evoking everyday lived experiences; it can present audiences with the filmmaker's imaginaries of those lived experiences, some of which may be built upon ethnographically-inspired reflection. It is for this reason that Suhr and Willerslev (2013: 5) elsewhere suggest the need for transposing the filmic technique of montage to anthropological theory-making, which is often so heavily oriented towards producing a transparent argument that it occludes the invisible. They make the important point that:

> The disruptive power of montage is especially in need when a theory's desire for laying bare and illuminating the invisible has become so dominant that it is driven towards total and unambiguous visibility. As scholars who have undertaken long-term training in making other peoples' worlds intelligible, anthropologists are perhaps especially disposed to the dangers of such total luminosity. It is not necessarily pleasant or comfortable to allow the invisible and its alterity to play its part in analysis. (Suhr and Willerslev 2013: 5)

Besides montage, there are other 'disruptive' techniques that filmmakers can harness in the service of revealing their imaginaries to audiences. Consider, for instance, how filmic imaginaries may follow a storyboard, script or ad hoc filmmaking choices, including the use of 'fictional' staged scenes. These devices may even be used in cases where filmmakers wish to allow the ethnography, rather than its storyboard, to surface. As Zamorano Villarreal (this volume) observes, both ethnographic film and what is called 'indigenous film' take many forms. There is no one consensus on how to make a good film, while any film may potentially reveal relationships of affinity and alterity. To paraphrase Suhr and Willerslev (2013: 5) again, though, it is not necessarily a drawback if these relationships are never shown in full and unambiguous terms to an audience. Ethnographic films that become world-making are likely, I propose, to showcase a unique imaginarium that blurs the boundaries between self/similarity/affinity and other/difference/alterity rather extensively (see Figure 3.4).

I borrow the term 'imaginarium' explicitly from the title of Terry Gilliam's (2009) film, *The Imaginarium of Doctor Parnassus*, which features the surrealistic imagination of a 'Doctor' who stars in a travelling caravan show. Gilliam's film pivots around the Doctor's stage performances, where he is seated on a glass pedestal, ostensibly levitating in an act of meditation that makes his imagination visible to audiences. Flanked by co-performers who soar aloft on Victorian theatre wires, the mechanics of the Doctor's imagination appear to be simple products of old-fashioned stagecraft. But as some audience members learn by going backstage, where they penetrate the inner workings of the show, the Doctor's imagination is more complex than it had appeared to be. Audience members who go backstage inadvertently enter the Doctor's imagination, where they witness the landscape transform from Victorian theatre to a surrealistic virtual reality that no one can fully control. All the invisible elements of the Doctor's imagination are not only made visible, but freely merge with – and even become a platform for – the imaginations of these audience members. Wayward audience members are thus forced to co-author with the Doctor (and anyone else who has entered his imagination) altogether new imaginaries that exceed themselves.

Now I suggest there are some rather anthropological conceptualizations of affinity and alterity at work in Gilliam's film. On the one hand, showing the Doctor's imagination on stage provides light entertainment to audiences, who can relate to the images they see on their own terms – much like Otto (2013: 197) suggests happens with the reception of any image. In these moments, no effort is made to jointly craft an imaginary that exceeds the biography or authorship of a single person. But on the other hand, when audience members gain backstage access to the Doctor's imagination, the collective imaginings of the Doctor and his audience give rise to surreal, and rather filmic, world-making effects. Distinctions between self and other (or affinity and alterity) are no longer in anyone's full control. Audience members no longer simply watch a production, but are transported by it in ways that mimic the vertiginous effects of a film. Bruce Kapferer (2014) highlights how film enfolds audiences within the specific imaginaries that it unleashes, through his admirable study of the affinities between Sri Lankan exorcism rituals and Stanley Kubrick's (1968) *2001: A Space Odyssey*. In yet another work that builds chiefly on Gilles Deleuze, Kapferer reminds us that cinema operates through special technologies that envelop audiences within the filmic imaginary:

> Most especially, Deleuze argues that in cinema, while the audience (as in theatre) is in a fixed relation to the screen, the movement of images across the screen operates to continually shift subject positions and realign their relations. That is, through the movement of images on the screen subject positioning and perspective is continually changing – the subject in the situation of the audience is routinely re-positioned through the organization of images. The audience is not always in a reflective distanced situation but becomes one with the changing images on the screen. (Kapferer 2013b: 10; see also 2013c)

Seen in this light, Gilliam's plot for *The Imaginarium of Doctor Parnassus* presents audiences with a slippage between theatrical imagination and the filmic imaginarium. His work plays with the theatre/film distinction, where the understanding is that film moves images on screen (often through montage) at a much more continuous pace than tends to occur in theatre – except, of course, in cases where theatrical productions incorporate film.

Whereas theatrical imaginaries tend to be enjoyed at a distance by performers and audiences who occupy distinct physical spaces, these spaces break down entirely in the filmic imaginarium, where performers and audiences co-produce a mutually enveloping vision that blurs the boundaries between them. What Gilliam's film offers anthropologists, then, is the potent suggestion that – through their filmic imaginariums – they can evoke relationships of affinity and alterity in ways that exceed themselves, their interlocutors and their audiences. To show how this works, I now return to the discussion of how our filmmaking team produced an imaginarium of Alan Winnington's legacy among the Nuosu of Ninglang.

Shooting the Imaginarium: The Anthropologist on Film

In the early days of our filmmaking project, Jiarimuji and I chose the film's title, which was designed to do several things at once. The film is titled *1956. A Briton in the Cool Mountains of China*, which we translated into Chinese (1956. 一个英国人在凉山) and Nuosu (1956. ꆏꉢꀕꇖꊪꑌꁨꆏꈐꑭ). Jiarimuji wanted '1956' to be the main title of the film, since in China it evokes the watershed year in which the Democratic Reforms were launched across the nation's southwest. Alan Winnington is the Briton referred to in the title, who reached Ninglang in December 1956 to conduct research for his book, *The*

Slaves of the Cool Mountains, after which the film was also named. On another level, the term 'Briton' applies to me too, as an anthropologist based in the United Kingdom who came to document Winnington's legacy among the Nuosu. Finally, the film's title evokes the Nuosu residents of the Cool Mountains, who appear in both Winnington's book and the film. We wanted the title to specifically evoke the relationships of affinity and alterity between ourselves, the persons we filmed and Winnington. Our full 'cast' was thus an assemblage of persons from 1956 to the present day. However, we had only vague ideas then about the kind of footage we would receive.

From the very start, we envisioned that our conversations on screen would reveal not only local memories of Winnington, but how (if at all) Nuosu nowadays connect their experiences of 'internationalization' (Ch. *guojihua* 国际化) to Winnington's journalism, Nuosu ethnology and even anglophone anthropology. Our filmmaking project explicitly thus cross-cut different moments in time and space, by bringing Winnington's journalism into dialogue with life in present-day Ninglang. It also required marrying together quite different ethno-historical and anthropological approaches that could reveal, as Ty Tengan (this volume) suggests for Oceanian anthropology, how 'the pasts and the lived genealogical relationships to such pasts [become] generative for' all those involved in its production. This was a rather ambitious programme, given our low budget, two-month production time, and inexperience in collaborating on a film.

Our total filmmaking team was comprised of a Nuosu anthropologist (Jiarimuji), a 'British' anthropologist originally from Los Angeles (myself), a Nuosu ethno-historian (my co-director), a Chinese PhD student in ethnology at Minzu University of China (our main cinematographer) and my co-director's two daughters, one of whom did our main editing and Nuosu translation, the other of whom was our driver and second cinematographer. Although Jiarimuji had produced and taken part in several ethnographic films in China, he could only offer his input from a distance, as he was conducting fieldwork in a town that was several hours' drive from Ninglang. As I was a complete novice at filmmaking, and my co-director's understanding of it was drawn from watching ethnological films that informed his writing, it was our good fortune to recruit the student ethnologist as our cinematographer. Her visions of the film were foundational to its narrative, as well as to how it was shot, edited, screened and eventually emerged in its final form.

My co-director got straight down to business, saying that we would need to know the 'storyboard' (Ch. *gushi* 故事) of the film in advance. He was echoed by our cinematographer, who had made a couple of short ethnographic films before, and his elder daughter. Each of them felt that a film is only successful when the filmmakers have a clear narrative in mind before they shoot any footage. They were concerned that none of our team members, except for myself or Jiarimuji who was away from Ninglang, had read any of Winnington's book in advance. I did not consider this to be especially problematic, given that our interlocutors were unlikely to have read Winnington either. But the rest of the team insisted on learning everything about Winnington's book – even (so I felt) to the point of understanding it with the aforementioned 'total and unambiguous visibility' that is prized by anthropologists (Suhr and Willerslev 2013: 5). On several occasions, I was requested to provide an offhand spoken synopsis of Winnington's book, which followed the map he took to reach Ninglang, what he did when he arrived, who he met, where he went in the county and so forth (see Figure 3.5). Due to time constraints, though, we only discussed a few key points of Winnington's book and made a list of the persons and places named within it, before charting an organic path into the shooting process.

We shot the main footage within just six days. Over the remaining weeks of the project, we obtained additional footage at Ninglang's Old Museum, New Museum, and its recently opened Luguhu Airport. The Ninglang television station also kindly shared with us their footage of the airport, which we used to produce the film's closing sequence. Our main shooting unfolded rapidly, although I was ill with a heavy cold throughout it. Footage was obtained in the Ninglang County centre, several Nuosu villages on its outskirts, and neighbouring Yongsheng County. In total, we filmed eleven interviewees who shared memories of Winnington, the persons and places mentioned in his book, the Democratic Reforms and the years that followed them, and the internationalization that gradually unfolded through sixty years of change in Ninglang.

While shooting the film, my co-director already started to envision how our unseen footage could be transformed through the editing process into a storyboard narrative. He anticipated that our greatest difficulty would be finding anyone who had heard of, let alone known about, Winnington. Most of our interlocutors would have been young children sixty years ago, which meant that any memories of Winnington's visit were likely to have been fuzzy. It was also possible that our interlocutors would only vaguely recall the Nuosu persons in Winnington's book, many of whom were slaves given common first names, which meant they could be easily mistaken for someone else. We thus chose to make a virtue of necessity, by incorporating the uncertainty surrounding memories of Winnington into the film, making it one of our key imaginaries. Early into the shooting, my co-director already suggested that the film's opening vignette could unfold through clips we had just filmed, in which we had asked our interlocutors if they had heard of or seen Winnington before (see Figure 3.6). Building on this, my co-director and our driver approached the rest of our shooting work with several recurrent questions in hand. Genuinely excited by what we were uncovering, this father-daughter team sought to emulate the journalistic approach of the local television station or even of Winnington. I was advised to routinely follow a list of scripted questions about Winnington's visit, internationalization, sixty years of change in Ninglang and so on. Although I had reservations about this, as did our cinematographer, we found that whenever I failed to ask scripted questions, our driver and co-director quickly leapt in to ask them. They wanted to shape the interviews in ways that aligned with Nuosu perspectives on what a good film happens to be.

As we progressed with the shooting, we uncovered local memories that intersected with Winnington's book. These unfolded through interviews held at the homes (or, in one case, the office) of persons who could share knowledge that evoked Winnington's narrative. Often seated at the host's request, I simultaneously 'was' and 'acted' the role of the foreign anthropologist on film, while my co-director and his elder daughter 'were' and 'acted' the roles of local Nuosu experts. But on the third day of shooting, our cinematographer quietly complained to me that this interview-based, ethno-historical approach gave the film a false veneer, under which a much 'truer' anthropological film could have emerged, if we had the additional time to plan, film and edit a much longer version (our film is sixty-eight minutes long). Initially, she had envisaged adding behind-the-scenes clips of our filmmaking, to reveal the debates underpinning our work of evoking alterity and affinity on screen. I agreed that she had suggested a brilliant approach to the film, although it would have required exponentially more production time.

Our cinematographer's complaints resurfaced throughout the day, before she finally delivered an extended monologue on anthropology and film over dinner at a village restaurant. She argued that an ethnographic film should avoid brisk sit-down interviews, give more time to unobtrusive filming that uncovers the local's point of view, and thereby reflect an anthropological perspective. After listening for some time, our driver insisted there are merits to the 'native' (Ch. *bentu* 本土) perspective that she and her father had on the filmmaking. It did not matter, she said, whether the film aligned with an anthropological or ethnological approach. The filmmaking had already enabled her to see Nuosu cultural history and memory in a far fuller light, as she anticipated would be the case for our local audiences, given the linguistic and cultural fluency that she and her father brought to the team. Finally, she reminded our cinematographer that, as she was not Nuosu and hailed from Beijing, she was less informed about local history and culture. While it was obvious that our driver had presented an essentialized picture of Nuosu, which elided the differences between urban ethno-historians and rural non-scholarly laypersons, we all agreed to accept the filmmaking would have limitations. To finish on a note of humour, our cinematographer added that I should have filmed the debate that had just unfolded, as footage of it would have enabled our anthropological imaginaries to surface on screen, in tandem with the Nuosu ones.

Each of us, then, acquiesced to the plan that Nuosu ethno-historical imaginaries would be more prominent than the anthropological imaginaries in our film. Intrigued that our film would showcase a Nuosu ethno-historical imagination, I wondered whether it might reveal how – as Gey Pin Ang and Caroline Gatt observe (this volume) – 'collaboration affords mutual learning' about what anthropology can be. Yet I also did not want to relinquish the possibility that our film might speak to what João de Pina-Cabral (this volume) calls the anthropological 'ecumene', which is comprised of both ordinary persons and the scholars of diverse anthropological, ethnological, ethno-historical and other disciplinary traditions.

Following my co-director's suggestions – which our cinematographer increasingly came to echo – I therefore hesitantly agreed to stage several clips that mimicked Chinese journalistic filmmaking. Their idea was to prepare transitional takes between frames, so that during the editing we would be equipped to enable our storyboard to surface. Although no one knew what this storyboard might entail, my co-director encouraged me to speak in English for several additional clips, where I introduced key places that Winnington visited (see Figure 3.7). He and I also produced an entirely contrived clip, in which I suggested that we should visit a person whom we had just interviewed (see Figure 3.8). Over the next few days, I involuntarily slipped into a popular mode of reportage, and wondered afterwards if I had inadvertently honed this style when judging the Torch Festival with television cameras pointed at me a week earlier.

Certainly, this quasi-journalism was more intrusive than observational ethnographic filmmaking. But my co-director grounded his approach on what he felt was an intelligible and imaginative platform for our interlocutors. Some of our interviews were illuminating, even if they were quasi-scripted by leading questions. Yet other dialogues were more natural, but less useful for the film. Our interlocutors appeared to view us as anthropologists and ethnologists trailing after and, to some extent, mimicking Winnington on his trek through Ninglang sixty years earlier. As though to underscore this, our cinematographer filmed many clips of Winnington's book. She was already envisioning how we would enable transitions between frames, while evoking the layers of ethno-history that connected us to Winnington's volume. It was not until the editing phase, though, that we assembled our filmic layers of ethno-historical and anthropological imagining.

Editing Imaginaries: Layers of Ethno-history and Anthropology

After the shooting, we devoted several days to selecting the scenes we would edit. During this time, my co-director wrote his storyboard for the film. Following the chronology of our footage, he stressed the resonances between it and key themes or persons mentioned in Winnington's book. My co-director's second daughter, who had trained in filmmaking at university, became our main editor. She started the initial selection of scenes at night, when the television station's machines were available for us to use. Much of our work was done in 'night shifts', from 6 p.m. until 10 p.m., or on weekends. As we had chosen to make the film trilingual, with Chinese and English subtitles throughout, she also produced the Nuosu to Chinese subtitles. I then produced the Chinese to English subtitles. We started to run out of time, but were nonetheless beset by power outages caused by monsoon rains or the summer repair work to Ninglang's electrics.

On one particularly late evening of editing, I discussed the film with both our cinematographer and editor. We had already completed the subtitles and selected the best scenes. All we had left to do was complete the opening and closing credits, music and subtitles. At that point, we paused to ask whether we had indeed made our filmic imaginaries surface. Both our cinematographer and editor felt that something invisible was missing. But they did not know how we could further illuminate how our Nuosu interlocutors conceptualized their history, internationalization or involvement in contemporary ethno-historical and anthropological scholarship. Having watched the film, I also felt it was flat. While the footage revealed points in common between the stories of the Nuosu persons we filmed, these were not yet explicitly linked to Winnington's work. We made the collective decision to telephone my co-director, who had been in Kunming throughout the editing process. He had not seen the edited film and we wanted to ask his advice on how to make our filmic imaginaries surface.

Over the telephone, an extended debate unfolded between myself, my co-director, our cinematographer and editor about how we were going to make the 'invisible' quality of our film come to light. We all agreed that a 'good film' must evoke the invisible in some way. In our case, this meant revealing new ethno-historical and anthropological imaginaries. But we wondered how our footage would enable this. My co-director tried to reassure us by suggesting that it is nearly impossible to reveal the filmic imaginaries in an ethno-historical film, which is comprised mostly of sit-down interviews. Echoing the views of the television station reporters, he added that any ethnographic film is tediously 'long-winded' and 'troublesome' (Ch. *luosuo* 啰嗦) to make. Promising to return soon to Ninglang, he agreed to comment more fully on the edited footage. Once we ended the phone call, our editor and cinematographer said that we should forget what my co-director had just said. The three of us decided that more needed to be done to unleash our imaginarium for the audience.

Under pressure to complete in time, and with no one else offering fresh ideas, I suggested a way forward. I pointed out that while my co-director's storyboard contained key scenes, it did not show how they unfolded in tandem with Winnington's travels. Nor did it reveal how the dialogues we held with our interlocutors pivoted around layered experiences and conceptualizations of affinity or alterity. We wanted to show, through filmic imaginaries, the layers of ethno-historical and anthropological scholarship that connected ourselves, our interlocutors and (potentially) our audiences to Winnington's volume. My proposal, then, was that we re-sequence the film in line with Winnington's itinerary. This would mean presenting our footage anachronistically and allowing it to deviate from the order in which we filmed the interviews. Following this simple technique of montage would allow our imaginaries to surface, but only if we incorporated title card 'signs' with captions that would signpost the stops Winnington made in his travels through Ninglang (see Figure 3.9). Some of these signs could be made by producing film clips of photographs from Winnington's book. Our cinematographer and editor agreed this was our best solution, although it would be labour-intensive.

Layering Winnington's 'roadmap' onto our footage was a significant move. Through it, we created an anthropological imaginarium that showcased our behind-the-scenes efforts at evoking affinity and alterity. Our title cards of Winnington's stops were a classic use of montage that invited viewers to consider how our imaginaries might connect them to Winnington's volume. Much like our interlocutors in Ninglang, who cross-cut different moments in time and space when reflecting on Winnington's legacy, our audiences were encouraged to imagine having both a relationship of affinity with Winnington (by learning details about him through the film) and a relationship of alterity with him (as they witnessed his life and work being objectified as an ethno-historical project). They were also invited to reflect on our imaginaries of the relationships between ethno-history, anthropology and life in present-day Ninglang. The decision to produce the film in this comparatively 'staged' and quasi-journalistic light may not have presented Nuosu life according to the conventions of observational cinema, but our anachronistic editing and use of montage did enable us to offer up an imaginarium of the multiple ways in which the Winnington project evoked alterity and affinity within and beyond Ninglang.

When my co-director arrived in Ninglang several days later, he was pleased with the new storyboard, which echoed his original wish to thoroughly understand Winnington's roadmap and project before we started the shooting. He also was satisfied with the quasi-journalistic style of the film, including our editor's decision to incorporate the staged clip between the two of us so that the storyboard would flow well. Declaring that the film would bring to light the ethnographic imaginaries we had in mind, he felt that it would further increase the fame of Ninglang County. To be sure the whole team agreed, I raised several questions with my co-director, editor and cinematographer, namely: did the film evoke our efforts, with our interlocutors, to traverse sixty years of memories about Alan Winnington? Had we revealed the changes to Ninglang that followed on the heels of the Democratic Reforms? On another level, had we shown our interlocutors' perceptions of us, as ethnologists and anthropologists, whose research perhaps echoed Winnington's study? The team collectively agreed that the film was not bad, given our production time and means. Delighted with the film, my co-director even exclaimed with gusto: 'Thirty years after Alan Winnington's death, we have made him famous'!

Screening the Invisible: The Imaginarium in the Round

Perhaps an hour after we had completed the film, my co-director suggested that he and I give the film's premiere at a rural school in Ninglang that very evening. Driving to the school would only take a couple of hours and would enable me to fit in several screenings in Ninglang, and another scheduled in Kunming, within my remaining time in China. Over the next five days, then, my co-director and I screened the film at two local schools and the Ninglang television station. We planned to do the final edits after the screenings in Ninglang, so that we could incorporate audience suggestions and our own notes on the film.

We held the first screening at a village middle school with a classroom of around fifty children aged ten, many of whom become engrossed in the film. When it ended, they politely applauded the film, and following my co-director's encouragement, added responses to a brief questionnaire I had made on how the film might have affected them. Their teacher also filled out the questionnaire, congratulated us for our work on the film, and seemed to enjoy it overall. As these were younger children, their impressions of our imaginarium were difficult to gauge, but they did understand that the film was meant to bring them into dialogue with sixty years of local history and scholarship.

The second screening was held at a prestigious high school in the Ninglang County centre, for a classroom of over one hundred students aged sixteen to eighteen. These local students found certain scenes highly amusing, and given both the intricacy of Nuosu lineage politics and the status acquired through storytelling, they were curious to find out who said what. At the end of the screening, some students critiqued the noisy cockerels and motor sounds in certain scenes. While my co-director replied that an ethnographic film is enhanced by the local context, I wondered how accessible our ethnographic imaginaries were to this county-based audience of elite students. However, the students appeared to enjoy the film, took care in adding their thoughts to the questionnaire, and several congratulated us for making a film on their history.

Our third screening was held at the Ninglang television station for a small audience of mostly elderly persons who appeared in the film, or their immediate family members. As my co-director stated that 'older people' should not be burdened with writing too much on forms, they only volunteered their names on the questionnaire. During the screening, though, these persons appeared to be intrigued at watching themselves and their peers on film. A few audience members even alternated between watching the film and looking at the person who was speaking on screen. When the film ended, one elderly man suggested a correction to the Chinese subtitles that named a long-dead person mentioned in one of our interlocutor's stories. The son of a noble family who appeared in our film also requested a copy of it, explaining that it was a new repository of his family history that could be screened at home. After promising that my co-director would get him a copy that included our final edits, we added the final corrections to the subtitles and completed the film.

When I left Ninglang in early September 2016, I travelled to Kunming, where I stayed on the campus of Yunnan Minzu University. Jiarimuji had already arranged our next screening in an ethnographic film class. We had an audience of over one hundred entrance-level undergraduate students, including my co-director's son who was studying at a different university in Kunming, and members of the general public with an interest in Nuosu culture. Like the high school students in Ninglang, this audience found certain scenes highly amusing. Jiarimuji even burst out laughing at the staged take between my co-director and myself, whispering that he knew the moment he saw us talking on screen that the scene was a fictional device 'arranged for the camera' (Ch. *baipaide* 摆拍的). The screening was followed by a half-hour question-and-answer session in Chinese, where we received feedback on our imaginarium. Some students wondered what the film's message was meant to be, and, as in the high school student screening, critiqued the loud cockerels and motors. Others engaged with the film in ways that revealed our imaginarium had provoked reflections about alterity and affinity.

One student at Yunnan Minzu University wondered if the film reflected an 'Orientalist' view, as if it had been shot entirely through the lens of my own imaginary. I replied that, since the film was created by a team of mostly Nuosu, it was meant to showcase the imaginaries of both local Nuosu persons and myself. Yet the student's question was apt, given that my co-director and cinematographer ensured I would appear in as many takes as possible, thereby simulating my lead role in the interviews. Through our imaginarium, we evoked the ambiguities underpinning relationships between ethno-history, anthropology and life in present-day Ninglang (and indeed, across wider China) – ambiguities which, to cite Suhr and Willerslev again, reminded us that 'it is not necessarily pleasant or comfortable to allow the invisible and its alterity to play its part in analysis' (2013: 5). In this case, the invisible and its alterity that I evoked on screen, through my role as the white 'British' anthropologist foregrounded by our cinematographer, with Nuosu colleagues at my side, would seem to reflect an anglophone anthropology that positions its interlocutors on a different plane of alterity or even humanity (see Figure 3.10). As Liana Chua and Nayanika Mathur (this volume) suggest, anthropologists from the anglophone tradition bear within their purview 'the lingering prejudices and power structures embedded in their own thought and society', namely the very power relations that Edward W. Said's (1978) *Orientalism* 'made uncomfortably clear'.

The student's query was unsettling enough to have resurfaced in the tea that followed the question-and-answer session, which I had with several academics and master's students. We discussed the ambiguities in our film, which were meant to evoke how each member of our 'cast' (including Winnington) mutually produced our experiences of affinity and alterity. Ironically, this had been invisible to some audience members. However, the anthropologists at Yunnan Minzu University felt that our imaginarium would be visible to the trained anthropologist, even if it was not accessible to new anthropology students. They envisioned that, with extra production time, our film could more fully reveal the imaginaries shared by a team of Nuosu ethno-historians, a Chinese ethnologist and a 'British' anthropologist.

Two months passed before I screened the film's UK premiere on 11 November 2016, as part of the Chinese Visual Festival Club in association with King's College London Film Studies. We had a small audience of roughly fifteen persons, most of whom were Chinese and Euro-American scholars in film studies. They felt the memories, imagination and oral history surrounding Winnington's visit and scholarship were 'wrapped up' in the film. There were also two unexpected visitors at the screening. One was a person who had read Winnington's book shortly after it was first published; the other person was extremely familiar with Winnington's biography. Having agreed to help me contact persons who knew Winnington, they introduced me by email to several of Winnington's friends and former colleagues in Beijing and London. I learned by watching the flow of emails that our imaginarium had taken a whole new, and delightfully unexpected, turn. I was corresponding with members of the British Communist Party, some of whom appeared to have worked with Winnington during the 1950s at *The People's Daily/Morning Star*, a left-leaning British newspaper. Not long after, one of Winnington's Beijing-based contacts requested that I send him a copy of the film, so that he could watch it and perhaps screen it to Party members there.

He also offered to help make the second part of the film, as originally envisioned, by extending an invitation to Jiarimuji to interview him and Winnington's old friends in Beijing. Perhaps the most remarkable feature of our film's imaginarium is that it enabled us to make this unexpected connection to Winnington, which could unleash yet further imaginings of alterity and affinity.

Concluding Remarks: Producing Filmic Imaginaries of Affinity and Alterity

Let me conclude by returning to my earlier point that ethnographic filmmakers can evoke multiple relationships of affinity and alterity. Drawing on Terry Gilliam's (2009) concept of an imaginarium, I have suggested that our filmmaking team's imaginaries were meant to show how Nuosu conceptualize their history, internationalization and involvement in contemporary ethno-historical and anthropological scholarship. To this end, our filmmaking team made ample use of montage, a storyboard that presented our footage anachronistically, and even the quasi-journalistic style favoured by my co-director, who is a Nuosu ethno-historian. Filmic imaginariums, such as the one we produced, do not fall in line with the conventions of observational cinema that are typically preferred by ethnographic filmmakers. What imaginariums instead evoke are relationships of affinity and alterity that unfold behind the scenes, between ethnographic filmmakers and their interlocutors, thus revealing the often-invisible relationships that underpin a film's conceptualization and production. Anthropological imaginariums invite audiences to reflect on questions about alterity and affinity in filmmaking, such as: how was this film made? Whose visions have appeared on screen? What anthropological (or other) imaginaries were unleashed in this work? Was this film Orientalist? Can I relate to the film, its filmmakers or their interlocutors? What voices were mobilized in this film?

Every anthropological work, whether film or prose, is to some extent an imaginarium. This is why ethnographic films are open to the same critical debates that have shaped ethnographic writing for more than thirty years, which start from the premise that there is always an imaginative reconstruction of ethnographic experience (Geertz 1973; Clifford and Marcus 1986). But just how imaginatively ethnographic experience should be (re)presented to audiences and readers remains an open question. Anthropologists may endeavour to produce the closest approximation of an ethnographic 'original', or they may evoke it through imaginaries that exceed the total ethnographic experience. I have suggested that ethnographic films are particularly likely to have world-making effects where they can reveal the imaginaries of alterity and affinity that enabled their production in the first place. But evoking these imaginaries is a tall order, which probably requires that the anthropologist appears on camera and allows herself to be crafted by all those who envision, shoot, edit and screen the film. Typically invisible elements of the anthropologist on film – and her alterity – may then be evoked by filmmakers. I found this to be perhaps the most surreal element of our filmmaking in Ninglang, but then I knew from the start that my Nuosu colleagues and interlocutors wanted our film to attract fame and opportunities for them. They therefore crafted imaginaries of my biography and my relationships to them on film in ways that could have world-making effects in the future.

Figure 3.1 Title card from *1956. A Briton in the Cool Mountains of China* (Swancutt and Jiarimuji 2016). An introductory moment of the film, showing Alan Winnington's book.

Figure 3.2 Title card from *1956. A Briton in the Cool Mountains of China* (Swancutt and Jiarimuji 2016). Alan Winnington and a group of newly released slaves in Ninglang, circa 1957.

Figure 3.3 Still from *1956. A Briton in the Cool Mountains of China* (Swancutt and Jiarimuji 2016). A photograph of two former slaves wearing their Nuosu finery, which appears in Alan Winnington's book. Off screen, Nuosu villagers suggest the mountains in the distance are probably the same as those which appear behind these former slave girls, whose portrait was taken sixty years ago.

The Anthropological Imaginarium 121

Figure 3.4 Still from *1956. A Briton in the Cool Mountains of China* (Swancutt and Jiarimuji 2016). Nuosu villagers try to recall the two former slaves photographed in Alan Winnington's book. My hands support the book, but I am otherwise off camera.

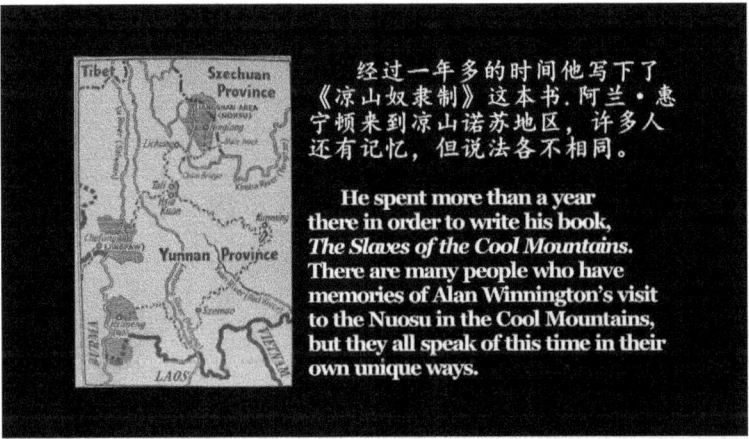

Figure 3.5 Title card from *1956. A Briton in the Cool Mountains of China* (Swancutt and Jiarimuji 2016). Alan Winnington's map from Lijiang to Ninglang.

Figure 3.6 Still from *1956. A Briton in the Cool Mountains of China* (Swancutt and Jiarimuji 2016). Part of the film's opening vignette, where I asked nearly a dozen Nuosu persons if they had heard of or seen Alan Winnington before.

Figure 3.7 Still from *1956. A Briton in the Cool Mountains of China* (Swancutt and Jiarimuji 2016). I introduce Boluo village to our film audience. According to Alan Winnington (1959: 25), Boluo (which he writes as 'Bolo') was the first place in Ninglang that he visited.

The Anthropological Imaginarium 123

Figure 3.8 Still from *1956. A Briton in the Cool Mountains of China* (Swancutt and Jiarimuji 2016). The staged clip, in which my co-director and I discuss how we will visit a person whom we had just finished interviewing.

Figure 3.9 Title card from *1956. A Briton in the Cool Mountains of China* (Swancutt and Jiarimuji 2016). The 'sign' indicating the fifth stop in both Alan Winnington's book and our film. Echoing Winnington (1959: 97–119), the film offers local Nuosu reflections on how freed slaves were formed into work teams during the Democratic Reforms.

Figure 3.10 Still from *1956. A Briton in the Cool Mountains of China* (Swancutt and Jiarimuji 2016). My co-director jokes with a Nuosu woman about my 'foreigner' looks, after she had told us her childhood memories of hiding from Alan Winnington in the highlands of her village. There were local rumours at the time that Winnington was a Tibetan lama who would eat people. As the scene unfolds, this woman confirms that she no longer fears foreigners and is used to seeing them on television. Embarrassed, I laugh at how my alterity, which was often invisible to (or forgotten by) me, surfaces uncomfortably through the 'Orientalism' invoked by my co-director's joke.

Acknowledgements

Fieldwork and filmmaking for this chapter were funded by the Faculty of Arts and Humanities International Collaborations Fund and the REF QR Fund at King's College London. Earlier versions of this chapter benefitted from comments received in the Anthropology Seminar at the University of Roehampton and at the second Culture and Identity workshop between King's College London and Shanghai Jiaotong University on 'Discourse, Life-Writing and Memory'.

Katherine Swancutt is Senior Lecturer in the Anthropology of Religion in the Department of Theology and Religious Studies, King's College London. She is the author of *Fortune and the Cursed: The Sliding Scale of Time in Mongolian Divination* (Berghahn Books, 2012) and co-editor of a special issue of *Social Analysis* titled 'Animism Beyond the Soul: Ontology, Reflexivity, and the Making of Anthropological Knowledge' (2016). Her main area of interest is Inner Asia, where she has conducted fieldwork among Buryat Mongols, Deed Mongols, and the Nuosu of Southwest China. Currently, her work focuses on the ethnographic dreams and fame-building projects of Nuosu scholars, religious specialists and laypersons, which is part of her ongoing contribution to debates within the 'new animism' in anthropology.

References

Abramson, Allen, and Martin Holbraad (eds). 2014. *Framing Cosmologies: The Anthropology of Worlds*. Manchester: Manchester University Press.
Balzer, Marjorie Mandelstam. 2011. *Shamans, Spirituality, and Cultural Revitalization: Explorations in Siberia and Beyond*. New York: Palgrave MacMillan.
Bamo, Ayi, Stevan Harrell and Lunzy Ma. 2007. *Fieldwork Connections: The Fabric of Ethnographic Collaboration in China and America*. Seattle, WA: University of Washington Press.
Chao, Emily. 2012. 'Dongba Culture and the Authenticization of Marginality', in *Lijiang Stories: Shamans, Taxi Drivers, and Runaway Brides in Reform-Era China*. Seattle, WA: University of Washington Press, pp. 49–81.
Chua, Liana. 2015. 'Troubled Landscapes, Troubling Anthropology: Co-Presence, Necessity, and the Making of Ethnographic Knowledge', *Journal of the Royal Anthropological Institute* 21(3): 641–59.
Clifford, James, and George E. Marcus (eds). 1986. *Writing Culture: The Poetics and Politics of Ethnography*. Berkeley, CA, Los Angeles and London: University of California Press.
Deger, Jennifer. 2006. *Shimmering Screens: Making Media in an Aboriginal Community*. Minneapolis, MN: University of Minnesota Press.
Geertz, Clifford. 1973. *The Interpretation of Cultures: Selected Essays by Clifford Geertz*. New York: Basic Books.
Gilliam, Terry (director). 2009. *The Imaginarium of Doctor Parnassus*. Film. Distributed by Metropolitan Filmexport, Lionsgate, and Sony Pictures Classics. (123 minutes).
Goulet, Jean-Guy A., and Bruce Granville Miller (eds). 2007. *Extraordinary Anthropology: Transformations in the Field*. Lincoln, NE: University of Nebraska Press.
Holmes, Douglas R., and George E. Marcus. 2008. 'Collaboration Today and the Re-imagination of the Classic Scene of Fieldwork Encounter', *Collaborative Anthropologies* 1: 81–101.
Humphrey, Caroline. 2008. 'Reassembling Individual Subjects: Events and Decisions in Troubled Times', *Anthropological Theory* 8(4): 357–80.
Kapferer, Bruce. 2013a. 'How Anthropologists Think: Configurations of the Exotic', *Journal of the Royal Anthropological Institute* 19(4): 813–36.
Kapferer, Bruce. 2013b. 'Portrait: Ritual Practice and Anthropological Theory', *Religion and Society: Advances in Research* 4(1): 3–40.

Kapferer, Bruce. 2013c. 'Montage and Time: Deleuze, Cinema, and a Buddhist Sorcery Rite', in Christian Suhr and Rane Willerslev (eds), *Transcultural Montage*. New York: Berghahn Books, pp. 20–39.

Kapferer, Bruce. 2014. 'Cosmology and the Mythic in Kubrick's *2001*: The Imaginary in the Aesthetic of Cinema', in Allen Abramson and Martin Holbraad (eds), *Framing Cosmologies: The Anthropology of Worlds*. Manchester: Manchester University Press, pp. 278–309.

Kraef, Olivia. 2013a. 'The Yi and the Internet: Promoting Ethnicity and Ethnic Identity in Chinese Virtuality', *Pacific Geographies* 39: 26–30.

Kraef, Olivia. 2013b. 'Building Yi (M)other Tongue: Virtual Platforms, Language Maintenance and Cultural Awareness in a Chinese Minority Context', in E. Kasten and T. de Graaf (eds), *Sustaining Indigenous Knowledge: Learning Tools and Community Initiatives for Preserving Endangered Languages and Local Cultural Heritage*. Fürstenberg/Havel: Kulturstiftung Sibirien, pp. 219–48.

Kraef, Olivia. 2014. 'Of Canons and Commodities: The Cultural Predicaments of Nuosu-Yi "Bimo Culture"', *Journal of Current Chinese Affairs* 43(2): 145–79.

MacDougall, David. 1998. *Transcultural Cinema*. Princeton, NJ: Princeton University Press.

Mittermaier, Amira. 2011. *Dreams that Matter: Egyptian Landscapes of the Imagination*. Berkeley, CA, Los Angeles and London: University of California Press.

Otto, Ton. 2013. 'Ethnographic Film as Exchange', *The Asia Pacific Journal of Anthropology* 14(2): 195–205.

Poirier, Sylvie. 2005. *A World of Relationships: Itineraries, Dreams, and Events in the Australian Western Desert*. Toronto: University of Toronto Press.

Rappaport, Joanne. 2008. 'Beyond Participant Observation: Collaborative Ethnography as Theoretical Innovation', *Collaborative Anthropologies* 1: 1–31.

Said, Edward W. 1978. *Orientalism: Western Conceptions of the Orient*. London: Routledge & Kegan Paul.

Stewart, Charles. 2012. *Dreaming and Historical Consciousness in Island Greece*. Cambridge, MA: Harvard University Press.

Suhr, Christian, and Ton Otto (directors and producers) with Steffen Dalsgaard. 2009. *Ngat Is Dead – Studying Mortuary Traditions*. Film. Moesgaard Film. Distributed by Documentary Educational Resources and the Royal Anthropological Institute. (59 minutes).

Suhr, Christian, and Rane Willerslev. 2012. 'Can Film Show the Invisible? The Work of Montage in Ethnographic Filmmaking', *Current Anthropology* 53(3): 282–301.

Suhr, Christian, and Rane Willerslev (eds). 2013. 'Introduction. Montage as an Amplifier of Invisibility', in *Transcultural Montage*. New York: Berghahn Books, pp. 1–15.

Swancutt, Katherine. 2016a. 'The Art of Capture: Hidden Jokes and the Reinvention of Animistic Ontologies in Southwest China', in Katherine Swancutt and Mireille Mazard (eds), *Social Analysis* 60(1), special issue on 'Animism Beyond the Soul: Ontology, Reflexivity, and the Making of Anthropological Knowledge', pp. 74–91.

Swancutt, Katherine. 2016b. 'Religion through the Looking Glass: Fieldwork, Biography, and Authorship in Southwest China and Beyond', *Religion and Society: Advances in Research* 7(1): 51–67.

Swancutt, Katherine. 2016c. 'The Anti-Favour: Ideathesia, Aesthetics, and Obligation in Southwest China', in Nikolette Makovicky and David Henig (eds), *Economies of Favour after Socialism*. Oxford: Oxford University Press, pp. 96–116.

Swancutt, Katherine, and Jiarimuji (producers). 2016. *1956: A Briton in the Cool Mountains of China*. [Chinese Title: 1956. 一个英国人在凉山; Nuosu Title: 1956. ꀉꀉꀉꀉꀉꀉꀉꀉꀉ]. Film. (68 minutes).

Swancutt, Katherine, and Mireille Mazard (eds). 2016. 'Animism Beyond the Soul: Ontology, Reflexivity, and the Making of Anthropological Knowledge', special issue of *Social Analysis* 60(1).

Vitebsky, Piers. 2008. 'Loving and Forgetting: Moments of Inarticulacy in Tribal India', *Journal of the Royal Anthropological Institute* 14(2): 243–61.

Vitebsky, Piers. 2012. 'Repeated Returns and Special Friends: From Mythic Encounter to Shared History', in Signe Howell and Aud Talle (eds), *Returns to the Field: Multitemporal Research and Contemporary Anthropology*. Bloomington: Indiana University Press, pp. 180–202.

Wellens, Koen. 2009. 'Negotiable Rights? China's Ethnic Minorities and the Right to Freedom of Religion', *International Journal on Minority and Group Rights* 16(3): 433–54.

Willerslev, Rane. 2012. *On the Run in Siberia*, trans. Coilín ÓhAiseadha. Minneapolis: University of Minnesota Press.

Winnington, Alan. 1959. *The Slaves of the Cool Mountains: The Ancient Social Conditions and Changes Now in Progress on the Remote South-Western Borders of China*. London: Lawrence & Wishart.

Chapter 4

THE RISKS OF AFFINITY

INDIGENEITY AND INDIGENOUS FILM PRODUCTION IN BOLIVIA

Gabriela Zamorano Villarreal

Indigenous film projects throughout Latin America result from an intersection of three different historical developments during the last three decades. First, most indigenous media projects have emerged in countries where native struggles have gained presence in national politics. For example, in Bolivia this presence ensured the electoral triumph of an indigenous president in 2005, a Constituent Assembly from 2006 to 2007, and a new national constitution and the proclamation as a plurinational state in 2009. Second, since the 1990s, indigeneity as a global discourse on native peoples' rights has increasingly become influential among international institutions, governments and non-governmental organization (NGO) policies, and has been instrumental for the emergence and development of indigenous media projects.[1] And third, indigenous media projects are highly informed by the involvement of the anthropological discipline in defining the 'indigenous', as well as by its relatively recent concerns with the epistemological and political impacts of collaboration and dialogue between anthropologists and their research subjects.

This chapter centres on this last element to explore how the phenomenon of indigenous film production in Bolivia relates to anthropological developments on issues like indigenous struggles, indigeneity, collaboration, epistemological authority, and politics and representation. I pay particular attention to the celebrated notion of affinity, which is central to these anthropological debates.

My analysis draws from two anthropological trends that have been influential in anthropological approaches to indigenous media and indigenous struggles in Latin America. First, I reflect on the emphasis that 'other' anthropologies, such as the literature on 'world anthropologies' and 'anthropologies of the South', place on collaboration and affinity with research subjects (Ribeiro and Escobar 2006; Ribeiro 2014; Krotz 2008, 2010). Second, I engage with anthropological explanations of indigenous media as a turning point in the history of anthropology and ethnographic film (Ginsburg 1995).

Aside from highlighting the inarguable contributions of these debates, throughout this conversation I seek to challenge dichotomous approaches that celebrate affinity as an intrinsically good notion for anthropology, as opposed to alterity as inherently colonial and bad. Through examples of how indigenous media practices speak to the complicated relationship between anthropology and indigeneity, I suggest that alterity is much more present in anthropological practice than most of 'us', contemporary anthropologists concerned with challenging the colonial legacies of the discipline, would like it to be.

I pay particular attention to what I identify as a risk in the anthropological search for *affinity* with its subjects, namely, that it might result in alterizing forms of celebration or even condescension – notions that bring us dangerously close to the discipline's colonial roots that Isak Niehaus and David Sneath discuss in the first chapters of this volume.

The Inescapability of Alterity/the Risks of Affinity

An implicit issue at stake in the analysis of alterity and affinity within anthropology is the complicated epistemological and political impact of collaboration and dialogue between anthropologists and their research subjects. This issue points at a broader tension within influential debates in current anthropology. As a reaction to the fact that most contemporary anthropologists consider *alterity* to be one of the most problematic colonial legacies of the discipline, many scholars draw on *affinity* as a kind of moral value that could break with the colonial and political distances that have historically separated researchers from their research subjects. Concurring with the editors of this volume, this is how many recent anthropological debates, including those within 'other', 'world' or 'South' anthropologies, emphasize the need for a more participative, plural and politically committed anthropology.

For example, while some of these perspectives acknowledge that alterity is central for the development of anthropology, they suggest that the discipline needs to engage with it in more respectful ways (Krotz 2002: 2). Alternatively, these approaches explicitly position research in terms of political affinity and action (Krotz 2010: 13), or of 'valuing of nonacademic knowledge [such as theories and debates] that appreciate the emergence and visibility of indigenous theories' (Ribeiro 2014: 494). Similarly, indigenous film studies advocate for collaborative or participatory methodologies that could arguably allow people who have traditionally been anthropological subjects to 'speak for themselves' (e.g. Gauthier 2008: 71). While acknowledging the invaluable contribution of this disciplinary shift for contesting anthropology's hierarchical roots, this chapter points to the dangerous potential of affinity to flatten the critical possibilities of anthropological research. When cultivating affinity or collaborating with ethnographic subjects means prioritizing empowerment and resistance over critical analysis, then such a strategy risks becoming another, politically correct, form of alterizing anthropological subjects.

As the editors of this volume note, the critical proposals that these anthropological currents have developed build necessary continuities with the epistemological and political crises that have shaken anglophone anthropology for over thirty years (Clifford 1983, 1988; Clifford and Marcus 1986; Marcus and Fischer 1996; Behar and Gordon 1995). I suggest that the examples of indigenous media tensions that I discuss below are illustrative to reflect on the limitations and contradictions of these disciplinary efforts.

A point of departure for my discussion is an essay by Bolivian historian Rossana Barragán (2008). In 'Bolivia, Bridges and Chasms', she problematizes the relationship between indigenous struggles and the production of anthropological knowledge in Bolivia. Drawing from this title, in this chapter I suggest that projects like 'world anthropologies' and 'anthropologies of the South' are optimistically paying too much attention to the possible *bridges* that collaborative and politically engaged anthropology can build. Nevertheless, we also need a more critical, less optimistic reflection that pays attention to the *chasms*, limitations or conflicts of this proclaimed collaboration. Looking at the *chasms* is helpful for unpacking the claims through which some of these currents reshape an anthropological 'we'. This mutually constitutive relationship between indigenous struggles and anthropological knowledge has been instrumental for articulating the locally based language of indigeneity that is so influential in current Bolivian politics.

An event that I experienced at the beginning of my fieldwork on indigenous media production in Bolivia in 2005 is useful to illustrate how my research was shaped by the tensions just addressed. For this purpose, it is relevant to explain my approach to this research subject as a Mexican, middle-class white woman who at the time had been a graduate anthropology student for five years in North American universities. My own regional identity as a Latin American scholar looking comparatively at a Latin American country different than mine, my previous experience working with indigenous media projects with a women's peasant organization in Oaxaca, Mexico, my collaboration at the time in organizing indigenous film festivals at the National Museum of the American Indian of the Smithsonian Institution in New York City, and my own political affinity with indigenous struggles both in Mexico and Bolivia strongly informed my doctoral research interests.

One year before my arrival in Bolivia to start my fieldwork in September 2005, I had discussed with some indigenous media-makers and project coordinators the possibility of developing a research project on the Plan Nacional Indígena Originario de Comunicación Audiovisual (National Plan of Indigenous Audiovisual Communication), the strongest indigenous media initiative of Bolivia and one of the most representative experiences of this kind in Latin America.[2] Although all my hosts were welcoming and aware of the reasons for my visit, I was not immediately given access to their work. While they asked me with curiosity about the focus of my project, they also asked straightforward questions about the use of my research and its potential risks for their own political process. They mentioned previous experiences with anthropologists and researchers who met with organizations and communities to obtain people's information in order to 'take it away' and publish it in other languages. They also talked about cases of 'well-intentioned' anthropologists who end up damaging the organizations' internal political processes by publishing their data without being aware of possible political consequences. At certain points they also subtly asked what the use of my research was, considering that one of their own goals was to produce knowledge about indigenous communities and political processes in Bolivia.

In the midst of this conversation, I remembered that the Plan Nacional emerged as a response to the work of anthropologists and filmmakers who authoritatively portrayed the life of indigenous peoples, without considering the possible impacts that such works could have on them, and without considering them as interlocutors. The questions of my interlocutors about the possible use of my research for their own process forced me to rethink my questions and goals in relation to their political work. These questions also led me to redefine my methodological approach so I could 'collaborate' on specific tasks during my observation of their activities, discuss some of my research questions with Plan Nacional members through a series of workshops on indigenous visual representations, and find ways to share with them my research results for their own uses. Something that contributed to them finally agreeing to my research project was that Plan Nacional members acknowledged my previous work on indigenous communication in Southern Mexico.

These attempts to develop a more collaborative research process did not necessarily guarantee an accurate or comprehensive representation of the Plan Nacional's work. Yet this frank questioning at the beginning of my field research, and the process of collaboration that ensued, contributed to building an engaged dialogue with my research subjects, which provided key insights and questions for my own research and which, in many ways, reshaped my own understanding of the anthropological endeavour.[3]

At the same time, this first, somehow confrontational encounter with my research subjects highlighted a tension, a *chasm*, that has prevailed throughout my academic work about how much political and emotional affinity with research subjects should result in celebratory findings that contribute to their particular struggles despite the risk of silencing potential critical questions. Acknowledging the relevance of anthropology for analysing the texture of social and political relations, I propose that exploring the contradictions and tensions that anthropological subjects experience in their daily lives and works is not detrimental to their political goals, but rather allows understanding of how these take place within larger, more complex histories and power structures that often limit their coherence. In this regard, I suggest that collaboration and affinity are invaluable qualities of anthropological practices, but these should not be detrimental to the critical spirit of the discipline.

Aside from these examples of the concrete tensions and possibilities of collaboration that I found in my own fieldwork, a question that persisted throughout my research was what made particular kinds of film production 'indigenous'. As discussed in the following sections, I find this issue to be a central site for examining how local definitions of 'indigenous film' dialogue with anthropological approaches to indigeneity, participatory film and ideas about political commitment and collaboration. I suggest that all these aspects inform specific forms of understanding affinity in relation to indigenous film practices.

Indigenous Film

A first, perhaps obvious, finding of my research on the Plan Nacional was that the quality of 'indigenous' in its kinds of films was not an automatic imprint of a pre-existing ethnic identity among media-makers.[4] Rather, processes of indigenous affiliation are shaped by interwoven experiences of race and class that constitute regional and personal histories and forms of interacting with the state and with other indigenous and non-indigenous peoples.

A related finding was that Plan Nacional film instruction was not only about technical training on the use of equipment, but also a space for debating and reflecting on the meaning and implications of producing indigenous media.[5] Although many media-makers already identified themselves as indigenous people before attending the Plan Nacional workshops through previous participation in their communities and organizations, for many of them their reflection on indigenous identities started only through their participation in the Plan Nacional. Some media-makers acknowledged that although in their communities they 'live as indigenous peoples',[6] it was only within the Plan Nacional that they started analysing the question of indigenous identity in great depth. Others explained that their participation in workshops helped them acknowledge an indigenous affiliation that was previously unclear due to migration and discrimination issues.[7] The Plan Nacional workshops were also instrumental for some media-makers to reflect on their own ethnic identity as they became conscious of the cultural diversity of their regions.[8] In doing so, the Plan Nacional media initiative, as many other native intellectual, audiovisual and activist projects worldwide, exemplify what Ty Tengan's contribution in this volume explains as the 'we shift' among Oceanian indigenous anthropologists.

These initial debates on ethnic affiliation among indigenous media-makers worked as spaces in which the language of indigeneity became articulated and reproduced in dialogue with anthropological, sociological and NGO discourses of experts who were in charge of instruction. According to Canessa, indigeneity is 'a globalized discourse of rights which are accessed by peoples engaged in local struggles' and 'a "claim to justice" ... based on awareness of historical injustice the consequences of which have been inherited by contemporary people' (Canessa 2012: 10–11).

Therefore, as in many other Latin American media initiatives, in the case of the Plan Nacional ethnic affiliation becomes a common ground to define the objectives and methodologies for producing 'indigenous films'. This common ethnic ground is learned and articulated 'in a dialogic manner' (Wortham 2013: 148) in relation to activist, institutional and academic discourses on cultural identity that have been highly informed by anthropology.

In addition to issues of ethnic affiliation, indigenous film has raised interest about its argued participatory and collective character. During the last three decades, anthropological research has depicted indigenous media as a turning point in the history of ethnographic film and as a challenge to conventional anthropological perspectives. Indigenous media are often celebrated by media scholars and anthropologists for their ability to destabilize the foundational relationship of anthropology with alterity because they are claimed to enable indigenous subjects to 'represent themselves' or to 'serve their own needs and ends' (Ginsburg 2002: 40). This phenomenon, often explained as 'a reconceptualization of "the native voice"' (Ginsburg 1992: 359), involves a series of film production and distribution practices that differ from conventional ethnographic cinema and fieldwork, for instance through an emphasis on collective or collaborative authorship, through a specific 'embeddedness' or positioning within indigenous cultures (Ginsburg 1994; Wortham 2013) and through distribution strategies to build heterogeneous audiences that include indigenous communities. Indigenous media have also been acclaimed for their instrumentality in making visible indigenous peoples' political struggles and for objectifying 'their own culture[s]', thereby for conveying 'more vividly and directly than any other form of communication that their "culture" had value' (Turner 1991: 305–6). Furthermore, according to Ginsburg, indigenous media contest the authority of ethnographic film because they 'help to realign a long-outdated paradigm of ethnographic film built on the assumption of culture as a stable and bounded object, and documentary representation as restricted to realist illusion' (1995: 73).

At the same time, indigenous media as an anthropological creation arose partly out of the ambition for more participatory methods among ethnographic filmmakers. Some of these filmmakers, such as Jean Rouch, were active promoters of Direct Cinema or *Cinema Verité*'s premise that the situation produced by the subjective interaction between the filmmaker and the subject could produce knowledge and truth (Wood 2005). For this purpose, this movement widely experimented with collaborative and subjective film techniques that implied a break with conventional ethnographic and documentary methods, for example by promoting small filming teams and the involvement of local people in decisions related to script-writing, mise-en-scène, shooting and editing; promoting the immersed presence of the camera in ethnographic situations through handheld camerawork; or by including the voices of ethnographic subjects in film narration (De Brigard 1995: 36–37; Rouch 2003).

From this perspective, in the early 1970s, a decade before audiovisual technologies allowed for a wider access to film production and distribution, Jean Rouch envisioned a future in which 'ethnographic film will help us to "share anthropology"' (2003: 46). Rouch predicted the technological possibilities that 'a camera can so totally participate that it will automatically pass into the hands of those who, until now, have always been in front of the lens', and which would therefore make possible that 'anthropologists will no longer control the monopoly of observation' (2003: 46). Similarly, in his attempts for 'multiple authorship' in ethnographic film, renowned filmmaker and anthropologist David MacDougall suggested 'intertextual cinema' as an approach in which 'film may be in a better position to address conflicting views of reality, in a world in which observers and observed are less clearly separated and in which reciprocal observation and exchange increasingly matter' (MacDougall 1998: 138).

Political Commitment

Often in dialogue with anthropological concerns for reciprocal observation and exchange (MacDougall 1998: 138), between the 1970s and 1980s other realms of filmmaking were experimenting with collaborative methods towards more explicit political goals. Broadly speaking, Latin American militant or revolutionary cinema developed in places like Argentina, Bolivia, Brazil, Colombia, Cuba, Chile and Mexico and borrowed *Cinéma Verité*'s experimentation with collaborative possibilities for approaching political realities in documentary or fictional films, including strategies such as working with non-professional actors, participating with the camera in improvised situations, and re-enacting and recreating conflictive political issues in order to make visible problems that conventional film and media would not address. Likewise, trusting in the possibilities of film for approaching truth, both movements relied on the idea that 'knowledge . . . emerges . . . from the creative process at the intersection of filmmaker and subject' (Wood 2005: 150). Yet, as Wood notes, various Latin American revolutionary filmmakers such as Jorge Sanjinés, Marta Rodríguez and Jorge Silva also 'revolutionized'

Cinéma Verité. Unlike *Cinéma Verité*'s emphasis on subjectivity and its aim to produce knowledge, the 'Marxist political commitment' of most Latin American filmmakers led them to use film both to demonstrate a material reality and to transform it (Wood 2005: 149–50; Burton 1986).

With the proliferation of video technologies, since the 1980s documentary filmmaking throughout the world has used elements from *Cinéma Verité* to work with social projects in developing countries or with subaltern groups. Inspired both by participatory ethnographic film and by the strong history of militant cinema, indigenous media emerged in Latin America in the late 1980s, often with the participation of anthropologists within *indigenista* state projects (i.e. Mexico and Brazil), and/or in collaboration with indigenous organizations (i.e. Ecuador, Colombia and Bolivia). In all of these cases, much of the discursive and technical training for indigenous media production is rooted in identity politics debates and their definition of indigenousness, which are nourished by various processes related to indigeneity. These include the attention of academic studies to indigenous issues from the 1960s (Barragán 2008), the growing emphasis of international institutions on indigenous rights, the globalization of indigenous struggles, as well as contemporary constitutional processes that stress the participation of indigenous peoples in national politics. At the same time, most indigenous media initiatives emerged as a more urgent political response to ethnographic film production.

The following account of a conflict within the Latin American Council of Indigenous Peoples' Film and Communication CLACPI (Consejo Latinoamericano de Cine y Comunicación de Pueblos Indígenas) in 1992 is a concrete example of the kinds of tensions between anthropologists and ethnographic filmmakers who defended the utility of ethnographic film for producing scientific knowledge, and ethnographic and indigenous filmmakers who argued for using film for social transformation. In an interview in 2007, Iván Sanjinés, the founder of the Centro de Formación y Realización Cinematográfica (CEFREC) of Bolivia, explained that he participated for the first time in the Fourth Indigenous Film and Video Festival organized by CLACPI in the cities of Lima and Cuzco in Peru in 1992. He mentioned that CLACPI was created in 1985 in Mexico by a group of ethnographic filmmakers with the idea of having a space to screen and discuss films about indigenous peoples. Nevertheless, in the Fourth Festival in Peru, CLACPI suffered a crisis due to ideological differences between a group of ethnographic filmmakers who proposed to continue doing films *about* indigenous peoples, and a group of filmmakers and organizations that sought to do films *by* indigenous peoples. 'CLACPI had its own value from its foundation in 1985, it was the first festival, there was no other space to see films of indigenous peoples',⁹ Iván Sanjinés affirmed.¹⁰

> Even when films were not produced by indigenous people themselves, there were interesting people in that group who wanted to change things. But there was also a group that wanted to continue doing their films, their research. They wanted to continue doing anthropological and ethnographic film. And we hooked up more with the people who had a more committed vision, more political. Then CLACPI changed and became a space for building processes. I think we are part of a broader energy that gets together and grows bigger.¹¹

Iván Sanjinés underlined the significance of CLACPI for the Bolivian process:

> Then in 1992, as we became closer to CLACPI, we participated in the Lima and Cuzco Festival. We arrived in the most interesting moment, at the time for definitions. And we were also going through a reflection process because it was more a matter of commitment, about how this could be useful to transform things, than an issue about skin, about being indigenous people, miners, or urban people. We arrived in Peru and there was all that crisis at the Festival. And we obviously joined the group that wanted to change things.¹²

This account speaks to a crisis within ethnographic film and within anthropology in general. In anthropology, this 'crisis of representation' questioned the issue of 'ethnographic authority', which referred to all kinds of ethnographic representations, including ethnographic writing and film (Marcus and Fischer 1996). The debate that Iván Sanjinés describes within CLACPI relates to these kinds of discussions: should the ethnographic voice in film remain in the charge of an observing author or ethnographer? Or should film work as a tool to 'build processes' and contribute to transforming political realities through training subaltern subjects – who most of the time serve as ethnographic 'informants' – so that they use video technologies to express 'their own voices' and to 'depict their own realities'? This debate also questioned the limits and possibilities of academic research for political action.

As Iván Sanjinés explained, the idea of using film for 'building political processes' did not mean working with indigenous peoples per se. He argues that beyond being 'an issue about skin' or about being 'indigenous peoples, miners, or urban', their concern was to diversify the possibilities of expressing different voices as a political 'commitment' to 'transform things'. This reflection emphasizes indigenous communication not so much as an ethnic or cultural issue, but as a political 'commitment' to contribute to transformation processes that are taking place in different Latin American countries, which include but are not limited to indigenous struggles.

Challenges of Collaboration

In many ways, indigenous media envisage similar goals to those of 'other' anthropologies in terms of their engagement with social transformation, their political positionality, their emphasis on collaboration and their search for expressing a multiplicity of voices that have historically been silenced. In this regard, for example, the contribution of Katherine Swancutt (this volume) on her experience of ethnographic film production in Southwest China is insightful for reflecting on the implications and challenges of collaboration, in this case for developing a native 'imaginarium' of the anthropological endeavour and identity. The conflicts that I have described above, as well as the further tensions regarding collaboration, authorship and political representation in indigenous media projects after the 1992 CLACPI festival, complicate anthropological celebrations of indigenous media as one of the strongest sites for contesting hegemonic knowledge production and circulation. As in 'world' (Ribeiro and Escobar 2006; Ribeiro 2014) and 'South' (Krotz 2008, 2010) anthropologies, indigenous media constitute some kind of peripheral, marginal or 'provincial' initiatives. As with 'world' and 'South' anthropologies, indigenous media also seek to break with alterizing and objectifying practices, and therefore destabilize the conventional role of anthropologists as the unique, authoritative producers of knowledge.

In her analysis of the state-sponsored project of Indigenous Media Transference to Indigenous Communities in Mexico, Erica Wortham exemplifies how the language of indigenous media is learned and articulated in relation to activist, institutional and academic discourses on cultural identity. She notes that a video production workshop organized by the *Indigenista* National Institution INI 'transferred more than video production equipment and basic skills for its use. The workshop also transferred the institution's discourse about the role culture plays in the development of indigenous communities and how self-representation through the use of video can strengthen community identity' (Wortham 2013: 147). Yet she also nuances this affirmation by explaining that indigenous mediamakers did not mechanically appropriate institutional or anthropological discourses, but adapted them to their daily practices, therefore 'demonstrating how video *indígena* is produced in a dialogic manner' (ibid.: 148).

Both the case of Plan Nacional media workshops presented at the beginning of this chapter, as well as Wortham's analysis of video workshops in Mexico, allow us to identify two related aspects of indigenous media practices. On the one hand, these practices have undeniably contributed to anthropology, ethnographic film methods and debates about ethnographic authority, reflexivity, alterity and objectivity. On the other hand, their conflictive bond with identity politics debates often results in essentializing, and therefore alterizing, approaches to ethnic identity.

As Rouch, MacDougall, Ginsburg and other anthropologists and filmmakers predicted, indigenous peoples' use of media does constitute a structural and formal challenge to authoritarian or alterizing practices within anthropology and ethnographic film. Examples of this are the strategies that the Plan Nacional has developed for emphasizing collective authorship, for contesting the figure of film director, and for operating under very low budgets. Additionally, in most indigenous media projects, there is an increasing involvement in film production, control of audiovisual technologies, and even professional film training among people from indigenous communities and organizations. There is a growing number of productions spoken in indigenous languages in different regions of the world, and indigenous media projects have developed creative distribution strategies to build different publics, including those from indigenous regions.

These and other practices are instrumental for most indigenous media projects to explicitly or implicitly challenge 'hegemonic epistemologies' (Schiwy 2009: 13) by questioning the argued political neutrality and objectivity of ethnographic film, as well as the 'ethnographic authority' or authoritative forms of interpreting and representing cultures within anthropology (Clifford 1983). Many of these projects, such as the one described in Bolivia, and others developed in places like Colombia, Brazil, Mexico and Ecuador, seek to take part of major indigenous movements' political agendas that include struggles for self-determination, land and territory, and traditional law, and to 'intervene' or transform political realities through their production and distribution methodologies (Zamorano Villarreal 2009; Wortham 2013; Schiwy 2011). All these practices, which constitute much of indigenous media production in Latin America and worldwide, have assuredly informed the practices and perspectives of anthropologists who have somehow participated in these kinds of projects. Either in terms of explicit affinity with indigenous media projects' political agendas, or through their direct involvement in indigenous media projects' design, training, production, management and distribution activities, anthropologists and professional filmmakers related to indigenous media are contributing to arguments against anthropological practices based on objectivity, political neutrality and authoritative representations.

Yet despite these significant contributions, indigenous media projects are not free from tensions. Issues like collective or individual authorship, ethnic affiliation and political representation are intensively debated among media-makers from the region. In terms of authorship, for example, the relationship between personal expression and collective authorship represents a tension within the Plan Nacional in Bolivia. Indeed, as positive as this notion sounds, the process of collective authorship is far from the friendly attribute that some media-makers have even described as 'the essence of indigenousness'.[13] This notion is the tip of an iceberg filled with numerous tensions concerning issues of property, recognition and status, the media-makers' relationship with funders and distributers, and authenticity. For example, although most media-makers work under a collective principle, there is always some ambiguity between personal learning and satisfaction that media-makers feel, for example when finishing a video or when it wins awards at international festivals, and their commitment to all the people who made it possible. Likewise, this principle raises the question of how much the collective label conceals the actual relations of competition among media-makers, which is reflected, for instance, in the anxiety and tensions regarding who will be selected to attend an international festival, or in eventual jokes and feelings of resentment that some media-makers express against those who stand out. Similarly, the notion of collective authorship conceals the individual quests of some media-makers for recognition. While most media-makers acknowledge that they do not work for money, or to become 'film stars', some have expressed concerns regarding the scarce monetary compensation they receive for their work. Finally, the emphasis on collective authorship introduces the question of how much a collective production strengthens or limits the creative possibilities of specific individuals, as well as the critical role of negotiation in defining such collectiveness.

Alternatively, in terms of the concern that most media-makers express for depicting indigeneity in fair and dignified ways, there is a continuous debate among indigenous video-makers in Bolivia about what makes their films explicitly indigenous, or about the possibilities for developing an indigenous film language. In this regard, indigenous media-makers' efforts to explicitly include elements of their own cultures, aesthetics and realities have motivated them to experiment in terms of narrative structure, recreation based in storytelling and oral history, length, use of natural locations, and aesthetic references to indigenous life. At the same time, these efforts to stamp their films as indigenous are shaped by other political and economic aspects, such as technical expertise, distribution and negotiation within production teams, as well as the current political urge for expressing indigeneity.

What these complexities point to is the need to question the idea that there are intrinsically indigenous features that make their way into film aesthetics. Instead, I suggest that the mobilization of storytelling, mythology, concepts and values attributed to indigenous cultures in films and their production respond in a more contentious and dynamic way to a political need for expressing indigeneity, rather than to inherent features of indigenousness that reveal themselves at the moment of filmmaking.

Aside from these kinds of debates around authorship and indigenous aesthetics, indigenous media practices are inevitably immersed in power processes that include tensions between economic compensation and political commitment; competition for status and economic benefit; and the reproduction of hierarchical relations, for instance in terms of gender (Wortham 2013; Zamorano Villarreal 2009; Zamorano Villarreal and Wammack 2014). These issues permeate indigenous media-makers' work on a daily basis in Bolivia. For example, they often joke that in order to work for the Plan Nacional, 'you have to remain single'. 'And if you are not', they go on, 'you'll become single again soon'. Far from being funny, this joke rather refers to the trouble that most media-makers face when trying to balance their family responsibilities with the highly demanding schedules and low economic compensation at the Plan Nacional. The issue of monetary compensation differently impacts young media-makers who take their work as part of their education, and those who have family responsibilities and who, therefore, have a stronger need to juggle their communication job with other activities. The work of media-makers is not a regular job, but demands availability to take trips of a month or more during workshops, shooting, editing or distribution periods. Hence, besides the need for monetary compensation, the work commitment implies leaving community or family responsibilities in other people's hands. The impact of this can be seen, for example, in the higher dropout rate among female media-makers; while male family heads can live through periods of economic pressure through family support, women can hardly stay away from domestic responsibilities such as child care for long periods of time.

Tensions around economic compensation also relate to a common assumption in Bolivia that actual political commitment involves an economic sacrifice, as if having fair financial compensation contradicted political or moral responsibility. As it comes out, this assumption has resulted in further stress in the work, often because media-makers feel that they do not obtain fair compensation for their efforts. Nevertheless, it is worth noting that not even half of the Plan Nacional's achievements would be possible if it were not based on this economic dynamic. It is not the case, as in many NGOs, that 'professional' staff salaries are incommensurate with those of interns and community promoters. Still, economic compensation tensions within the Plan Nacional speak about concrete structural limitations that complicate the often-celebrated revival of arguably indigenous-based practices such as collectivity and reciprocity.

Despite these kinds of internal tensions, the effective challenge that indigenous media have posed to ethnographic authority has led some scholars to adopt celebratory approaches that reflect the anthropological dream of freeing the discipline from its alterizing roots. As mentioned earlier, the fact of labelling a kind of film practice as 'indigenous' raises a series of issues related to the imbricated relationship between anthropology and indigeneity. By this I mean, in agreement with Rossana Barragán (2008), that all processes of indigenous struggle, including indigenous media practices, as well as the institutionalization of indigeneity within state projects and international agencies, are influenced by, while also informing, anthropological knowledge. Yet, at the moment of referring to indigenous peoples, it is still an anthropological challenge not to take this term as a self-contained category from which subjects speak and act. As stated through my introductory question to this chapter about what makes this kind of film 'indigenous', I think I can also speak for other colleagues researching indigenous media when I acknowledge that I still struggle with the temptation of taking for granted, for instance, that there is an indigenous film aesthetics, or of assuming that just because they are produced by indigenous peoples, their films have the intrinsic power to coherently contribute to 'intervene in reality' (Zamorano Villarreal 2009) or to anticolonial, autonomic or sovereign claims (Schiwy 2009; Wortham 2013; Raheja 2013). In this regard, I concur with Poole that 'by ignoring the broader political and discursive landscape within which categories such as "the indigenous" emerge and take hold', our academic production on this subject might 'en[d] up defending an essentialist or primordial notion of identity. . .' (2005: 170).

In other words, an emphasis on the ethnic aspect of particular media projects risks distracting attention from their contributions both to anthropology and to media practices, as well as reproducing alterizing hierarchies within anthropology. These media are effective because they are experimenting – and often struggling – with many other elements such as collective work, 'imperfect' aesthetics (Salazar and Córdova 2008), low-budget strategies, and explicitly subordinate political positioning that, although often attributed to indigenousness, might as well be characteristic of community projects, subaltern movements or 'citizens' media' (Rodríguez 2001).

In the past three sections, I have discussed how indigenous film practices converge with influential anthropological debates around indigenousness, political commitment and collaboration. In doing so, I have tried to point to a paradox, namely the possibility that far from emancipating indigenous filmmakers from their anthropological ghosts, efforts of both anthropologists and media-makers to explain indigenous media as inherently indigenous ways of representing their own cultures and identities may give rise to new, essentializing constructions of indigenous peoples as 'Others'.

Conclusion

Throughout this chapter, I have proposed that indigenous media projects constitute a complex case to discuss the possibilities and limitations of the celebrated notion of affinity because they complicate the relationship between collaboration, epistemological authority, politics and representation; because they have a mutually constitutive relationship with indigeneity; and because this phenomenon has itself been the subject of anthropological reflection.

During the last three decades, disciplinary debates have contested the ways in which anthropological constructions of alterity have contributed to colonial, imperial and state projects (Krotz 2002). As Krotz suggests, the notion of alterity involves an initial scientific curiosity sparked by the 'contact between cultures' (ibid.: 12), and therefore implies establishing a distance, justified in epistemological terms, between social scientists and their research subjects. Yet, as we have also learned from Krotz and other research on the history of anthropology, this apparently innocuous scientific positioning generally conceals the political implications of establishing many other kinds of distances, in terms of power relations, through alterity. These include, for example, an assumed epistemological superiority of scientists over their subjects, and their consequent objectification through exoticizing, racializing, sexualizing or essentializing perspectives.

As a way to reverse the historical impact of alterity over anthropological practice, many contemporary debates coincide with the idea that epistemological and political affinity with research subjects can break with the hierarchical roots of the discipline. Affinity then involves epistemological and methodological elaborations to make possible, for instance, a closer and more equitable collaboration between anthropologists and their research subjects, a disciplinary engagement with social transformation, and a clear positioning with respect to research subjects' politics. The notion of affinity also involves taking seriously the fact that there have been 'changes in the subject position of anthropology's "object"' (Ribeiro and Escobar 2006: 1). Such changes include, for example, the fact that some of those who used to be conventional anthropological subjects are now themselves making anthropological or historical research about their own realities, as the example of the Taller de Historia Oral Andina in Bolivia (THOA), to name just one among many other cases, demonstrates (Stephenson 2002).

Similarly to the case of 'native' anthropologists, indigenous media projects challenge the ways in which knowledge and debate about indigenous realities are produced and authored. By analysing some Latin American experiences of indigenous media production, this chapter has pointed at the risks of the anthropological tendency to privilege and cultivate affinity flattening out epistemological and political intricacies. In terms of knowledge production, I contend that in 'our' anthropological attempts to establish affinity with marginal subjects, we often prioritize presenting the positive impacts of their resisting practices over the contradictions in which they are embedded, therefore concealing the conflicts that could help us to understand the historical and political limitations, in this case, of indigenous struggles. Alternatively, a political risk of celebratory approaches is reproducing essentializing categories – which are easily adopted by all kinds of social actors – and which often turn out to be more constraining than liberating for their own purposes, as various media-makers, such as Carlos Efraín Pérez and Pedro Daniel López from Mexico, have suggested when referring to their own uneasiness with the 'indigenous media' term.

Finally, this tension leads us back to the question of 'who are "we"?' that brings this volume together. 'Other' anthropologies debates have rightly attempted to distance themselves from what Ribeiro explains as 'imperial' or dominant anthropologies (2014). In this effort, groups of scholars have struggled to define different anthropological communities that prioritize affinity, collaboration and a political positioning with social peripheries through terms like 'radical anthropology' (ibid.). Although these debates are undeniably contributing to the reshaping of anthropological practices and to the establishment of alternative dialogues, my concern is that these new forms of delineating a 'we' through a common affinity with marginal social subjects might, again, flatten out crucial differences. For instance, as much as 'we', critical anthropologists, seek to break with the epistemological and political distances when interacting with 'our' subjects, we cannot obliterate the ways in which our privileges, as members of academic institutions with far more stable salaries than those of most of our research subjects, still draw irreconcilable gaps with their own realities and struggles. In this regard, I suggest that 'our' search for affinity should not make 'us' assume that 'our' urge for social transformation is exactly the same as 'theirs'. Likewise, the search for affinity might turn into a fascination for testifying to the ways in which conventional anthropological subjects now 'speak for themselves'. These issues point at possible ways in which affinity might dangerously conceal new forms of alterity.

Acknowledgements

I would like to thank Liana Chua and Nayanika Mathur for inviting me to take part in this project and for their support in editing this text. The presentations and debates we had during the workshop 'Who Are "We"? Reimagining Alterity and Affinity in Anthropology' in September 2014 were of great inspiration for this piece. Parts of this chapter appear in G. Zamorano Villarreal, *Indigenous Media and Political Imaginaries in Contemporary Bolivia* (University of Nebraska Press, 2017). Reprinted with permission.

Gabriela Zamorano Villarreal is a researcher at the Centro de Estudios Antropológicos in El Colegio de Michoacán. After having received her Ph.D. from the Anthropology Department of the City University of New York in 2008, she conducted postdoctoral research on racial photography in Bolivia at the Musée du Quai Branly in Paris in 2009. She is the author of *Indigenous Media and Political Imaginaries* in *Contemporary Bolivia* (University of Nebraska Press, 2017), and co-author of *De Frente al Perfil: Retratos Raciales de Frederick Starr* (Colmich, 2012), as well as various articles and book chapters in publications in Latin America, the United States and Europe. Her research has been funded by the National Science Foundation and the National Council for Science and Technology in Mexico. Her current research includes work on popular photographic and audiovisual archives in Michoacán, Mexico, and the direction of a documentary film project on the photographic archives of Bolivian photographer Julio Cordero.

Notes

1. To legally determine who can be considered indigenous populations, official definitions of indigeneity first emerged within international institutional debates at the United Nations Working Group for Indigenous Peoples in the early 1970s. This definition has been re-elaborated by the International Labour Organization Convention 169 in the 1980s and, later, by the World Bank in the early 1990s (http://johansandbergmcguinne.wordpress.com/official-definitions-of-indigeneity/, accessed 22 November 2013).
2. After the Constituent Assembly, the Plan Nacional defined itself in 2009 as a communication system and changed its name to 'Sistema Plurinacional de Comunicación Indigena Originario Campesino Intercultural' (Indigenous, Originario, Peasant and Intercultural Plurinational System of Communication).
3. A concrete example of this dialogue is a publication I prepared in collaboration with the Plan Nacional presenting preliminary data and findings of my research, which include a written account of the history and characteristics of the Plan Nacional, as well as fragments of interviews with media-makers about how their personal and political trajectories have informed their understandings of indigenous media (Zamorano Villarreal, Ticona and Gutiérrez 2008). Another form of collaboration was to organize a series of workshops on visual representations of indigenousness in Bolivia with media-makers and leaders. This activity was very insightful for analysing the contradictions and questions that media-makers faced both as image consumers and as producers seeking to avoid negative or stereotyping representations. At the same time, this activity was useful for media-makers' communicational training processes.
4. The ethnographic information presented in this section was obtained during my two-year field research in Bolivia from 2005 to 2007 as part of my doctoral dissertation project. The results are published in *Indigenous Media and Political Imaginaries in Contemporary Bolivia* (Zamorano Villarreal 2017).

5. I was able to attend some of these workshops from April to June 2006 as part of the training activities at the centre created by the Plan Nacional's Communication Strategy, which since 2010 has operated as the School of Integral Training of Indigenous Leadership in Rights, Gender, and Communication in the city of Cochabamba.
6. Humberto Claros, interview with the author, La Paz, May 2006. All translations from the Spanish are my own.
7. Regina Monasterios, interview with the author, La Paz, July 2006.
8. Ariel Yáñez, interview with the author, La Paz, September 2006.
9. Iván Sanjinés Savedra, interview with the author, La Paz, May 2007.
10. See also Sanjinés Saavedra (2013).
11. Iván Sanjinés Savedra, interview with the author, La Paz, May 2007.
12. Ibid.
13. Franklin Gutiérrez, interview with the author, La Paz, May 2007.

References

Barragán, R. 2008. 'Bolivia: Bridges and Chasms', in D. Poole (ed.), *A Companion to Latin American Anthropology*. New Jersey, NJ: Wiley-Blackwell, pp. 32–55.
Behar, R., and D.A. Gordon (eds). 1995. *Women Writing Culture*. Oakland, CA: University of California Press.
Burton, J. (ed.). 1986. *Cinema and Social Change in Latin America*. Austin, TX: University of Texas Press.
Canessa, A. 2012. *Intimate Indigeneities: Race, Sex, and History in the Small Spaces of Andean Life*. Durham, NC and London: Duke University Press.
Choque Quispe, M.E. 1998. 'Reconstitución y fortalecimiento del ayllu: Una experiencia de participación desde el pueblo aymara', In-house document. La Paz: THOA.
Clifford, J. 1983. 'On Ethnographic Authority', *Representations* 2: 118–46.
Clifford, J. 1988. *The Predicament of Culture*. Cambridge, MA: Harvard University Press.
Clifford, J., and G.E. Marcus. 1986. *Writing Culture: The Poetics and Politics of Ethnography*. Oakland, CA: University of California Press.
De Brigard, E. 1995. 'The History of Ethnographic Film', in P. Hockings (ed.), *Principles of Visual Anthropology*. Berlin: Mouton de Gruyter, pp. 13–43.
De la Cadena, M. 2008. 'La producción de otros conocimientos y sus tensiones: ¿de una antropología andinista a la interculturalidad?', in G.L. Ribeiro and A. Escobar (eds), *Antropologías del Mundo: Transformaciones disciplinarias dentro de sistemas de poder*. Mexico: The Wenner-Gren International, Centro de Investigaciones y Estudios Superiores en Antropología Social, Envión, pp. 249–78.
De Sousa, B. 2009. *Una epistemología del Sur: La reinvención del conocimiento y la emancipación social*. Mexico: CLACSO y Siglo XXI.

Gamio, Manuel. 2006. *Forjando Patria*. Mexico: Porrúa.

Gauthier, J. 2008. '"Lest Others Speak for Us": The Neglected Roots and Uncertain Future of Maori Cinema in New Zealand', in P. Wilson and M. Stewart (eds), *Global Indigenous Media: Cultures, Poetics and Politics*. Durham, NC: Duke University Press.

Ginsburg, F. 1992. 'Indigenous Media: Faustian Contract or Global Village?', in E. Marcus (ed.), *Re-reading Cultural Anthropology*. Durham, NC: Duke University Press, pp. 356–76.

Ginsburg, F. 1994. 'Embedded Aesthetics: Creating a Discursive Space for Indigenous Media', *Cultural Anthropology* 9(3): 365–82.

Ginsburg, F. 1995. 'The Parallax Effect: The Impact of Aboriginal Media on Ethnographic Film', *Visual Anthropology Review* 11(2): 64–76.

Ginsburg, F. 2002. 'Screen Memories: Resignifying the Traditional in Indigenous Media', in F.D. Ginsburg, L. Abu-Lughod and B. Larkin (eds), *Media Worlds: Anthropology on New Terrain*. Oakland, CA: University of California Press, pp. 39–57.

Krotz, E. 1997. 'Anthropologies of the South: Their Rise, Their Silencing, Their Characteristics', *Critique of Anthropology* 17: 237–51.

Krotz, E. 2002. *La otredad cultural entre utopía y ciencia: Un estudio sobre el origen, el desarrollo y la reorientación de la antropología*. Mexico City: Fondo de Cultura Económica-UAM.

Krotz, E. 2008. 'La antropología mexicana y su búsqueda permanente de identidad', in G.L. Ribeiro and A. Escobar (eds), *Antropologías del mundo: Transformaciones disciplinarias dentro de sistemas de poder*. Mexico City: UAM-CIESAS- Universidad Iberoamericana, pp. 119–143.

Krotz, E. 2010. 'Evolution of the Anthropologies of the South: Contributions of Three Mexican Anthropologists in the Latter Half of the Twentieth Century', *Histories of Anthropology Annual* 6: 1–17.

MacDougall, D. 1998. *Transcultural Cinema*. Princeton, NJ: Princeton University Press.

Mamani Condori, C. 1989. *Metodología de la historia oral*. La Paz: THOA.

Marcus, G.E., and M.M. Fischer. 1996. *Anthropology as Cultural Critique: An Experimental Moment in the Human Sciences*. Chicago, IL: University of Chicago Press.

Pérez Rojas, C.E. 2005. Video comunitario y Autorrepresentación. Interview by Gabriela Zamorano. www.redesindigenas.si.edu.

Poole, D. 2005. 'An Excess of Description: Ethnography, Race and Visual Technologies', *Annual Review of Anthropology* 34: 159–79.

Raheja, M.H. 2011. *Reservation Reelism: Redfacing, Visual Sovereignty, and Representations of Native Americans in Film*. Lincoln, NE: University of Nebraska Press.

Rama, A. 1984. *La Ciudad Letrada/The Literacy City*. Hanover: Ediciones del Norte.

Ribeiro, G.L. 2006. 'World Anthropologies: Cosmopolitics for a New Global Scenario in Anthropology', *Critique of Anthropology* 26(4): 363–86.

Ribeiro, G.L. 2014. 'World Anthropologies: Anthropological Cosmopolitanisms and Cosmopolitics', *Annual Review of Anthropology* 43: 483–98.
Ribeiro, G.L., and A. Escobar. 2006. *World Anthropologies: Disciplinary Transformations within Systems of Power*. New York: Berg Publishers.
Rivera-Cusicanqui, S. 1993. 'La Raíz: colonizadores y colonizados', in X. Albó & R. Barrios (eds), *Violencias encubiertas en Bolivia (1), Cultura y Política*. La Paz: Cipca- Aruwiyiri, pp. 27–139.
Rivera Cusicanqui, S. 2003. *Oprimidos Pero no Vencidos. Luchas del Campesinado Aymara y Qhechwa 1900–1980*. La Paz: Yachaywasi.
Rodríguez, C. 2001. *Fissures in the Mediascape: An International Study of Citizens' Media*. New Jersey, NJ: Hampton Press.
Rouch, J. 2003. 'The Camera and Man', in *Cine-Ethnography*. Minneapolis, MN: Minnesota University Press, pp. 29–46.
Salazar, J.F., and A. Córdova. 2008. 'Imperfect Media and the Poetics of Indigenous Video in Latin America', in P. Wilson and M. Stewart (eds), *Global Indigenous Media: Cultures, Poetics, and Politics*. Durham, NC: Duke University Press, pp. 39–57.
Sanjinés Saavedra, I. 2013. 'Usando el audiovisual como una estrategia de sobrevivencia y de lucha, de creación y recreación de un imaginario propio', *Revista Chilena de Antropología Visual* 21: 32–50.
Schiwy, F. 2009. *Indianizing Film: Decolonization, the Andes, and the Question of Technology*. New Brunswick, NJ: Rutgers University Press.
Schiwy, F. 2011. 'Todos somos presidentes / We Are All Presidents', *Cultural Studies* 25(6): 729–56.
Stephenson, M. 2002. 'Forging an Indigenous Counterpublic Sphere: The Taller de Historia Oral Andina in Bolivia', *Latin American Research Review* 37(2): 99–118.
Turner, T. 1991. 'Representing, Resisting, Rethinking', in G.W. Stocking, Jr. (ed.), *Colonial Situations: Essays on the Contextualization of Ethnographic Knowledge*. Madison, WI: University of Wisconsin Press, pp. 285–313.
Warman, A. 1970. *De eso que llaman antropología mexicana*. México: Editorial Nuestro Tiempo.
Warman, A. 1976. *Y venimos a contradecir Vol. 2*. México: Ediciones de la Casa Chata.
Wood, D.M.J. 2005. 'Revolution and Pachakuti Political and Indigenous Cinema in Bolivia and Colombia', Ph.D. thesis. London: University of London.
Wortham, E. 2013. *Indigenous Media In Mexico: Culture, Community, and the State*. Durham, NC: Duke University Press.
Zamorano Villarreal, G. 2009. 'Intervenir en la realidad: usos políticos del video indígena en Bolivia', *Revista Colombiana de Antropología* 45(2): 259–85.
Zamorano Villarreal, G. 2017. *Indigenous Media and Political Imaginaries in Contemporary Bolivia*. Lincoln, NE: University of Nebraska Press.

Zamorano Villarreal, G., A. Ticona and G.F. Gutiérrez. 2008. *El Camino de Nuestra Imagen. El Plan Nacional: Un proceso de Comunicación Indígena Originaria en Bolivia*. La Paz: CEFREC/CAIB.

Zamorano Villarreal, G., and B. Wammack. 2014. 'El Audiovisual indígena en México y sus aportes al género documental', in *Reflexiones sobre cine mexicano contemporáneo documental*. Mexico: Cineteca Nacional.

Žižek, S. 1997. 'Multiculturalism, or, the Cultural Logic of Multinational Capitalism', *New Left Review* 0(225): 28–51.

Chapter 5

SHIFTING THE 'WE' IN OCEANIA

ANTHROPOLOGY AND PACIFIC ISLANDERS REVISITED

Ty P. Kāwika Tengan

In 1975, the Oceanian anthropologist, writer and philosopher Epeli Hau'ofa published 'Anthropology and Pacific Islanders', a critical reflection on the gulf between disciplinary practices and Indigenous projects in the postcolonial Pacific. Born to Tongan missionary parents working in Papua New Guinea (PNG), Hau'ofa attended school in Tonga, Fiji, Australia and Canada and carried out fieldwork in Trinidad for his M.A. at McGill before returning to the Pacific to do a Ph.D. in anthropology at the Australian National University based on ethnographic work in PNG, where he was also a university tutor (Thomas 2012; White 2008). As a Tongan man who considered himself Papuan for the first nine years of his life and was identified as Fijian by his university friends (Thomas 2012: 122), Hau'ofa straddled multiple and sometimes ambivalent – if always regional – identities. He first delivered 'Anthropology and Pacific Islanders' as an address to the Australian and New Zealand Association for the Advancement of Science while he was finishing his dissertation and reflecting on his looming status as only the second 'native professional anthropologist' (Hau'ofa 2008: 8) to come from the Pacific (excluding New Zealand Māori and Aboriginal Australians). Most anthropologists, he observed, 'involve Pacific peoples in our research projects only in the capacity of field assistants, which is paternalism in the extreme' (ibid.). He thus advocated the 'rise of fully trained local colleagues . . . in each Pacific country' as an antidote to the 'kinds of tokenism we have so far entrenched' (ibid.). This was crucial, for he argued that 'the longer that we, as outsiders, monopolise the research in the region, the stronger will be the feelings against us, and the more difficult will be our task of extricating our discipline from the taint of imperialism and exploitation' (ibid.).

'Anthropology and Pacific Islanders' was later included as the first chapter of *We Are the Ocean* (2008), a collection of Hau'ofa's academic and creative works published shortly before his untimely passing in 2009.[1] By then, Hau'ofa had become known for his visionary writings on Oceania as a place of expansive possibility, which he articulated precisely as he was shedding his identity as an anthropologist (and an 'outsider'). As he drove to a 1993 speaking engagement at the University of Hawai'i at Hilo following a meeting of the Association for Social Anthropology in Oceania (ASAO) on the other side of the island, he took inspiration from the vast lava fields and active volcano (and its deity) to pen his seminal 'Our Sea of Islands'. In it, he countered the belittling discourses that constructed the Pacific Islands and its peoples as small, isolated and dependent with a more optimistic view of Oceania as a space of possibility where lands and communities were *connected*, rather than separated, by the sea. Descendants of ancient navigators who settled over one-third of the globe, contemporary Oceanians continue a practice of 'world enlargement' (Hau'ofa 2008: 30) as they extend kinship and economic networks to new shores. He concluded: 'We are the sea, we are the ocean, we must wake up to this ancient truth and together use it to overturn all hegemonic views that aim ultimately to confine us . . . We must not allow anyone to belittle us again, and take away our freedom' (ibid.: 39).

This chapter seeks to pay homage to Hau'ofa by reassessing the shifting relations between Oceanians and anthropology with a particular focus on the ways in which a new generation of Indigenous anthropologists are wrestling with multiple intellectual, cultural and political genealogies in an effort to unsettle any stable notions of a 'we' in Oceanian anthropology. How are the pasts and the lived genealogical relationships to such pasts generative for us? How are they not? Under whose terms and what conditions do 'we' come to claim affinity or assert alterity? How do we also navigate other histories that divide as much as unite our Oceanian peoples? Heeding the call of this volume's editors to think through 'the question of who "we" are' in order to 'reach across anthropological spaces, to enter new ones and, in the process, to *reimagine* and transform existing forms and spaces of contemporary anthropology' (Chua and Mathur, this volume), this chapter explores the ways in which genealogical practice may engage the intersections and divergences among anthropological and Native Pacific pasts in order to generate a more just and decolonial future.

We Remain

Despite the modernist narratives that predicted the end of the Native, Indigenous peoples remain stubbornly sovereign. As Clifford (2013: 1) notes, the increasing volume of claims made under the banner of Indigeneity globally over the last forty years has shown the durability and adaptability of Natives whose 'returns' have led to a 'decentering of the West'. Part of this has entailed a direct challenge to anthropologists who would speak on behalf of Indigenous peoples to whom they claimed affinity, often by virtue of their 'deep immersion' and perhaps even 'adoption' into families. Quoting the punch line from a well-known joke about the fictional characters The Lone Ranger and Tonto, the Native Hawaiian scholar and activist Haunani-Kay Trask (1999: 123) entitled her 1993 critique of anthropological authority 'What Do You Mean "We" White Man?'[2]

Though one might assume that the answer to such colonial ventriloquism is to 'infiltrate the anthropological ranks' (so to speak) and become a certified member of the anthropological 'we', such a task is easier said than done, if it is at all in fact desired. As Abu-Lughod (1991: 140) has pointed out, the power-laden anthropological tradition of a masculine Western self-definition against the feminized non-Western Other often leaves feminist, 'halfie' and Indigenous anthropologists with 'a blocked ability to comfortably assume the self of anthropology' (cited in Uperesa 2010: 284). Indeed, as Chua and Mathur point out in their introduction, this volume in part arose from their 'confessional conversations' that led them to discover their shared 'alienation' – as 'women of colour hailing from Singapore and India respectively' – from the 'Malinowskian persona of the ambivalent European', as well as 'the "we" to which he spoke' (Chua and Mathur, this volume). Echoing these sentiments, the Samoan anthropologist Lisa Uperesa (2010, 284) recalled the shame she felt when reading Margaret Mead's representations of her people as an undergraduate and asked: 'Why would I want to be part of a discipline that saw me as a primitive, sexual, savage?'

Such questioning might usefully be framed as a kind of refusal. For the Mohawk anthropologist Audra Simpson (2014), the assertion of Indigenous sovereignty against settler erasure entails an 'ethnographic refusal' of the classical anthropological modes of theorizing and describing the 'disappearing Indian'. This refusal stems from the ways in which the people of the Kahnawà:ke reserve community in Quebec, Canada 'had *refused* the authority of the state at almost every turn and in so doing reinstated a different political authority. This practice ... includes ... how refusal worked in everyday encounters to enunciate repeatedly to themselves and to outsiders: "This is who we are; this is who you are; these are my rights"' (Simpson 2014: 106). Reflecting upon one interviewee's evasion of questions she posed on citizenship, Simpson argues that such refusals are rooted in a broader Mohawk resistance to political and intellectual forces that would take away their sovereign ability to define themselves as a 'we' (ibid.: 113–14).

I should be clear that when I use the terms Native and Indigenous (with the capital N and I), I am referring to the First Peoples that by and large have a blocked ability to exercise full sovereignty on their traditional homelands.[3] Thus, when I speak of Native anthropology, I am not merely referencing 'insider' (small n in native) anthropology as has typically been the case in meditations on the topic (Narayan 1993; Jacobs-Huey 2002; Tsuda 2015). Rather, I speak of the ways in which Native nations and their members have taken up anthropology for their own purposes, particularly by entering the field and seeking a Ph.D.

Like the terms Native and Indigenous, 'Pacific Islander' (as well as 'Pacific' and 'Islander') indexes historically and geographically situated notions of belonging and autochthony in Oceania (McGavin 2014: 134–35). In his 1975 essay, Hau'ofa narrowed his usage of the term by stating:

> I exclude from this paper the Maori of New Zealand and the Aborigines of Australia because these groups live in predominantly Western-type societies and their problems are different from those of the largely indigenous populations of the rest of the Pacific isles. (2008: 4)

His choice of these groups signalled not only their positions as (fourth world) Indigenous peoples in (first world) settler societies, but also the status of New Zealand and Australia as the dominant political and economic powers impacting the futures of the Island nations located in the cultural regions of Melanesia, Polynesia and Micronesia that he was most engaged with; to that end, he could have also mentioned Native Hawaiians – were Hawai'i not seen as so completely assimilated as to be no longer considered a Pacific society. These divisions also map onto distinctions that Māori, Indigenous Australians and Native Hawaiians themselves were making and continue to make between themselves and the other diasporic Islanders living in their homelands. In these situations, especially with Micronesians in Hawai'i, Pacific Islanders have often suffered racial discrimination and prejudice both from the state and from Indigenous groups who see them simply (and sometimes mistakenly) as 'immigrants' with separate and competing claims to place (Lyons and Tengan 2015b).

Against these tendencies, a new set of scholarly, artistic and political projects have worked to bridge these divides, as seen in Te Punga Somerville's (2012) reminder to Māori that they too 'once were Pacific' and Yamashiro and Goodyear-Kaʻōpua's (2014) hail of all Hawai'i's residents under the banner 'We are Islanders'. That same invocation in Australia, as heard by the Lovangi (PNG)/Pākehā (white New Zealander) anthropologist Kirsten McGavin (2014: 133), conversely signals a pan-ethnic identity for diasporic Pacific peoples that does not include Indigenous Australians.[4] Indigenous scholars such as Lisa Kahaleole Hall (2015) have also warned against the dangers of eliding the experiences and histories of specific Islander groups under conflating categories such as those used by the United States Census, including 'Native Hawaiian and Other Pacific Islanders', and its even more problematic predecessor 'Asian Americans and Pacific Islanders' (which is still used by a variety of national organizations).

Hauʻofa sought to expand the reaches of Oceania and the identities that emerged from it in his later writings. In 'Our Sea of Islands' (1993), Hauʻofa framed Oceania in a way that defied the arbitrary boundaries circumscribing and the associated smallness of Polynesia, Melanesia and Micronesia by extending Oceania out to 'the great cities of Australia, New Zealand, the United States, and Canada' (2008: 36). In 'The Ocean in Us' (1997), he problematized a 'Pacific Islander identity', questioning its viability given the various impacts of imperial/colonial/neocolonial state formations on the identities of Islanders, including 'the New Zealand Maori, Native Hawaiians, and Australian Aborigines' (2008: 50). Eschewing the frames of nationality and race, he wrote:

> As far as I am concerned, anyone who has lived in our region and is committed to Oceania is an Oceanian. This view opens up the possibility of expanding Oceania progressively to cover larger areas and more peoples than is possible under the term Pacific Islands Region... We have to search for appropriate names for common identities that are more accommodating, inclusive, and flexible than what we have today. (2008: 51)

Heeding the call to 'find appropriate names', Hūfanga ʻOkusitino Māhina (2010) and Tēvita O Kaʻili (2012) have been among the most prominent proponents of the use of the term Moana, which across several Pacific (mainly Polynesian) languages translates to 'ocean' (as well as Oceania and Oceanian), as a broadly inclusive identity and anthropological practice that foregrounds Indigenous epistemology (see also Kaʻili, Māhina and Addo 2017). Another related set of reimaginings includes the mobilization of an Austronesian identity defined by the language group that includes (most) Pacific Islanders, Aboriginal Taiwanese, Filipinos and others in Island Southeast Asia out to Madagascar (Odango 2015).

My primary concern in this chapter is to think about the experiences of those Oceanians who identify as Indigenous to the Pacific. I use Indigenous, Oceanian, Pacific and Islander interchangeably and in an open-ended way that is meant to highlight but not delimit Native Pacific identities, histories and politics while not delegitimizing Moana and Austronesian projects.[5] While I do not seek to exclude Indigenous Australians (including both Aboriginal Peoples and Torres Strait Islanders), their experiences receive less attention here. However, it should be noted that Hawaiian, Māori and Aboriginal Peoples have developed particularly strong trans-Indigenous alliances with each other and with American Indian, Alaskan Native and First Nations groups in North America that have their own histories and genealogies of affiliation that are sometimes separate from those that centre other Oceanians.

My present (selective) reflection on the genealogy of anthropology in Oceania builds upon a 2001 essay by Geoffrey White and myself that examined the ways in which the 'shifting politics and practices of cultural representation in the Pacific are challenging and transforming anthropology, as well as producing new possibilities' (White and Tengan 2001: 384). We observed then that the 'Pacific has been one of the most desired regions for traditional anthropology' with its 'anthropological mother lode of linguistic and cultural diversity' (ibid.: 383). 'The conventional western picture of the Pacific', we noted, 'is one of an area of a multitude of indigenous societies where both geography and culture appear as "islands" – small, bounded, and isolated' (ibid.: 384). Among other things, we argued that 'such metaphors have served to reproduce images of Pacific peoples as exotic and distant, located in geographic and cultural spaces wholly separated from the "us" of academic authorship and readership' (ibid.). Regarding Indigenous Oceanians' engagements with anthropology, we commented:

> Anthropology's ethos of fieldwork and 'will to otherness' has combined with Native readings of western domination to lead island scholars away from anthropology and toward a variety of fields such as literature, history, politics, and area study. Yet, native scholars are entering the field in a small but steady flow. As they do, they contribute to its ongoing transformation. (ibid.: 404)

While significant, the impact of these Native Pacific anthropologists needs to be tempered by the persistence of 'the ostensibly universal paradigm of "good" anthropology that continues to structure the academic world system', which 'is built around a particular [Western] "we" whose theoretical, methodological and socioeconomic attributes tend to reinforce each other and the structures in which they operate' (Chua and Mathur, this volume).

Recognizing the durability of a Western-generated 'disciplinary persona' (Chua and Mathur, this volume), it is nevertheless important to point to just a few ways in which Islanders have inserted themselves into and thus rewoven certain strands of these intellectual genealogies. The current cohort of Indigenous anthropologists constitutes a wide range of scholars inside and out of the academy with a variety of levels of training. Though I have not been able to verify specific numbers, the largest number of active Ph.D.s is Māori (over a dozen) and Papua New Guinean (about ten), with smaller numbers coming from Tongan, Hawaiian, French Polynesian, Samoan, Banaban and I-Kiribati communities.[6] Perhaps more significant than the numbers has been the active gathering of Indigenous anthropologists – both doctorates and graduate students – in a series of meetings at the ASAO over the course of four years that produced a special issue of the journal *Pacific Studies* (Volume 33, No. 2/3, August/December 2010) entitled 'Genealogies: Articulating Indigenous Anthropology in/of Oceania'. Co-edited by myself, Tēvita O. Kaʻili and Rochelle Tuitagavaʻa Fonoti, this is the first collection of writings edited and authored by Indigenous Oceanian anthropologists, with contributions from non-Indigenous allies. In our introduction, we suggested that 'articulating visions of anthropology's future ... can be done only through genealogical work – the search for, production, and transformation of connections across space and time' (Tengan, Kaʻili and Fonoti 2010: 140). Attending to such differences as race, ethnicity, class, gender, sexuality, Island origin, colonial history, nationality, institutional location and language, we were careful not to present an essentialized or homogenized view of either Indigeneity or anthropology. With Katerina Teaiwa (2004: 230–31), we took 'an approach that conceive[d] of Pacific peoples as specific, different, and connected individuals or groups ... with respect to *each other* in the past and present' (emphasis in original), and considered 'connections and differences (or the production of connections and differences)' between them. Acknowledging the diversity inherent to the Native Pacific, we engaged Indigenous anthropologists from Turtle Island (North America) in dialogue over 'emergent praxis' and 'strange affinities' in two roundtables at the 2015 meetings of the American Anthropological Association (AAA).[7] Here I would like to spend additional time commenting on the Indigenous anthropological 'we' in the Oceania.

We Shift

In a number of Oceanian languages, the pronoun 'we' has both inclusive and exclusive forms based upon the relationship of the speaker to the audience, and can mark number in different ways. In Hawaiian, there are four plural pronouns for 'we': *kāua* ('we two' including the hearer), *māua* ('we two' excluding the addressee), *kākou* ('we three or more' including those being addressed), and *mākou* ('we three or more' exclusive of the audience). Kākou has become a slogan for broad inclusivity and cooperation, as epitomized in the phrase 'it's a kākou thing' (cf. Hermes 2015). On the other hand, the term 'mākou' tends to have less circulation outside of Hawaiian language contexts; I would argue that this is because mākou refuses the settler assumption that Indigenous places and identities are open and available for all to claim.

Let me start with a statement that I will complicate shortly: it's a mākou thing. We – Indigenous Oceanian anthropologists – have our own set of complex and contradictory genealogies, but they are ours. In his essay 'Pasts to Remember' (2000), Hauʻofa oriented his masterful treatment of Oceanian time as a (partial) response to 'ideas propounded by certain anthropologists about the constructions of the past and the politics of culture' (2008: 61). Lyons (2017: 131) hears in Hauʻofa's use of 'we' and 'us' an 'echoing [of] ... mākou', issued loudly in the following passage:

> We could learn from the works of ethnographic historians and historical anthropologists, as well as from mainline historians, but we Oceanians must find ways of reconstructing our pasts that are our own. Non-Oceanians may construct and interpret our pasts or our present, but those are their constructions and interpretations, not ours. Theirs may be excellent and very instructive, but we must rely much more on ours. (Hauʻofa 2008: 64)

What stands out as particularly remarkable in this passage is the ways in which the dichotomy between anthropology and Pacific Islanders drawn first in Hauʻofa's 1975 essay remains, yet his 'we' has not only shifted but actually switched sides in an effort to repossess a remembered Oceanian past. 'We must resort very seriously to our ecologically based narratives' (2008: 64), he implores, and replace 'the linear processes that presently dominate modern society' with 'the notion of the spiral, which connotes both cyclic and lineal movements' (ibid.: 69) based on 'the regularity of seasons marked by natural phenomena' (ibid.: 67) and on genealogies that 'had much to do with assertions of rights for succession and inheritance, not, perhaps ever, with evolutionary development as we know it' (ibid.: 66).

Hauʻofa also explains that our histories are to be found in the landscapes and seascapes that are the 'maps of movements, pauses, and more movements' (2008: 73) of Oceanian societies across space and time. Thus, it is imperative that we regain what Goodyear-Kaʻōpua (2013: xvi) has called our 'land-based literacies' that include 'a range of critically engaged observational, interpretive, and expressive practices that put land and natural environment at the center'. She further expounds:

> Kānaka [Hawaiians] also recognize our connection to ʻāina [land] as genealogical because we are composed of ʻāina; the organic material of which we are made literally comes from the earth and is constantly returning to it. Our stories come from and are layered upon the land. Thus, many ʻŌiwi assert that we are not only related to but also a part of what is referenced to when one talks about ʻāina. (Ibid.: 33)

This crucial practice of reading and speaking the land and people entails not only an epistemological but an ontological shift (Salmond 2013: 24).

Viewed genealogically, the past generates new possibilities for the future, giving orientation and direction for present action while establishing frameworks for creating new and transforming old relationships. James Clifford, who drew great inspiration from Hauʻofa and honoured him in his writing,[8] explained that 'Hauʻofa's "spiral" is a figure for indigenous thriving, for transformations and returns in endless, genealogical development – a profoundly relational process' (2013: 43). Invoking Lilikalā Kameʻeleihiwa's (1992: 22–23) oft-cited explication of the Hawaiian view of the past as 'the time in front' (which Hauʻofa also references), Clifford (2013: 25) notes that 'she engages a generative, sociomythic tradition', where 'temporality' might be thought of as 'looping lines of recollection, and specific paths forward'; this 'past is about generativity, not recurrence'. Of course, these genealogies may generate as many differences as they do connections, particularly when embedded in contested landscapes. Hauʻofa (2008: 72) writes that 'our important traditions pinpoint particular spots as', among other things,

> markers of more localised mobility out of one's own into other people's territories, which made much of the land throughout our islands enduringly contested by parties deploying not only arms but also oral narratives, including genealogies, to validate their claims and counterclaims.

This insight applies not only to mobilizations on/through Indigenous lands/seas, but also the discursive and physical spaces claimed that comprise the halls of anthropology. Drawing inspiration from Hauʻofa in a 2009 distinguished lecture to the ASAO, Clifford wrote that Oceania 'and some of its distinctive problems and theorists have been generative for thinking about broad issues', including 'differential histories' or 'ways of telling large-scale stories about where we – always a contested pronoun – have come from and are going, separately and together' (2013: 196). It is precisely through tracing the intersections and divergences of Indigenous and anthropological genealogies that we (Indigenous anthropologists and allies) remain active and present in the field, committed to redefining and reshaping a decolonial future for the discipline (Tengan, Kaʻili and Fonoti 2010).

Clifford (2013: 61–62) suggests that one way of thinking about contemporary Indigeneity is through an 'articulation' approach (from Stuart Hall and Antonio Gramsci):

> In articulation theory, the whole question of authenticity is secondary, and the process of social and cultural persistence is political all the way back. It's assumed that cultural forms will always be made, unmade, and remade. Communities can and must reconfigure themselves, drawing selectively on remembered pasts. The relevant question is whether, and how, they convince and coerce insiders and outsiders, often in power-charged, unequal situations, to accept the autonomy of a 'we'.

Pacific Islanders articulating Indigeneity with anthropology in Oceania are thus engaging in tactical alliances of positions in order to assert continuity of and responsibility over community and lands (Tengan, Kaʻili and Fonoti 2010: 154). Based upon the context, the mākou (us, not you) may switch to a kākou (all of us together). This tactical 'clusivity' of Oceanian pronouns indexes shifting relations of power and knowledge that frame Indigenous insistence and persistence. Moreover, the mākou and kākou shift over time as the construction of boundaries around Indigeneity and anthropology variously expands and contracts, reconfiguring relations between Natives and anthropologists. This kind of shifting is consistent with the kinds of genealogical practice I am invoking as the ground for a distinctively Oceanian anthropology. Indeed, there is much we can learn from Indigenous genealogists such as Māori experts in *whakapapa* (genealogy and oral history) who, as Amiria Salmond (2013: 25–26) explains,

> are experienced handlers of ... apparent incommensurabilities – expert translators of alterity into affinity, and of alliance into otherness. Accustomed to shifting between worlds and to scaling their networks strategically, they are schooled in traditions geared to facilitating smooth transitions between alternative universalisms and to the creative encompassment of those who (at least initially) appear as other. Within whakapapa's terms, indeed, 'incommensurability' and 'untranslatability' – and what might be termed 'ontological alterity' in general – are relational states, open to generative transformation like all the nexi and threads (people, landscapes, taonga [ancestral treasures], etc.) that make up its inherently mobile fabric.[9]

This generative ability to interweave or unravel distinct relational lines characterizes an important strand of Oceanic genealogical practice,[10] which relies heavily on the multiplicity of meaning found in Indigenous lexical terms.[11]

Paul Lyons' insightful reading of Epeli Hau'ofa's 'pronominal poetics' (2017: 119) is instructive here. In contrast to his writing in 'Anthropology and Pacific Islanders', which consistently located 'we' and 'us' in the realm of outsider anthropology, Hau'ofa's later essays (including 'Our Sea of Islands', 'The Ocean in Us' and 'Our Place Within'[12]) employed these terms in what Lyons notes are 'mobile and multi-phonic' (2017: 117) ways that show 'how possessive pronouns resonate with issues relating to possession and dispossession in multiple senses of these words' (ibid.: 115). At times, Hau'ofa's 'we' includes 'anyone who has lived in our region and is committed to Oceania', while at other times it references 'autonomous peoples within the new international order' (Hau'ofa 2008: 51, 76). Pointing to the kākou/mākou and kāua/māua distinctions, Lyons (2017: 121) explains that 'Pacific pronouns are marked in ways that indicate proximity and direction, establishing the relationship between speakers and listeners much more precisely and appropriately'.[13]

Drawing from the work of linguistic anthropologists focusing on indexicality in the wake of Silverstein's (1976) work on how speakers creatively deploy subtle and nuanced linguistic resources to work within and transform social contexts and relations, we can think of

Pacific personal pronouns as 'shifters' whose meaning exceeds the grammatical function of marking the number and person involved. Not only does the actual referent of 'we' shift 'from one context to the next' (Duranti 1997: 345), but the use of 'we' and especially the strategic use of inclusive and exclusive variants of 'we' or 'us' may also actively shift the context of the discourse, redefining and transforming relations through speech acts.[14] Clifford finds the Indigenous staying power of such pronominal shifts in a revision of the last words of Ishi, the Yahi Indian who famously lived and died at the University of California's Museum of Anthropology (1911–16). Seeing in the 'different retellings of Ishi's story' a challenge to the 'all-or-nothing outcomes' of settler colonialism, Clifford asserts that 'Ishi's "You stay, I go" becomes: "We remain. You make room"' (2013: 189).

But what happens when 'you' don't make room? And whose room is it anyway? Under what conditions and for what purposes do 'we' and 'you' become an 'us'? Which genealogies do we recount and revise in order to find our collective way forward while honouring the distinctions that matter? In solidarity with the confessional conversations that engendered this volume (see Chua and Mathur's introduction), I offer just a few genealogical stories here as a way of thinking through the 'tangle of historicities' (Clifford 2013: 210), both Indigenous and anthropological, that we (kākou, all of us) must always account for.

We Encounter

When I was a freshman at Dartmouth College, I took a 'Peoples of Oceania' anthropology course because it appeared to be the only class in Hanover, New Hampshire that addressed my central motivating question: what does it mean to be Hawaiian? To my chagrin, our primary text for studying Hawai'i was Captain Cook's journals. The instructor was elated to have a Native Hawaiian student in class, and he took every opportunity to 'let' me speak. A number of my Native American friends were in the class with me, and they would frequently joke about me being the live-in Native, much like Ishi. When Cook's 1779 arrival at Hawai'i Island's Kona coast was discussed, the professor wrote the bay's name 'KEALAKEKUA' on the board and said it aloud. He then turned to me and asked if it was pronounced correctly, to which I said yes. Then with wide eyes and his chalk still in hand, he pointed to me and said with an anticipatory smile, 'No, no, no, no, no. *You* say it'. I couldn't believe my ears (which happened to pick up the snickers of my Indian friends who would for years later repeat those same words at random times to elicit raucous laughter). I want to say that I refused the request, but I have something of a blocked ability to recall exactly what role I ended up playing in that 'command performance' (Clifford 2013: 131). Despite all of that, I somehow ended up majoring in anthropology, with the important modification of adding Native American Studies as part of a combined bachelor's degree, and returned home to earn my Ph.D. (2003) at the University of Hawai'i at Mānoa under the generous mentorship of Geoffrey White and with the guidance of Noenoe Silva, Christine Yano, Vilsoni Hereniko and Ben Finney.

Students coming from Indigenous communities that have been the classical subjects of ethnography inevitably encounter and struggle with the 'weight' of the anthropological genealogies that precede and prefigure their presence in the halls of the academy (Uperesa 2010). Lisa Uperesa, whose story I briefly mentioned above, explains that when her undergraduate professor at the University of California at Berkeley learned she was Samoan, he asked her to read Mead's *Coming of Age in Samoa* and give him her impression of it. 'It is hard to describe my response to the book – it provoked a visceral reaction of shame, indignation, and disgust' (Uperesa 2010: 282). She notes: 'The impact of this first encounter with anthropology was powerful because I went quickly from the position of "amateur anthropologist" to "primitive Native" in one fell swoop and felt the full weight of the anthropological gaze turned upon me' (ibid.: 284). The experience was enough to dissuade her from taking up anthropology as a major. She eventually returned to the field as a graduate student at Columbia where she was attracted to the critical and elegant writing of Lila Abu-Lughod; at the same time, the work of the Māori scholar Linda Tuhiwai Smith in Aotearoa/New Zealand 'reconfirmed my belief that research is not always already a colonizing project but can be driven by local needs and desires' (ibid.: 285).

Perhaps ironically, Indigenous critique that helped Uperesa to imagine a new kind of anthropology had a very different impact in Aotearoa/New Zealand. Amiria Salmond notes that despite a long and rich genealogy of Māori anthropology, the move to decolonize knowledge practices in the academy 'contributed to the departure of Maori from the discipline – many because they felt their intellectual resources better spent elsewhere' (Henare [Salmond] 2007: 104; see also Te Awekotuku 2012). Lily George, one of the few contemporary Māori to follow in the footsteps of the early twentieth-century leader Sir Apirana Ngata and take up anthropology as one of 'the tools of

Europeans' (Henare [Salmond] 2007: 100), asserts that, 'as indigenous people, we have the right to use those tools in ways that suit our needs. *We* decide how we use them; I believe we have that power, and therefore we have the attendant responsibility and accountability to those we research with and for' (George 2010: 253, emphasis in original). For George, anthropological practices are articulated with Indigenous ones, particularly '*whakapapa* (genealogy/history)', which she explains is a methodological framework and 'the bridge that carries us from one experience to another, from one being to another' (ibid.: 241).

Yet again we find blockage here, specifically in the ability and right to freely move from 'one being to another' and assert the co-presence of multiple ontologies in the practice of Indigenous anthropology. The writings of Mārama Muru-Lanning, the first Māori to receive a Ph.D. (2010) at the University of Auckland since Māori Studies separated from Anthropology in 1993, are particularly instructive on this front. Her book *Tupuna Awa: People and Politics of the Waikato River*, based on her dissertation, shows how linguistic shifts in debates over ownership and guardianship of the Waikato River are 'indicative and expressive of ... struggles for influence, prestige and power' (Muru-Lanning 2016: 6).[15] She describes how prior to embarking on her doctoral research, her father and other elders from Waikato took her on a *hīkoi* – a 'spiritual and ethical journey' (ibid.: 27) – to ask permission from her own ancestors (both living and deceased), the various elders from the descent groups living along the river's banks, and the very source of the river itself (ibid.: 27–28). Muru-Lanning notes that 'my anthropology supervisors who were recent arrivals from Britain were unable to see the cultural (and ethical) importance of the hīkoi to my research and any future work I might undertake in relation to the Waikato River', and they had her remove the story from her methods section.[16] In her book, she places that powerful story squarely in the text of the second chapter as a way of opening up a discussion of 'The Landscape We Create' (ibid.: 29). Her 'we' in that section shifts between her Māori and her anthropological identities by at once arguing that 'landscape theory is valuable because it provides a nucleus of debate and discussion for examining the multiple ways of seeing and being in an environment' and then qualifying her use of it primarily as a way of 'explaining why Māori and indigenous scholars design research projects that involve their whānau [extended family] and why respectful and long-term relationships with research participants are valued' (ibid.: 29). Muru-Lanning ends that section with a further caveat: 'While landscape anthropology offers some promise in its intent to deny the primacy of a Western viewpoint, the reality is that most Western-trained scholars rarely question the sources of power and disciplinary productions of knowledge that legitimate their existence' (ibid.: 31). In contrast to that 'reality', her discussion here (as well as her entire monograph) recreates the anthropological landscape from a Native Pacific vantage point that foregrounds genealogical practices of enacting and negotiating relations with ancestors, families, lands, waterways and other anthropologists and anthropologies.

Reviewing Western anthropological critiques of Māori who foreground Indigenous ways of being, Salmond writes: 'One reason why scholars might find it difficult to take their pronouncements seriously is not simply that the terminology deployed is somewhat dated – the often-used "Maori world view" springs to mind – but that we are unwilling to acknowledge even the *potential* alterity of what is being put forward' (Henare [Salmond] 2007: 108, emphasis in original; see also Salmond 2013: 13–14). Salmond's analysis helps to advance a deeper consideration of colonial erasures of co-presence while raising new questions. Rather than thinking of '*potential* alterity', we (the kākou inclusive of all 'scholars') should recognize that 'Indigeneity – Indigenous difference – is fundamentally the condition of "before", of cultural, philosophical, and political life that connect to specific territories and of the political exigencies of this relatedness in the present', and that 'the difference that is Indigeneity is the maintenance of culture, treaty, history, and self within the historical and ongoing context of settlement' (Simpson 2011: 208). Within this context, assertions of we-ness in anthropology deal with nothing less than the continuity of Oceanian peoplehood and the Indigenous lands and seas from which we descend and to which we return.

We Return

In 2014, I gave the distinguished lecture at the annual meeting of the Association for Social Anthropology in Oceania in Kona, Hawai'i. This came as something of a surprise to many, including myself. I had left the association in 2011 after they denied a request that my co-editors and I had made to hold a launch of our special journal issue on Indigenous anthropology at the Honolulu meetings that year; we were told, 'there is no spare room or break in the program'. We felt, once again, like we did not belong.

In 2013, Lisa Uperesa, who at the time was my colleague at the University of Hawai'i, was voted chair-elect of the ASAO. She and her predecessors Edvard Hviding and Paige West had worked hard to make positive changes in the association. Writing in the ASAO newsletter in 2013, West reflected on the most recent of flare-ups on the ASAO listserve on the question of members' experiences of the most recent meeting and suggestions for 'adjustments' at the next one. While she found some emails constructive, she 'was stunned and appalled by the lack of consideration for the inclusion of divergent perspectives in some of the messages' (West 2013: 4). Noting that 'the world of scholarship is changing' and that many researchers (particularly Indigenous ones) in Oceania were 'not anthropologists', West argued, 'We must figure out how to open our world to our colleagues', engage 'questions of sovereignty' and 'make sure that ASAO is a welcoming and productive place for our Pacific Islander colleagues' (ibid.: 4–5). While the 'we' in this message echoed more of Hau'ofa's 1975 usage than his later, the election of Uperesa as the next chair signalled a tangible shift. Indeed, it was Uperesa who convinced me to come back, which I agreed to do with the explicit understanding that I would be speaking to the major issues that I thought the organization needed to address.

As I began working on the talk, I did research into the genealogy of the King Kamehameha's Kona Beach Hotel at which the meeting would be held. It was built on an area known traditionally as Kamakahonu (the Eye of the Turtle), which was the first capitol of the Hawaiian Kingdom unified under Kamehameha in 1810. Kamehameha's personal temple Ahu'ena (Burning Altar) still stood there, now as a backdrop for the evening *lū'au* feasts and cocktail parties. The hotel was the very same site from which Hau'ofa, after delivering a fairly conventional distinguished lecture at the 1993 meeting of the ASAO, departed when he embarked on his trip across the volcanic expanse of Hawai'i Island that inspired him to write 'Our Sea of Islands'.

The traditional custodian of the Ahu'ena, a Hawaiian woman by the name of Lamakū Mikahala Roy, had in recent years come into conflict with the new management. No one on the ASAO board knew of this situation, and so I decided to bring forth these histories (and others) and create a space for Roy to be present at the lecture and share her own thoughts with the audience. In addition, Roy and I organized a special welcoming ceremony at Ahu'ena where a small group of us (Pacific Islanders, including Uperesa) presented offerings to the land and ancestors on behalf of all of ASAO and requested permission to be at Kamakahonu.

As it had become custom to publish the distinguished lecture in the journal *Oceania*, I invited Roy to co-author with me (Tengan and

Roy 2014). The experience was a challenging and rewarding one, particularly as we decided to maintain two distinct voices in the piece and decline a blind reviewer's suggestion to consistently adopt a 'we' voice that might have 'positioned the *best* of contemporary Pacific anthropology as always already in dialogue with our selves, our colleagues, our non-academic yet expert community members'. While we saw that as a potentially generative move, Roy and I felt that even as they intersected, our genealogies needed to also be kept distinct and intact. The most important part was that they were *both* represented and that neither was erased.

There are important relations of respect that are enacted and created in the selective use of plural pronouns, choices that reflect deeper-seated understandings of seniority and genealogical precedence. The different use of kākou and mākou in two Hawaiian proverbs illustrates this. The first goes, 'I paʻa i kona kupuna ʻaʻole *kākou* e puka / Had our ancestress died in bearing our grandparent, *we* would not have come forth' (Pukui 1983: 136, emphasis mine). As Mary Kawena Pukui explains, this is 'said to remind a member of the family to respect the senior line, because they came first' (ibid.). By including the addressee in the kākou/we, generational affiliation and positioning is established and performed through deference to the elders. The second proverb states, 'Nana i waele mua i ke ala, mahope aku *mākou*, nā pōkiʻi / He [or she] first cleared the path and then *we* younger ones followed' and is 'said with affection and respect for the oldest sibling' (ibid.: 247, emphasis mine). Here the mākou/we marks a double separation, the first between speaker and listener(s) and the second between younger siblings and eldest (referred to in the third person). As a junior to Roy, and as a part of the group following on the path that she had cleared for 'us', I knew that my place was 'mahope' (behind).

Extending the conversation on pronominal shifts to relations between Indigenous and non-Indigenous anthropologists, I quote at length my colleague Alex Mawyer, the ASAO programme coordinator:

> That the non-indigenous (hopefully respectful, thoughtful) colleague is *not always part of the inclusive 'we'* should simply be ok, that part of the play of language seems worth pointing out if only for how obvious it should be to everyone engaged in the study of culture and groupness....
>
> Here's another thought. The fact of the kākou/mākou distinction is not itself inherently political or weighty. And speakers of Hawaiian or Tahitian or Mangarevan often use it as part of showing respect to their interlocutors, the folks they're talking to, making it clear by choosing the right 'we' for that moment, that they appreciate all the shared or

not-shared experiences or action, or thoughts, or contextual whatever that came before the conversation. Choosing the right 'we' for the speaker can be a way of showing respect and giving honor to everyone for where they are coming from.

So, could you even imagine an indigenous anthropologist giving respect to non-indigenous anthropologists by *not* including them in the 'inclusive-we'? I absolutely can under some circumstances! Of course, it's also easy to imagine excluding the non-indigenous anthropologist because she/he *has to be excluded* because of what's being communicated, marked out, specified as part of the appropriateness, (in)felicity of the moment. (Alex Mawyer, email, 20 August 2014, emphasis in original)

I quote Alex at length because he is quite smart, and I like him a lot. I also think that our dialogue responds (perhaps at a different register than imagined) to Paige West's injunction: 'We must, as an organization, be able to have open, honest, and collegial conversations about change, inclusion, and the future' (West 2013: 5).

Lisa Uperesa spent her year as chair working with Paige, Alex and others to continue to shift the culture of the association towards one of a deeper collaboration with Indigenous and interdisciplinary interlocutors (personal communication with the author, 2 June 2015). In large part, this comes through her repossession of 'we' and 'us' when writing in the ASAO newsletter. Inspired by the way in which the Kona meetings 'allowed us to respectfully engage, learn from, and share with local scholars and community members in a way that was both organic and revitalizing' (Uperesa 2014a: 2–3), she framed the meeting site of Santa Fe (New Mexico) as one in which the ASAO would be 'mindful of the place we are in and of the relevant connections, both existing and yet to be made, to the Pacific' (Uperesa 2014b: 2). In her final message from the chair, she 'had the pleasure to welcome incoming members Saʻiliemanu Lilomaiava-Doktor and Marama Muru-Lanning to the ASAO Board' (Uperesa 2014c: 2). In 2016, Mārama Muru-Lanning followed Helen Lee as chair and Albert Refiti (Samoan) succeeded Mary Good as chair in 2018. It seems, at least for the moment, that 'we' may be finding new places in anthropology after all.

We Hope

Over forty years have passed since Epeli Hauʻofa called anthropologists (himself included) to task, insisting that 'we must devise ways – or, better still, widen the horizon of our discipline – in order to tap instead of suppress the subjectivity [of Pacific Islanders] to which I have referred and thereby humanise our study of the conditions of the peoples and cultures of the Pacific' (2008: 9). Today, it appears that many of the same conversations are still taking place. That said, a new generation of Indigenous anthropologists in/of Oceania (and their allies) are significantly shifting the dialogue in Pacific anthropology through subtle and not-so-subtle pronominal repossessions of the terms 'we' and 'our' (e.g. Kaʻili, Māhina and Addo 2017: 14).

Given this state of affairs, one might find cause for hope. Should we? Let's get real, ethnographically and historically. Or in Clifford's words:

> To take seriously the current resurgence of native, tribal, or aboriginal societies we need to avoid both romantic celebration and knowing critique. An attitude of critical openness is required, a way of engaging with complex historical transformations and intersecting paths in the contemporary world. I call this attitude realism. (2013: 13)

A significant inspiration for Clifford's ethnographic and historical realism was Hauʻofa's utopic vision of an interconnected and expansive Oceania based in such real-life examples of Islanders moving through the diaspora for work and dwelling in homes marred by armed conflict. The future was uncertain, and that was OK. History did not move on a teleological one-way street to a predetermined end in Oceania. Rather, as Hauʻofa (2008: 69, 72) noted, time spirals and moves in cycles, presenting us with what Clifford calls an 'open-ended conjuncture' and the possibilities of generative pasts. It is in this space that *we* might think of new and old forms of representation to multiple audiences.

I end this chapter by discussing Hauʻofa's choice for the final chapter in his 2008 book: the reprinting of his 1975 poem 'Blood in the Kava Bowl', a response to the historian Ronald Crocombe in their debate over the value of insider/outsider positionality that Hauʻofa articulated in his 'Anthropology and Pacific Islanders'. The poem begins:

> In the twilight we sit
> drinking kava from the bowl between us.
> Who we are we know and need not say
> for the soul we share came from Vaihi.
> Across the bowl we nod our understanding of the line
> that is also our cord brought by Tangaloa from above,
> and the professor does not know.
> He sees the line but not the cord
> for he drinks the kava not tasting its blood. (Hauʻofa 2008: 180)

Like the spiralled ecological time that Hauʻofa looped before us, this poem comes back to live a second life as a commentary on possessing pronouns. A (possibly) shared lineage to the place of 'Vaihi' might allow Hauʻofa and Crocombe to occupy the silent knowingness of 'who we are', defined in their engagement of 'drinking kava from the bowl between us'. However, one sees a shift away from we/us when Hauʻofa writes, 'He sees the line but not the cord'. Selina Tusitala Marsh (1999: 166) posits:

> The metaphorical umbilical cord connects all Pacific peoples genealogically to their spiritual parent, the Polynesian god Tangaloa. The familial relationship between those of common spiritual, mythological parentage means shared identities and knowledge of which the professor is ignorant.

Perhaps even more significant than the invisibility of the cord is the visibility of 'the line'. Were he drinking the kava and 'tasting its blood', perhaps the professor would grasp the generative possibilities of the cord; instead, his limited view of the line creates division rather than connection. And yet Hauʻofa's play on 'we' and 'our' can be read as ambiguous; does he deploy those terms in the inclusive or exclusive sense? The first two lines that place 'we' and 'us' in the context of the kava drinking seem to be inclusive of the listener (the professor). Yet one could read into the third and fourth lines an exclusive 'we' that refuses the queries of identity and 'need not say'. The 'our' in line five seems to include the listener 'across the bowl', but line six might shift back to the exclusive form when flagging possession of 'our cord'. These pronominal shifts continue to mark varying levels of affiliation and alterity throughout the poem. So too does his playfulness throw all of it into question as he ends it in a characteristically clowning crescendo:

> The kava has risen, my brother,
> drink this cup of the soul and the sweat of our people,
> and pass me three more mushrooms which grew in Mururoa
> on the shit of the cows Captain cook brought
> from the Kings of England and France! (Hauʻofa 2008: 181)

Where, then, does this subversion of ceremony, which is itself a ceremonial subversion, leave us? Perhaps all that we can say is that accounting for the Indigenous and the anthropological together, we may generate new futures from shared pasts.

Acknowledgements

I would like to thank Geoffrey White, Lisa Uperesa, Mārama Muru-Lanning, Alex Mawyer, Paul Lyons, Liana Chua, Nayanika Mathur, Amiria Salmond and the blind reviewers of this chapter for their helpful suggestions. All errors are my own.

Ty P. Kāwika Tengan is Associate Professor of Ethnic Studies and Anthropology at the University of Hawai'i at Mānoa. He is author of *Native Men Remade: Gender and Nation in Contemporary Hawai'i* (Duke University Press, 2008), co-editor of special issues on Indigenous anthropology and Native Pacific studies that appear in *Pacific Studies* (2010) and *American Quarterly* (2015), and co-editor of *New Mana: Transformations of a Classic Concept in Pacific Languages and Cultures* (ANU Press, 2016). He is presently working on a manuscript on Native Hawaiian veterans.

Notes

1. I will cite each of Hau'ofa's chapters as they have been reprinted in his 2008 book, though I will note the original date of publication in the text.
2. As Tobin (1994: 132n56) explains, 'Here, Trask is borrowing Tonto's response to the Lone Ranger's query: "We're surrounded by Indians. What are we going to do?"'
3. I am here suggesting a broad working definition that should in no way be seen as limiting the claims to Indigeneity made by others who feel their sovereignty has never been blocked (as I have heard from some of my Tongan friends who identify as Indigenous but remind me that Tonga was never formally colonized), nor do I wish to force the label on anyone who does not want it (as is the case with some of my Hawaiian friends who say we are *not* Indigenous because we too were never colonized, at least in accordance with international law). For a recent anthropological treatment of Indigeneity in Oceania, see Gagné and Salaün (2012).
4. Te Punga Somerville (2012: 232n25) remarks: 'Despite its proximity to the Pacific region, Australia is often excluded from "the Pacific" because of the cultural and linguistic distinctiveness of Aboriginal communities from Melanesian-Micronesian-Polynesian communities. Torres Strait Islanders are a distinct case and do share links with Melanesians in Papua New Guinea'. McGavin (2014: 130, 148n4) includes South Sea Islanders (descendants of Pacific Islanders brought to Australia in the

mid to late 1800s under conditions of forced or indentured servitude known as 'blackbirding' and recognized as a distinct ethnic group in 1994) but excludes Torres Strait Islanders 'because of their classification as Indigenous', though recognizing that some 'may identify as Pacific Islanders' (ibid.: 148n8).

5. On the articulation of an interdisciplinary Native Pacific Studies project in the context of the American academy, see Lyons and Tengan (2015a).

6. A broadly circulated email request was sent on 11 June 2014 with a long list of names inclusive of Pacific Islanders regardless of degree who were actively engaged with anthropology. I am currently in the process of separating out those who have Ph.D.s from those who do not, and in what fields. I have as yet not been able to adequately research Indigenous Australian anthropologists.

7. Leslie Sabiston and Kalaniopua Young organized the graduate student roundtable 'Strange Affinities of Indigenous Anthropology: Alter-Natives and Ethnographic Refusals' that included themselves and Claudia Serrato, Kristen Simmons, Patricia Fifita, Paratene Hirini Tane and Nanise Young-Okotai as participants, with P. Joshua Griffin and myself as co-chairs. Bernard Perley and I organized and chaired the session 'Indigenous Anthropology: Emergent Praxis against Anthropological Deliriums' that also included ourselves, Marama Muru-Lanning, Darren Ranco, J. Kēhaulani Kauanui, Merata Kawharu and Lisa Uperesa as participants. As the AAA conference was in Denver that year, we acknowledged first the Cheyenne, Arapaho, Kiowa and Ute peoples and territories of Colorado and gave thanks to the welcome that the association had received from the Kiowa and Arapaho elder John Emhoolah, Jr. A recording of the second roundtable was posted on YouTube at https://www.youtube.com/watch?v=TQt7DNVCKRA.

8. The chapters 'Indigenous Articulations' and 'Hau'ofa's Hope' that appear in Clifford's collection of essays, *Returns: Becoming Indigenous in the Twenty-First Century* (2013), were both previously published, the latter as Clifford's own homage to the Oceanian thinker's work. The newly written chapter 'Among Histories' draws heavily upon Hau'ofa. In this chapter, I am citing the book rather than the individual chapters or previously published versions.

9. I thank Amiria Salmond for pushing me to think on the way that 'appearing in one instant as the living face of one line, and in the next as the living face of quite another relational constellation, is common practice and does not necessarily imply the sacrifice of one identity for another (as might be assumed when thinking such issues through from the position of a more classically modern, post-Enlightenment subjectivity)' (email correspondence with author, 1 October 2015).

10. While Salmond invokes the metaphor of 'fabric' to represent whakapapa ways of relating, Tēvita Ka'ili, Rochelle Fonoti and I have argued that

cordage is also a productive way of thinking about genealogical practices of Oceanian anthropology (Tengan, Ka'ili and Fonoti 2010).

11. In her reconstruction of Hawaiian intellectual history, Noenoe Silva (2017) has shown how a mo'okū'auhau (genealogical) consciousness and deft usage of kaona (figurative and layered meanings) has characterized the writings of Hawaiian scholars both in the past and in the present, and all with an eye towards extending these forms of intellectual sovereignty into the future.

12. Published in 1993, 1997 and 2003 respectively, these essays are included as chapters in Hau'ofa (2008).

13. Furthermore, Hawaiian (and other Polynesian) linguistic forms of pronominal possession index an even deeper set of cultural and social distinctions in relationships through the use of 'a' and 'o' classes of possessive pronouns and genitives. Generally speaking, 'a' class marks relationships that are alienable, which the possessor controls; 'o' class marks inalienable relationships that the possessor does not control (Wilson 1976; Shutz 1994: 247). Baker argues that the a/o classes are better analysed as a part of the Hawaiian genitive system in which possession is only one function. He writes that 'the accurate definition of *o*-class genitives is that they are unmarked with respect to control and/or effectiveness, and *a*-class is the marked form. *A*-class marks, i.e., specifies, the referent of the genitive as being agentive within the scenario' (2012: 29–30). As my analysis here deals specifically with possessive pronouns, I will refer to them as such. However, I suggest that a fuller discussion of pronominal possession could readily be developed to further tease out how speakers of Hawaiian and other related languages creatively and strategically deploy subtle linguistic resources to navigate complex social relationships and realities.

14. I thank Alex Mawyer for his editorial suggestions here and throughout this chapter, and for directing me to this literature and helping me to understand shifters and anthropological/human 'shiftiness' more generally.

15. Though Muru-Lanning was not attending to the same kind of linguistic shifters that I attend to here in reference to different ways of expressing 'we' in Polynesian languages, she agreed that her arguments about language and claim-making that she interrogates in her book are applicable to the ways that 'we' marks contextualized inclusions and exclusions in assertions of mana (power and authority), both in Native Pacific communities and in anthropology (personal communication with author, 1 July 2017).

16. Even though she could not include it in the methods section, she 'surreptitiously insert[ed] the encounter into the appendices' (Muru-Lanning 2016: 29).

References

Abu-Lughod, Lila. 1991. 'Writing against Culture', in R.G. Fox (ed.), *Recapturing Anthropology: Working in the Present*. Santa Fe, NM: School of American Research Press, pp. 137–62.

Baker, C.M. Kaliko. 2012. 'A-Class Genitive Subject Effect: A Pragmatic and Discourse Grammar Approach to A- and O- Class Genitive Subject Selection in Hawaiian', Ph.D. dissertation. Department of Linguistics, University of Hawai'i at Mānoa.

Clifford, James. 2013. *Returns: Becoming Indigenous in the Twenty-First Century*. Cambridge, MA: Harvard University Press.

Duranti, Alessandro. 1997. 'Indexical Speech across Samoan Communities', *American Anthropologist* 99(2): 342–54.

Gagné, Natacha, and Marie Salaün (eds). 2012. 'Indigeneity in Oceania Today: A Conceptual Tool, a Battle Cry and an Experience', special issue of *Social Identities: Journal for the Study of Race, Nation and Culture* 18(4).

George, Lily. 2010. 'The Interweaving of People, Time, and Place: Whakapapa as Context and Method', *Pacific Studies* 33(2/3): 241–58.

Goodyear-Ka'ōpua, Noelani. 2013. *The Seeds We Planted: Portraits of a Native Hawaiian Charter School*. Minneapolis, MN: University of Minnesota Press.

Hall, Lisa Kahaleole. 2015. 'Which of These Things Is Not Like the Other: Hawaiians and Other Pacific Islanders Are Not Asian Americans, and All Pacific Islanders Are Not Hawaiian', *American Quarterly* 67(3): 727–747.

Hau'ofa, Epeli. 2008. *We Are the Ocean: Selected Works*. Honolulu, HI: University of Hawai'i Press.

Henare [Salmond], Amiria. 2007. 'Nga Rakau a te Pakeha: Reconsidering Maori Anthropology', in J. Edwards, P. Harvey and P. Wade (eds), *Anthropology and Science: Epistemologies in Practice*. Oxford: Berg, pp. 93–113.

Hermes, Karin Louise. 2015. 'The Spaces between "Us" (Inclusive) and "Them" – Aloha 'āina Is a Kākou Thing', *Critical Ethnic Studies* Weblog, 10 August. Retrieved on 11 January 2018 from http://www.criticalethnicstudiesjournal.org/blog/2015/8/10/the-spaces-between-us-inclusive-and-them-aloha-ina-is-a-kkou-thing.

Jacobs-Huey, Lanita. 2002. 'The Natives Are Gazing and Talking Back: Reviewing the Problematics of Positionality, Voice, and Accountability among "Native" Anthropologists', *American Anthropologist* 104(3): 791–804.

Ka'ili, Tēvita O. 2012. '*Felavai*, Interweaving Indigeneity and Anthropology: The Era of Indigenising Anthropology', in J. Hendry and L. Fitznor (eds), *Anthropologists, Indigenous Scholars, and the Research Endeavour: Seeking Bridges toward Mutual Respect*. New York: Routledge, pp. 21–27.

Ka'ili, Tēvita O. (Maui-Tāvā-He-Ako), 'Okusitino Māhina (Hūfanga) and Ping-Ann Addo (Kula-He-Fonua). 2017. 'Introduction: *Tā-Vā* (Time-

Space): The Birth of an Indigenous Moana Theory', *Pacific Studies* 40(1/2): 1–17.

Kameʻeleihiwa, Lilikalā. 1992. *Native Land and Foreign Desires: Pehea Lā e Pono Ai? (How Shall We Live in Harmony?)*. Honolulu, HI: Bishop Museum Press.

Lyons, Paul. 2017. 'ʻEpeli Hauʻofa's Pronouns', in H. Huang et al. (eds), *Ocean and Ecology in the Trans-Pacific Context*. Kaohsiung: National Sun-Yet University Press, pp. 115–34.

Lyons, Paul, and Ty P. Kāwika Tengan (eds). 2015a. 'Pacific Currents', special issue of *American Quarterly* 67(3).

Lyons, Paul, and Ty P. Kāwika Tengan. 2015b. 'COFA Complex: An Interview with Joakim "Jojo" Peter', *American Quarterly* 67(3): 663–679.

Māhina, Hūfanga ʻOkusitino. 2010. 'Tā, Vā, and Moana: Temporality, Spatiality, and Indigeneity', *Pacific Studies* 33(2/3): 168–202.

Marsh, Selina Tusitala. 1999. 'Here Our Words', in M. Rapaport (ed.), *The Pacific Islands: Environment and Society*. Honolulu: Bess Press, pp. 166–79.

McGavin, Kirsten. 2014. 'Being "Nesian": Pacific Islander Identity in Australia', *The Contemporary Pacific* 26(1): 126–54.

Muru-Lanning, Marama. 2016. *Tupuna Awa: People and Politics of the Waikato River*. Auckland: Auckland University Press.

Narayan, Kirin. 1993. 'How Native is the "Native" Anthropologist?', *American Anthropologist* 95: 671–85.

Odango, Emerson Lopez. 2015. 'Austronesian Youth Perspectives on Language Reclamation and Maintenance', *The Contemporary Pacific* 27(1): 73–108.

Pukui, Mary Kawena. 1983. *ʻŌlelo Noʻeau: Hawaiian Proverbs and Poetical Sayings*. Honolulu, HI: Bishop Museum Press.

Salmond, Amiria. 2013. 'Transforming Translations (Part I): "The Owner of These Bones"', *HAU: Journal of Ethnographic Theory* 3(3): 1–32.

Shutz, Albert. 1994. *The Voices of Eden: A History of Hawaiian Language Studies*. Honolulu, HI: University of Hawaiʻi Press.

Silva, Noenoe K. 2017. *The Power of the Steel-Tipped Pen: Reconstructing Native Hawaiian Intellectual History*. Foreword by Ngũgĩ Wa Thiong'o. Durham, NC: Duke University Press.

Silverstein, Michael. 1976. 'Shifters, Linguistic Categories, and Cultural Description', in K.H. Basso and H.A. Selby (eds), *Meaning in Anthropology*. Albuquerque, NM: University of New Mexico Press, pp. 11–56.

Simpson, Audra. 2011. 'Settlement's Secret', *Cultural Anthropology* 26(2): 205–17.

Simpson, Audra. 2014. *Mohawk Interruptus: Political Life across the Borders of Settler States*. Durham, NC: Duke University Press.

Teaiwa, Katerina. 2004. 'Multi-sited Methodologies: "Homework" in Australia, Fiji, and Kiribati', in L. Hume and J. Mulcock (eds), *Anthropologists in the Field: Cases in Participant Observation*. New York: Columbia University Press, pp. 216–33.

Te Awekotuku, Ngahuia. 2012. 'Re-imagining Indigenous Anthropology: Maori and Pacific Perspectives', keynote lecture at the Association of Social Anthropologists of Aotearoa/New Zealand Conference, Victoria University of Wellington, 8–10 December.

Tengan, Ty P. Kāwika, Tēvita O. Ka'ili and Rochelle Tuitagava'a Fonoti. 2010. 'Genealogies: Articulating Indigenous Anthropology in/of Oceania', *Pacific Studies* 33(2/3): 139–67.

Tengan, Ty P. Kāwika and Lamakū Mikahala Roy. 2014. '"I Search for the Channel Made Fragrant by the Maile": Genealogies of Discontent and Hope', *Oceania* 84(3): 315–30.

Te Punga Somerville, Alice. 2012. *Once Were Pacific: Māori Connections to Oceania*. Minneapolis, MN: Minnesota University Press.

Thomas, Nicholas. 2012. '"We Were Still Papuans": A 2006 Interview with Epeli Hau'ofa', *The Contemporary Pacific* 24(1): 119–33.

Tobin, Jeffrey. 1994. 'Cultural Construction and Native Nationalism: Report from the Hawaiian Front', *Boundary 2* 21(1): 111–33.

Trask, Haunani-Kay. 1999. *From a Native Daughter: Colonialism and Sovereignty in Hawai'i*. Revised edition. Honolulu, HI: University of Hawai'i Press.

Tsuda, Takeyuki (Gaku). 2015. 'Is Native Anthropology Really Possible?' *Anthropology Today* 31(3): 14–17.

Uperesa, Fa'anofa Lisaclaire. 2010. 'A Different Weight: Tension and Promise in "Indigenous Anthropology"', *Pacific Studies* 33(2/3): 280–300.

Uperesa, Fa'anofa Lisaclaire. 2014a. 'From the Chair', *Association for Social Anthropology in Oceania Newsletter* #148.

Uperesa, Fa'anofa Lisaclaire. 2014b. 'From the Chair', *Association for Social Anthropology in Oceania Newsletter* #149.

Uperesa, Fa'anofa Lisaclaire. 2014c. 'From the Chair', *Association for Social Anthropology in Oceania Newsletter* #150.

West, Paige. 2013. 'From the Chair', *Association for Social Anthropology in Oceania Newsletter* #145.

White, Geoffrey. 2008. 'Foreword' in E. Hau'ofa, *We Are the Ocean: Selected Works*. Honolulu, HI: University of Hawai'i Press, pp. ix–xx.

White, Geoffrey M. and Ty Kāwika Tengan. 'Disappearing Worlds: Anthropology and Cultural Studies in Hawai'i and the Pacific'. *The Contemporary Pacific* 13(2): 381–416.

Wilson, William H. 1976. 'The o/a Distinction in Hawaiian Possessives', *Oceanic Linguistics* 15(1/2): 39–50.

Yamashiro, Aiko, and Noelani Goodyear-Ka'ōpua. 2014. 'We Are Islanders', in *The Value of Hawai'i 2: Ancestral Roots, Oceanic Visions*. Honolulu, HI: University of Hawai'i Press, pp. 1–8.

PART III

Where Do 'We' Go from Here?

Chapter 6

CRAFTING ANTHROPOLOGY OTHERWISE

ALTERITY, AFFINITY AND PERFORMANCE

Gey Pin Ang and Caroline Gatt

If anthropologists are ever to take [alterity] seriously, our discipline will have to become something more than a cognitive game played in our heads and inscribed in – let's face it – somewhat tedious journals. We will have to become performers ourselves, and bring to human, existential fulfillment what have hitherto been only mentalistic protocols.
 —Victor Turner, 'Dramatic Ritual/Ritual Drama: Performative and Reflexive Anthropology'

Introduction

In the quote above, we have replaced Turner's word 'ethnodramatics' with 'alterity'. Although it changes the intended meaning entirely, we feel justified in taking this textual liberty. The spirit of experimentation that infused Turner's exploratory work in ethnodramatics resonates with current, hopeful, concerns with alterity.

Alterity and affinity are the focus of this edited volume, and in this chapter we, the authors, direct our attention to the senses of affinity and alterity that anthropologists feel in relation to other anthropologists. Who do anthropologists imagine they are referring to when the pronoun 'we' is used to refer to other anthropologists? Does this 'we' get used in relation to the people anthropologists conventionally work with during fieldwork? This deceptively short 'we' implies a sense of belonging, most easily paired off against 'them', a 'them' who 'we' don't necessarily identify with. It evokes the persistent tension in anthropology between the diversity of human experience and its universality. Considered in this binary way – us/them, similarity/difference – the two concepts, alterity and affinity, have resulted in anthropological stances that range from a closed sense of 'us' to an all-encompassing 'humanity'.

In fact, today most anthropologists experience a *dual* pull, towards a sense of mutuality with their fieldwork colleagues and towards the career-complex of anthropology (Sanjek 2015). In the collaborative experience between an anthropologist and a theatre maker, an experience that we draw on in writing this chapter, we have encountered difference and affinity in surprising places. The experiences of familiarity and strangeness in our exchanges were not simple binary oppositions. For this reason, we explore alterity and affinity from a non-contrastive angle.

In this chapter, we propose that the 'we' of anthropology can be a heterogeneous 'we'. In such a heterogeneous 'we', the disciplined nature of anthropological work would not be judged according to its alignment with predetermined and rigid criteria. If 'we' think of a discipline as a community of practice (Lave and Wenger 1991), what defines it is ongoing engagement, not standardization and fossilization of practice. This opens up the possibilities for a discipline based on the 'we' of 'acquaintanceship' (Duferne, cited in Bowman 1998: 267), defined as affinitive or associative relations (Haraway 1991; Bird-David 1994) rather than genealogical ones (Bamford and Leach 2009). Thus, distinguishing this 'we' could be a shifting matter like Mol and Law's (1994) fluid topology, in which the disciplined and rigorous character of academic anthropological work remains a shared aim. Crucially, this makes space for a different sort of collaboration with the people anthropologists conventionally work with in fieldwork. We are exploring this approach between us, Ang as a theatre practitioner and practice-as-research scholar and Gatt as an anthropologist and theatre practitioner.

What is already emerging in our joint work is that despite imperfect understanding, collaboration affords mutual learning. However, for learning to become actually *mutual* and non-hierarchical, there is the need to challenge the conventional environments of legitimation and evaluation of anthropological scholarship, and more broadly academic knowledge practices (see also Blaser 2010; Rodriguez 2015). Also emerging from the joint work are anthropological artefacts that bear little resemblance to ethnographic texts and narratives (Herzfeld 2007). Ethnography might have become the hallmark of anthropological making, but in fact anthropologists have always managed a great deal of freedom in their practices (Escobar and Restrepo 2005). And yet disciplinary gatekeeping appears to be moving towards increased standardization, reducing the degree of freedom in academic contexts (Shore and Wright 2000). Therefore, the experimental task of revisiting the anthropological craft that we propose is embedded in current disciplinary tensions. The collaboration we explore in this chapter has depended on the possibility of open-ended inquiry and a willingness to test ways of working that we needed to devise to fit situations that arose. In other words, the character of our collaborative work is speculative and experimental.

Experimental approaches are at home in an anthropology that is located within 'forms of life that are at odds with dominant, and dominating, modes of life' (Povinelli 2011); in other words, we aim for an anthropology otherwise. Historically, anthropology has credited its experimental character to the great diversity of practices and epistemologies encountered through fieldwork (Pels 2000). However, within the academy these often-called 'non-academic' knowledges are more often than not invisibilized (Blaser 2010). Therefore, experimenting between theatre and anthropology is one way in which to converse across different ways of knowing without subsuming one to the other (Gatt 2015). As Escobar (2008) points out, other modes of life offer alternatives to currently dominant forms. In fact, our approach resonates also with Escobar and Restrepo's (2005: 114) anthropologies otherwise. In this way, a heterogeneous anthropological 'we' is also a possible way towards decolonizing expertise.

Postcolonial thought enabled anthropologists to recognize how the discipline was deeply embedded in the colonial system (Asad 1973). In a way, it is a testament to the discipline that as a result, anthropologists have repeatedly challenged facile demarcations of us and them. The reflexive turn that reshaped much anthropological work in the 1980s is evidence of the seriousness with which anthropologists took these postcolonial concerns (Whitaker 1996). However, these efforts were largely made in addressing the othering effects of *ethnographic writing* (Marcus 2001). The institutional environment and academic craft were otherwise not much altered by the crisis of representation. In fact, it can be said that it simply drove various forms of relativism underground, so much so that Dirlick (1997: 72) has warned 'enthusiasts of diversity' that they may be simply reproducing the logic of empire.

The hegemony of academic epistemology is so entrenched that we can say that contemporary anthropology is underpinned by relativism, which is a very specific way of managing alterity (Holbraad

2012). Rarely do ethnographic texts elaborate on the implications of what is learnt during fieldwork for the ethnographer's own assumptions of reality (Willerslev 2004: 414).[1] The issue here is that this unspoken relativism has led to a certain complacency (ibid.) and lack of confidence (Gatt 2010) as regards how anthropological conceptualizations of alterity actually have effect in the world.[2] To achieve the aims of disciplinary decolonization implied in anthropologies otherwise, we will argue that the *craft* of anthropology needs to be revisited, not only the content of conceptual work. This disciplinary complex encompasses the daily practices of anthropology in universities, including the audiences to whom anthropologists are accountable. Taking Holbraad's (2012) provocation seriously, why not take recursive anthropology a step further? We could take cues from what we learn in fieldwork to renew our ways of enacting, as well as our ways of thinking, anthropologically, which are anyway intrinsically enmeshed in one another.

In the sections that follow, we describe our ongoing collaborative experiment in doing anthropology otherwise. In effect, this means that both the anthropologist and the theatre maker allow themselves the possibility to learn and be changed by that experience of collaborative enquiry across any aspect of their work. Importantly, this necessarily includes how we value and judge our work. In the final section, we discuss in detail how this entails a shift in the legitimating environment – in other words, a shift in who anthropologists are accountable to.

Carrying out a collaborative enquiry that is based within an academic institution can change the dynamic of research away from a logic of instrumentality (Marcus 2001). We then briefly unpack the notion of collaboration in anthropological practice, because even though this has become something of an antidote for the colonialist underpinnings of anthropology (ibid.), we have found that even key examples of collaborative anthropology, which do not attend to the entire craft of the discipline, have tended to reproduce epistemic colonialisms. Collaborative anthropological projects, similarly to 'writing culture', as Chua and Mathur point out in their introduction to this volume, often incorporate the voices of 'others' '*on anthropology's own terms*' (italics in the original). Before concluding, we present a taste of the hope that, as with social movements (Bocock 1974), the experimental fringes can enable more mainstream work to adopt aspects of our heterogeneous anthropology and theatre associative enquiry that would otherwise be excluded from currently conventional anthropological 'terms'.

Crafting Anthropology Collaboratively

According to Ingold and Lucas (2007), the artefacts produced by any practice carry the traces of the frames of attention that were employed to make them. In other words, one can recognize in an artefact the particular education of attention needed to make that artefact. An anthropological study, then, also carries a particular type of attention. Therefore, they ask: 'could we not regard the artwork as a *result* of something like an anthropological study, rather than as an *object* of such study? . . . [c]ould they also include drawings, paintings, printwork or sculpture? Or works of craft? Or musical compositions? Or buildings?' (Ingold and Lucas 2007: 291, italics in the original). We suggest that the same can be considered of an experimental theatre and anthropology associative enquiry, a performance of sorts.

Gey Pin Ang has recently been awarded her Practice-as-Research Ph.D. and has worked as an associate lecturer (2014–16) at the School of Arts, University of Kent. A performer and pedagogue, she is a recipient of the Theatre Artist Award, Singapore. Ang graduated from the University of Hawaii with a BA in Theatre in 1992, and performed lead roles within the Project *The Bridge: Developing Theatre Arts*, of the Workcenter of Jerzy Grotowski and Thomas Richards, in Italy. Since 2006, she has taught internationally via Sourcing Within Worksessions (sourcingwithin.org/) and collaborates with intercultural and interdisciplinary artists. Ang's current research explores the notion of 'care of the self' and the discoveries of the performer's potentiality via one's physical and vocal embodiment in a performative work.

Caroline Gatt is a Research Fellow on the *Knowing from the Inside* European Research Council-funded project, based in the Department of Anthropology, University of Aberdeen.[3] In parallel with her undergraduate studies in social anthropology at the University of Malta (1998–2002), Gatt trained with a research theatre group in Malta and later in Italy, carrying out practice-based research (2001–06). She was struck by the resonance between certain anthropological principles and practices and those in her theatre work. When in 2013 as part of her ongoing theatre work Gatt participated in a Sourcing Within Worksession led by Ang, she was inspired not only by Ang's responses to her anthropologically informed questions, but also what felt like an enthusiasm to engage in these sorts of exchanges. A hope took hold to develop a collaboration between them.

In one of our very first meetings discussing our collaboration, Ang made a suggestion that was keenly anthropological. She suggested that to achieve the sort of collaboration Gatt was interested in, she (Ang) could be the anthropologist, and observe Gatt's theatre work that resulted from working with Ang in her Sourcing Within Worksessions. Depending on the way Gatt engaged in the group improvisations or her individual creations, Ang would be able to tell whether Gatt had, as an anthropologist, understood something about Ang and the 'tradition' she carried with her. She would evaluate whether Gatt's anthropological interpretations had grasped something that resonated with her, not only through the conventional texts Gatt produced, but also through Gatt's theatre work – that was, after all, where Ang's expertise lay. Here is a key reason for including ongoing theatre work as an integral part of the daily research process. Creating anthropological artefacts in addition to text, such as theatre improvisations or theatre pieces in this case, is an essential way for evaluation and assessment to be shifted to those we work with and to shift towards complicity and away from instrumental research.

Some two decades ago, Ang spent a year studying humanities subjects before deciding to do her theatre degree in the United States. Among the courses, she had chosen an introductory course on cultural anthropology. Her first assignment for that course was to choose an activity (at a community centre) and write her observation on it. She based her observations on the differences (ethnicity and gender) of the people present there, their interactions with one another, and the possible happenings, all through her observation from a distance. She enjoyed the reading materials of that course, mainly about different cultures and experiences, and fieldwork conducted by various anthropologists in remote communities. These uncovered a big and fascinating world for her. The course teacher was a very encouraging mentor. She was always positive on the perspectives that Ang adopted in her class work. English language was secondary for those assignments, in which what seemed to be important to the anthropology lecturer was coming to an understanding rather than a precise use of language. Though she did not take further anthropology courses, she experienced joy attending that course. After that year of exploration of humanities subjects, she decided to study theatre as an undergraduate. Only much later did she realize that this anthropology course, as well as other humanities subjects she had attended, had influential effects on her theatre studies in the following years. Most of all, she had learned to take on different perspectives while creating performances or viewing performative works. She is intrigued by, and has continued to regard human interactions as a primary concern in her theatre-making process.

Since 2013, Ang has had the opportunity to participate in Gatt's anthropological work in the context of the *Knowing from the Inside* project at the Department of Anthropology, University of Aberdeen. This has brought her back to her initial interest in anthropology, which she has always associated closely to 'human being' and as a sense of 'livingness'. Indeed, Ang's collaborative experience alongside Gatt so far has opened up new territories for Ang, transcending any scholastic and disciplinary concern. Our shared explorations venture between the boundaries of our differences, and challenge the way(s) in which Ang had previously learned about anthropology as well as theatre. The current research experience made her more aware of what and how, together with Gatt, she can measure and re-evaluate this collaboration. Stemming from a professional partnership, this cross-disciplinary research has expanded beyond our cultural and lingual differences, and has extended towards a new horizon for Ang's practice-based research. These shared human experiences have demanded a continuous renewed mode of doing research (independently and jointly), adapting to each other's methodologies, and this has proven to be a nourishing experience. This is an important point because it is how we can tell whether a joint work process is succeeding in not being extractive. While we measure our existence through years of achievements in life, these shared human moments serve to be unusual and special, especially within an academic environment.

Initiated by Gatt, this joint effort has brought Ang's practice-based work into dialogue with other so-called 'embodied' research and methodologies platforms also based in universities, beyond the confines of performance studies. From Ang's point of view, to introduce praxis work in an academia setting is still comparatively uncommon. It requires new standards in terms of presentation modes, among many other things, and this challenges the limits of how a collaboration can take place and be shared.

Gatt's anthropological context for Ang's theatre practice is an endeavour that, as they strive for the practice to be accessible and to be shared heuristically, emphasizes lived rather than vicarious experience. From the field of phenomenological research, Ang approaches her practice-based work on the self – that is, her embodiment of *taijiquan* or singing of songs from her cultural roots – as a process of heuristic inquiry. The linguistic root of the term *heuristic* comes from the Greek word *heuriskein*, meaning to discover or to find. It refers to a process through which one discovers the nature and meaning of a given experience, and develops methods and procedures for its further investigation and analysis (Moustakas 1990: 9).

On different levels, this collaboration between Gatt and Ang has opened up a new doorway, finding a good balance between alterity and affinity in our own work and selves.[4] Between our differences in disciplines and as persons, the challenges of difference soften through our continuous conversations and exchanges. Our understanding is gained through willingness for acquaintanceship, encounters and constantly letting go of our own ideas and approaches in our respective disciplines and fields of research. And yet what this allows is for difference to become part of personal experience. This is a key point that we are making. Here, neither difference *nor* sameness could be essentialized for long (as Zamorano Villarreal, this volume, notes tends to happen in the field of indigenous media). We found that once we committed and began to work together both 'difference' and 'sameness' were inevitable experiences that we had to navigate as part of the process. We both had an equal commitment to our individual practices (Ang theatre and Gatt anthropology) which meant that neither of us would be content if either one of the practices or approaches was subjugated or silenced for any length of time.

One proviso here is that we are not suggesting that anthropologists attempt to become specialists in the area of expertise of the people they collaborate with. Apart from defeating the purpose of a collaboration, the result of such an attempt can only be mediocre. For instance, Dell Hymes, whom Escobar and Restrepo (2005: 106) praise for an early attempt to 'reinvent anthropology' in a vein that resonates with their anthropologies otherwise, participated in the production of an anthology of poems by forty-two anthropologists called *Reflections* (Prattis 1985). One reviewer, although entertainingly harsh, calls the majority of the volume by and large 'a disaster', and most of the poems amateurish (Sapir 1988: 446). Writing poetry requires craft and discipline, he continues, 'discipline often far exceeding that we impose upon our anthropology' (ibid.). He concludes that any poetry should be submitted to poetry journals, and 'survive a higher critical level' before being published by an anthropological body (ibid.). Our suggestion to revisit the anthropological craft is done with this pointed critique in mind. A heterogeneous discipline would anyway require ongoing negotiation about rigour.

Ang's suggestion to anthropologically observe Gatt's theatre work was not only informed by her expert following of how Gatt had worked in her sessions as an anthropologist, but also from her long-standing interest in carrying out ethnographic-type fieldwork as part of her own research *prior* to her engagement with Gatt. All the more frequently, carrying out anthropological fieldwork does not entail that the anthropologist entering the field is the only one with expertise on how to do social research. It has become clear that the people with whom anthropologists work rightly feel ownership of the knowledge co-produced (see Loovers 2016; Zamorano Villarreal, this volume; Tengan, this volume). One reason is the sensitive issue of knowledge and identity politics that are crucial in places such as Canada (Neizen 2000; Brown and Nicholas 2012), Australia (Weiner 2007; Hanson 1997; Linnekin 1992) and New Zealand (Salmond 2013, 2014). In addition, we do well to remember Escobar and Restrepo's (2005) point that anthropology is only considered homogeneous from a specific position, the position of 'dominant anthropologies'. Finally, there are many others who have explored the experimental possibilities of anthropological practice. However, we have found that these experimental approaches tend to be found outside the academy, among artists especially,[5] and in other disciplines such as in the field of design (Donavan and Gunn 2012; Gunn, Otto and Smith 2013; Binder et al. 2016). Performance studies is a discipline that emerged from a collaboration between the theatre maker Richard Schechner and the anthropologists Victor and Edith Turner. However, since the 1980s this is only mentioned in conventional anthropological texts to distinguish an ethnographic approach from a performance studies approach (Schieffelin 1998).

Since anthropology is practised beyond the narrow confines of academic anthropology, the hope that a heterogeneous anthropological 'we' can influence mainstream academic anthropology ensures at least two things. First that 'academic anthropologists' do not 'miss the boat', so to speak, as anthropology is in continuous transformation whether anthropologists like it or not. This would be a pity, since the value of the work done in the privileged seclusion of universities and academic journals could be lost. However, secondly, finding a way for current-day academic anthropologists to remain involved without stifling the constantly morphing thing that anthropology may become, might hopefully entail that rigour remains important and that the heterogeneous anthropologists of the future do not become 'poor poets'.

With these issues in mind, our current project is intended to be collaborative from its inception through to the various artefacts we are producing together and alongside each other. Ang and Gatt met before the beginning of the *Knowing from the Inside* (KFI) project, for intensive preparatory work. We also corresponded via email and Skype on an almost daily basis, discussing our hopes, plans and interests and exchanging written project proposals for our respective institutions for each other's feedback and thoughts. We exchanged articles and books and funding proposals, and Gatt continued to participate in the theatre Worksessions that Ang leads in varying localities.

It is impractical, if not impossible, for any anthropologist to be flagging every moment in which she makes a record of joint experiences. Collaboration, when this includes co-design of the research, is a definite way to temper what Castaneda calls the 'impossibility of transparency' in fieldwork (2006: 82). In fact, Castaneda argues that this impossibility is partly derived from 'the teleology of production and dissemination of ethnographic knowledge' (ibid.) that governs fieldwork. The result of this is that our current collaboration may include the production of ethnographic publications, as this chapter partly includes, but not only. In fact, there is also the space for 'nothing' to emerge; for 'failures' to occur; for collaborative experiments to become dead ends.

Prior to the beginning of the KFI project, Gatt participated in three Sourcing Within Worksessions. We also held public conversations after Ang's performances in Barcelona, in January 2014. The Worksessions Ang normally runs began to change through our collaboration. In the week-long Worksession in Portugal, earlier in January 2014, Ang introduced Gatt and our joint interests. Ang repeatedly incorporated comments resulting from our conversations in the reflections she shared with the participants *as they were carrying out the theatre tasks she gave them*. During one of the afternoon sessions, Gatt invited the Worksession participants to interview each other with three open-ended questions about life history and their experience of working as performers. They recorded their replies and reflections on large pieces of card that they could use as presentation material when they fed back to the group, if they wanted to. However, the key of this experiment was to ask the performers to interpret the experience of the interview through their own skills and develop a short one-minute improvisation to share with the rest of the group. On the last day, we had a group discussion about their experiences and reflections on the work we did.

In the past year, we have also worked towards developing a 'mixed media' conversation, where, like bilingual speakers, the participants in such a conversation are able to draw on different forms of communication in order to convey the different qualities of experience (see Gatt 2017a, 2017b and Gatt et al. 2017 for emerging experimental examples of this). Architects (Lucas 2007) and designers (Suchman 2000: 9; 2001: 168) already employ this multiple mode of communication using speech, writing and drawing of different forms. Using gesture to add depth to our speech is already something commonly done (Hendry and Watson 2001); the skills of performance refine the use of gesture, rhythm and interpersonal responsiveness.[6]

In March 2014, we organized and held a Sourcing Within Worksession specifically for anthropologists in Aberdeen. Different to Ang's previous Worksessions, this event was much shorter, only three days instead of the normal six, and included many more group discussions.[7] The experimental approach we have taken in this project explicitly challenges the conventional input/output model of research. Ethnographic research typically consists in a phased approach, composed of a block of time dedicated to a literature review, a block for fieldwork and a block for writing up. Instead, due to the necessary openness needed in the constant negotiation involved in this collaboration, the project had to be iterative in nature. Each of the threads normally kept separate are and will carry on being active throughout the project. In theatre research, there are movements between risky activities with unknown outcomes and refinement activities during which work is crystallized. These movements typically take place several times in a creative process rather than just once, at several scales, with different interlocutors. The same is being tried out in this project, variously shifting between open experimentation and temporary crystallization. The form this crystallization is taking is multiple: Ang and Gatt have presented jointly at four conferences, written three joint articles, and further individually written pieces that emerge and develop our exchanges (Ang 2015, 2017a, 2017b; Gatt 2013, 2015, 2017d, 2017e). We have begun to experiment with academic performances, but we are not in any rush for this, since devising performances for a public is specifically the aspect of theatre that laboratory theatre puts in abeyance (Grotowski [1968] 2002).

The Sourcing Worksessions during which we work together are simultaneously 'risky' fieldwork moments, and crystallizations (moments of dissemination/presentation) themselves. The participants in each Worksession are both participants in Gatt's and Ang's ongoing research and critical audiences for our work up to that point. To an extent, a number of the participants in each Worksession have remained in contact with Ang and Gatt, both jointly and individually, and a wider group of collaborators has long been in the process of formation.

Heterogeneous Collaboration

What may be hidden by the report format that we have presented above is that the sorts of collaborative enquiry we experimented with above do not necessarily emerge when anthropological engagement is 'circumstantial' (Marcus 1995: 113). If such engagement is aimed at developing rapport, then the character of fieldwork remains instrumental. 'Rapport signaled instrumentally building a relationship with a participant or informant with *the predesigned purposes* of the anthropologist's inquiry in mind and without the possibility that those very purposes could be changed by the evolution of the fieldwork relationship itself' (Marcus 2001: 521, emphasis added). Marcus suggests that reflexive complicity is needed if what is conventionally considered collaborative research is to cease being instrumental (ibid.). However, without critical attention to the entire craft of anthropology, *even reflexive complicity in collaborative anthropology* has tended to reproduce academic hegemony and thus maintain a closed anthropological 'we'.

As we have intimated already, collaborative anthropology requires partners to be included in all stages of the work, from project design, to methods, to analysis, to theory-building, to presentation (Lassiter 2005). Using an example from Colombia, Rappaport (2008: 2) argues that collaborative ethnography can revitalize anthropological thought. An important feature about Colombian anthropologists is that they are citizen-researchers; they consider their scholarship to be acts of citizenship (Jimeno 2000, cited in Rappaport 2008: 3). The implication of this is that the audience to whom the anthropologist holds themselves accountable extends beyond academia. This shift is essential to and necessary for collaborative ethnography as it is currently being defined (see Lassiter 2005). Here, 'collaboration is more than "good ethnography" because it shifts the control of the research process out of the hands of the anthropologist and into the collective sphere of the anthropologist working on an equal basis with community researchers' (Rappaport 2008: 7). Fieldwork shifts from being a site for data collection to one of co-conceptualization (ibid.: 5). Describing the principles of collaborative ethnography in more detail, Rappaport argues that there is a need to go beyond the sort of complicity of which Marcus gives examples. Marcus's examples include collaboration only with educated, cosmopolitan elites (ibid.: 9).[8] The Colombian projects Rappaport reports on aim to include subaltern subjects as collaborators, a position made clear even in the title of the initiative: Other Americas/*Otros saberes* (other knowledges). The difference in the sort of work described by Rappaport (ibid.: 4) is that collaborative work creates a particular type of public anthropology, one that does not *only* include the reading kind.

Despite this attention to the positioned nature of collaborators in fieldwork, exhibiting an attention to hierarchy or social stratification, this experiment in collaborative anthropology may need to challenge further its implicit logocentrism. This is not so much in its focus on text, as Rappaport (2008) emphasizes that only little of the project work is transformed into monographs. However, the stated aim of Rappaport's collaborative project is to include those who were previously subjects of study, local researchers, as equal members of the team. In order to justify recognition for these local researchers by the academy, Rappaport appeals to 'the creation of abstract forms'. Such collaborative endeavours, Rappaport maintains, are not only of co-analysis, they are also collaborative instances of theory-building (ibid.: 4–5). In this, the notion of knowledge as abstractable, fundamental to logocentrism, is not questioned. Neither is the value of theory questioned, not only as separate from analysis, description and practice, but also as a supposed mark of 'true scholarship'. Rather than widening the anthropological 'we' through making space for alterity, this approach simply educates, or domesticates in Escobar and Restrepo's terms, more people to be academic anthropologists.

Stengers' (2011) discussion of comparison provides a way forward. She notes that in the discourse of Western science, knowledge needs to be rendered commensurable for it to be brought together for comparison (ibid.: 56). To avoid this dependence on commensurability, she insists that what is necessary is for partners, those who are involved in the comparison, to be equal but not necessarily semblable: 'We are returned here to the Latin etymology of "comparison": *com- par* designates those who regard each other as equals – that is, as able to agree, which means also able to disagree, object, negotiate, and contest' (ibid.: 63). Furthermore, 'no comparison is legitimate if the parties compared cannot each present his own version of what the comparison is about; and each must be able to resist the imposition of irrelevant criteria' (ibid.: 56). What we are exploring in our shared work is how to collaborate without attempting to render our different approaches commensurable, understood as a *reduction* to a similar logic. This is necessary in order not to 'domesticate' the alterity of our respective knowledges, and to achieve the heterogeneous discipline we suggest herein.

It is also essential to recognize that taking others seriously depends squarely on acknowledging the reflexivity of the people who are fieldwork collaborators (Marcus 2001). Working with Ang's heterogeneous groups of performers, it has become clear that there are also different refractions of reflexivity; other ways of knowing also have their own systems for analysis, critique and evaluation (Gatt 2015). It appears currently that we are working with the same generative premise as Viveiros de Castro, Holbraad and Axel Pedersen (2014), that action and thought have consequences for the world we share. However, rather than focusing on conceptual creation alone (ontography), we are experimenting with various forms of enquiry and subsequent forms of communication (including writing) and importantly here with various forms of evaluation, ones that include non-academic criteria for assessment.

What we describe above exemplifies the value that a heterogeneous discipline can offer. Doing anthropology *with* theatre makers, rather than *of* theatre, can offer tools for understanding and participating within enacted relationships. The discipline and practice of performance can inspire ways to make space for diversity that are different from those afforded by text, or rather by certain ways in which texts have become authoritative tools in academia. To reiterate a previous point, text itself does not *determine* the inclusion, sense of immediacy or otherwise of the reader (see Gatt 2017a). In working with online fora, Kelty (2005) re-describes writing as composition (of text, scores, performances) that can be part of 'recursive publics'. A key insight from performance, which could also influence our understanding of writing, is that anthropologists could therefore develop skills that move the practice of scholarship away from retrospective description to responsiveness in the midst of engagement (Gatt and Ingold 2013).

Experiential Practice and Affinity

By employing an empirical and heuristic approach, Ang hopes to present her practice in a way that conveys lived experience. She emphasizes that a written testimony for her practice-as-research can be pertinent, especially for those who are also practising theatre makers or who have keen interest from an insider's perspective. Any performative work is a process filled with adventures, mistakes, surprises; all of the unknowns. The pre-performance phase via training and rehearsals is unpredictable and uncertain before a work then becomes fully developed and presentable. It is the instinctive and organic self that needs to be awakened to guide oneself through this experience. Ang aims to reveal experiential insights as someone who is creating a performance work: what are the impulses behind my creative process? How do different materials come into place? What accumulative life experiences might have contributed to the complex trajectory involved in creating my work? Whether as a practitioner or a researcher, Ang feels it is important not to rely overly on intellect; rather, she would like to reveal her experiential practice:

> Experience is always necessarily embodied, corporeally constituted, located in and as the subject's incarnation. Experience can only be understood between mind and body – or across them – in their lived conjunction. (Grosz 1994: 95)

'Experience' is the key to the doorway of her performance that has to be 'lived' and understood through doing. Though performance knowledge can be passed from person to person, the actual creation and execution of a performance are always metamorphosing and non-transmissible.

To a certain extent, the one who performs relates and interacts *directly* with those present in her performance. This means an act that is to be 'done' by someone, the actor, in a common space faced with other human beings, the audience. The sense of 'livingness' in a performance would not be complete without some scrutiny of 'theatre [as] an encounter' (Grotowski [1968] 2002: 55), a shared communion, experienced between the one who acts and the one who watches. It is exactly in the living circumstances of a performance that human beings converse and think collectively or individually. It is through a close proximity with those present in the performance that they subsequently become Ang's acquaintances and associates. This sense of 'acquaintanceship' also finds a resonance in Dufrenne's philosophical view of 'music as acquaintance, as friend and ... the lived music as experience' (Bowman 1998: 267). As a musical performance, Ang's Practice-as-Research Ph.D. performance *Wandering Sounds* investigates, uncovers and establishes a mode of a receptive encounter and attentive listening, yet another form of 'affinity' among people and their differences.

The practical knowledge in performing, as Ang has experienced it heuristically, stems from an intuitive mode. Attempting not to interfere with a judgemental stance in moments of her own playing *while* creating, materials begin to appear and take shape. Unlike a discursive mode where words and texts are the means of understanding, performative work demands 'intuitive listening' (Petitmengin-Peugeot

1999: 26). While rehearsing, Ang spontaneously follows the body- and sound-scapes, and constantly in accord with the live instrumental and visual creation/execution by the musician of the performance, Nickolai D. Nickolov.

Music has the capacity to stimulate our various senses all at once. Ang's practical experience revolving around music has been sensorial, being enacted with her whole self. Music provokes all her senses, where her mental understanding *does not dominate*, although it participates, during her doing and executing of the performance. In such an instance, she is at the experiential core of 'practice'.

Performance with an embodied approach suggests an openness to continuous learning and effortless process to be experienced again and again. Through a performance structure, the life in a performer's scores can be renewed and refreshed if unlearning what is already known. *Wandering Sounds* allows Ang a refined and active mode of conversing and reflecting upon her deeper thoughts and questions. Performance is an intermediate space for her between her daily life and her inner streams of thoughts and associations. *It is manifesting and concretizing her thoughts in action.* It is precisely during the act of performing with people in that instant that one is not able to stop or rehearse again. The act has to happen *now* and there is no way to repeat or restart the performance. It is a 'wisdom [that] does not merely cause us to know: it makes us "be" in a different way' (Hadot 1995: 265). The liveness of performance requires that a performer allows the presence of the audience to affect them without stopping. For this, the disciplined spontaneity described above is essential because one needs to be *hic et nunc*, to live it to the fullest, as if for the first time and as if never again. It requires one to be unmistakably attentive throughout the interactive process of performing; it requires a deep sense of 'affinity' and 'alterity' with oneself.

Conclusion: Challenges for a Heterogeneous Discipline

Here we have suggested that by shifting our expectation of the anthropological 'we' towards a heterogeneous one, the discipline of anthropology has the potential to move towards taking both affinity and alterity seriously, without necessarily essentializing either. The implication of this associative understanding of a discipline is that it would allow the work anthropologists do with others, in what is conventionally considered fieldwork or interdisciplinary collaboration, to inform not only anthropological concepts, but any aspect of the craft of anthropology. This is the sort of experiential or heuristic approach that performers develop in order to cultivate a disciplined spontaneity.

First, a focus on disciplined spontaneity requires a shift in academic knowledge practices from retrospective to prospective (see Gatt and Ingold 2013). Second, it generates a type of reflexivity which enables the recognition of difference and affinity within one's own experience in the very process of relating and collaboratively contemplating, learning and experimenting. Specifically, if the aim of any particular anthropologist is the decolonization of their craft, collaborative approaches offer a way out of the instrumental character of fieldwork relationships. What we have offered here is a specific example that has been attentive to different ways of knowing: laboratory theatre and anthropology.

We believe that our proposal is based in disciplinary realities because on the whole anthropologists have shown themselves to be considerably experimental. In fact, early in the history of the discipline, a large number of anthropologists experimented with collaboration by writing with primary informants, and sharing with them the entire research process (Lassiter 2005). Lassiter identifies the process of professionalization as the reason why collaborative endeavours of the sort did not become mainstream practice. And yet, professionalization notwithstanding, there have been many other experimental moments throughout the history of anthropology. Examples are Victor Turner's experiments in ethnodramatics, Del Hymes' ethnopoetics, Diane and Jerome Rothenberg's *Symposium of the Whole* (1983), which brought together anthropologists, poets and performers. More recently, anthropologists have also been experimenting with installation (Stoller 2015; Lincoln 2014) and the *laboratorium* (Ssorin-Chaikov 2013), and the European Association of Social Anthropologists (EASA) introduced laboratory sessions in its biennial conferences in 2014.

However, with the entrenchment of audit culture (Strathern 2000), the majority of anthropology departments are experiencing pressures to standardize their practice more than ever before. In fact, Shore and Wright (2000: 74) record that in the mid 1990s the Quality Assurance Agency (QAA) declared that a discipline is a corporate entity, implying that each discipline should strive for internal homogeneity of practice. In order to achieve Geertz's (1984) hope that anthropology is willing to discard ways of working that are no longer useful for current disciplinary concerns, willingness to experiment is vital. The heterogeneous discipline we argue would be ideal in order to truly address questions of alterity will have a hard time in this atmosphere of audit. This is especially the case since audit is a result of risk society and the perceived need to 'process risk' (Shore and Wright 2000: 83), where risk is an inherent and necessary part of experimentation.

Over and above the institutional challenges to the ideal of a heterogeneous, open anthropological 'we', there are a number of disciplinary challenges. Here are just three questions in this dilemma:

- How to develop communication in which interpretation and argument in a heterogeneous practice are fruitful?
- How to ensure rigour?
- What would be the processes for evaluation or judgement?

In the light of our current experience, here are two concluding thoughts. First, there is a clear value in having disciplines that attempt to maintain a certain degree of coherence. One reason is the possibility of having concise discussions in which the various parties involved can refer to an overlapping body of literature/knowledge. As Pina-Cabral (this volume) argues, any science is actually omnivorous, heterogeneous in our terms, incorporating anything from anywhere in its process of being 'ever open to its own transformation', while at the same time the praxes of peer review, examination, citation, publication and so on are part of a technique that has a concrete effect in the world. This is the main reason we have presented our work here in a standard academic form. However, the possibility of mutual understanding between those who have read the same books, and had the same 'socialization' into a discipline, is far from automatic or necessary. Communication is a constant struggle in any context (Povinelli 2001).[9] Clarity of argument is therefore not an inherent quality of spoken or written language, it is rather the result, and a transitional result even then, of the work put into ecologies of practice. Secondly, since our partial ability to interpret and respond to each other is anyway always a matter of negotiation, an open and affinitive-based anthropological 'we' would simply require different types of ongoing negotiation.

In his appeal for a trickster anthropology as regards ethics, Pels (2000: 163) suggests an emergent ethics, one that is 'no longer tied to a specific community (such as a professional association) but which locates ethical discussion in the negotiation of individual or communal interest that is characteristic of the practice of fieldwork'. In our collaborative process, we are developing something similar together with every opportunity we have to share our work with any form of audience, whether composed of anthropologists or performance artists – or, as is becoming more and more common, anthropologists who are also performance artists of some sort. We are negotiating joint conversations through different forms of practice, which may be awkward at times, but necessarily so because 'we know *as* we go, not before we go' (Ingold 2000a: 230, emphasis in the original).

Postscript: Through the Mirror

A further reflexive thought. We have suggested the possibility of considering the sense of belonging to the discipline of anthropology to be based on affinitive rather than genealogical or attributional types of identification. Similar to the transient groups Ang brings together in her Sourcing Within platform, anthropology as a discipline could include different practices or crafts as the need arises, resulting in a more ephemeral or faster-changing disciplinary craft.

That said, the urge towards fluidity and flexibility is itself a characteristic of and fiercely promoted by global capitalism (Sue Wright, pers. comm.). It would be ironic if in an attempt to develop an anthropology otherwise the very step we are suggesting would itself reinforce the current and emerging forms of global domination. Therefore, it is possible that contra our own arguments, the way forward for an anthropology otherwise is to return to a monastic form of scholarship where the boundaries of the anthropological 'we' are not so much policed, as inward looking; not so much gregarious, as meditative. Ironically, we suppose, we can only know by experimenting with both, and more, approaches.

Gey Pin Ang is a Singaporean theatre practitioner. She has initiated Sourcing Within, comprising practice-based work sessions for theatre practitioners and students, as well as cross-disciplinary researches in embodied practice, performing arts and anthropology. A former member of the Workcenter of Jerzy Grotowski and Thomas Richards in Italy, Ang has performed lead roles and toured with the company across Europe and Asia. She teaches and performs internationally, and her works are featured in scholarly journals and books of intercultural theatre and anthropology. She holds a Ph.D. in Drama: Practice-as-Research from the University of Kent, UK.

Caroline Gatt is a research fellow (*Knowing from the Inside*) at the University of Aberdeen. She is the author of *An Ethnography of Global Environmentalism: Becoming Friends of the Earth* (Routledge, 2017), and editor of *The Voices of the Pages* (Knowing from the Inside, 2017). Her other publications include articles in *Anthropological Theory* and *Anthropology in Action*. From 2001, Gatt has also carried out training and research in laboratory theatre, with groups in Malta, Italy and the UK. Gatt's current work is a study of the relationship between epistemology, education and well-being, including a speculative and experimental study of how performance epistemologies might invite a shift in the current educational paradigm in higher education.

Notes

1. Uzendoski's (2008) somatic poetry is an example of how ethnographic texts could be unsettled. Ingold's body of work (particularly 2000a, 2007a, 2011) provides examples of drawing on other ways of life to propose a renewed understanding of ontology, understood as a continuous world we all share. However, Ingold's approach has been criticized by indigenous scholars for abstracting localized knowledge that has the effect of turning indigenous knowledge into another colonial tool (Watts, cited in Todd 2015).
2. See also Pina-Cabral (this volume) and Tim Ingold (in press) on how anthropology, indeed all human communication, depends on the basic requirement of sharing a common world.
3. We would like to acknowledge the University of Aberdeen and the European Research Council who funded this project and made the research possible. The first draft of this chapter was presented at the seminar 'Who are we? Alterity and Affinity in Anthropology' in Cambridge 2014, we would like to thank Liana Chua and Nayanika Mathur for organizing the Wenner Gren funded seminar and inviting Gatt, for all their valuable comments and suggestions in their role as editors, and to thank all the participants who gave enriching feedback during the seminar and in the subsequent discussions in preparation for this volume. We received generous and very helpful feedback from Tristan Partirdge, Jelle Van Dijk, Thorsten Gieser and Cesar Giraldo Herera in an Academia.edu open paper session, many thanks to them. We would also like to thank various anonymous reviewers for their feedback that helped us better attune the interdisciplinary nature of this chapter.
4. The work of finding this balance also depends on being able to recognize similarities and differences in the first place. This is something we don't have space to expand on here but which is also important to the question of alterity in anthropology. Being able to recognize affinity takes as

much work as recognizing differences; it is in our experience the same work, only with different results. However, the work of recognizing alterity is something slightly different, possibly not even something we can *work* at as such, but only something we can make space for. In other words, it is not possible to recognize difference beyond one's terms of the recognizable – this is what Bourdieu would have called the doxa. However, it is possible at times to put in abeyance what one considers to be certainties, to allow for an emergence, even a hint that things may be radically different. On this, see Ang and Gatt 2016; Blaser n.d.; and Gatt and Rasanayagam in Brock et al. 2017.
5. Marcus and Myers 1995; and Wright and Schneider 2006, 2010, 2013 are examples of edited volumes dedicated to such crossovers between art and anthropology. A double special issue of the journal *Critical Arts: South-North Cultural and Media Studies*, edited by Kris Rutten, An van. Dienderen and Ronald Soetaert (2013a, 2013b), identifies alterity and questions of representation as primary concerns in many contemporary collaborations across art and anthropology.
6. Gatt has experimented with this form of multiple modes of communication in previous contexts with anthropologists: at the Redrawing Anthropology conference in 2009, a workshop in St Andrews in 2011 and one in Cambridge organized by Cambridge University Social Anthropology Society (CUSAS) in November 2012, and finally as part of a fourth-year course on Myth that Gatt designed in Aberdeen in 2013.
7. See Paola Esposito's blog (http://paolaesposito.wordpress.com/) for a report on the workshop, and see Ang and Gatt 2017 for a photo essay of our collaborative experiments.
8. The examples Rappaport mentions are Marcus and Mascarenhas (2005) and Holmes (1993) cited in Rappaport (2008: 8). We would also add the 'para-site' experiments run by the Centre for Ethnography at the UC Irvine, which depend on the participants' experience and ease with reading and discussing in logocentric and academic modes (http://www.ethnography.uci.edu/ethno_para-site).
9. See also Povinelli 2001 for details on the discussion about incommensurability in the philosophy of language on communication.

References

Amit, Vered (ed.). 2000. *Constructing the Field*. London: Routledge.
Ang, Gey Pin. 2015. 'An Intuitive Walk: A Thread to Play Along', in *The Unfamiliar*, 5(1 and 2): 119–122.
Ang, Gey Pin. 2017a. *Sourcing Within: A Reflexive Investigation of a Creative Path*. Doctoral thesis submitted to the University of Kent, Canterbury.
Ang, Gey Pin. 2017b. '气 Chi', in R. Harkness (ed.), *An Unfinished Compendium of Materials*, Aberdeen: Knowing from the Inside, pp. 32–36.

Ang, Gey Pin, and Caroline Gatt. 2016. 'Collaboration and Emergence: The Paradox of Presence and Surrender', paper presented at the workshop 'Collaboration in the Making', Aberdeen, September.

Ang, Gey Pin, and Caroline Gatt. 2017. 'An Emerging Theatre Anthropology', in E. Hodson (ed.), *Imagination, Surfaces, Interiors*. Aberdeen: Knowing from the Inside, pp. 17–21 and 128–129.

Asad, Talal (ed.). 1973. *Anthropology and the Colonial Encounter*. London; Ithaca, NY: Ithaca Press.

Bamford, Sandra, and James Leach. 2009. 'Introduction: Pedigrees of Knowledge: Anthropology and the Genealogical Model', in *Kinship and Beyond: The Genealogical Model Reconsidered*. New York: Berghahn Books, pp. 1–23.

Binder, Thomas, Rachel Charlotte Smith, Kasper TangVankilde, Mette Gislev Kjærsgaard, Ton Otto and Joachim Halse (eds). 2016. *Design Anthropological Futures*. London; New York: Bloomsbury.Bird-David, Nurit. 1994. 'Sociality and Immediacy: Or, Past and Present Conversations on Bands'. *Man*, New Series, 29(3): 583–603.

Blaser, Mario. Forthcoming. 'On the Properly Political (Disposition for the) Anthropocene', *Anthropological Theory*.

Blaser, Mario. 2010. *Storytelling Globalization: From the Chaco and Beyond*. Durham, NC: Duke University Press.

Bloch, Maurice. 2005. 'Where Did Anthropology Go? Or the Need for "Human Nature"', in *Essays on Cultural Transmission*. LSE Monographs on Social Anthropology. Oxford: Berg Publishers, pp. 1–20.

Bocock, Robert. 1974. *Ritual in Industrial Society: A Sociological Analysis of Ritualism in Modern England*. London: Allen & Unwin.

Bowman, W.D. 1998. *Philosophical Perspectives on Music*. New York: Oxford University Press.

Brock, Brian, Caroline Gatt, Tim Ingold, and Johan Rasanayagam. 2017. 'Rethinking Difference: Anthropological and Theological Perspectives', SANECH Seminar Series, Aberdeen, 12 October.

Brown, Deidre, and George Nicholas. 2012. 'Protecting Indigenous Cultural Property in the Age of Digital Democracy: Institution and Communal Responses to Canadian First Nations and Maori Heritage Concerns', *Journal of Material Culture* 17(3): 307–24.

Castaneda, Quetzil. 2006. 'The Invisible Theatre of Ethnography: Performative Principles of Fieldwork', *Anthropological Quarterly* 79(1): 75–104.

Coleman, Simon, and Peter Collins. 2006. 'Introduction: "Being...Where?" Performing Fields on Shifting Grounds', in S. Coleman and P. Collins (eds), *Locating the Field: Space, Place and Context in Anthropology*. Oxford; New York: Berg, pp. 1–22.

Conquergood, Dwight. 2002. 'Performance Studies: Interventions and Radical Research', *The Drama Review* 46(2): 145–56.

Das, V. n.d.. 'Poverty, Suffering and the Moral Life', unpublished manuscript.

Das, V. 2010. 'Reversing the Image of Time: Technologies of the Self and the Task of Detachment', paper presented at the conference *Reconsidering Detachment: The Ethics and Analytics of Disconnection*, 30 June–3 July, Cambridge, UK.

Dirlik, Arif. 1997. *The Postcolonial Aura: Third World Criticism in the Age of Global Capitalism*. Boulder, CO: Westview Press.

Donovan, Jared and Wendy Gunn. 2012. *Design and Anthropology*. London; New York: Routledge.

Escobar, Arturo. 2008. *Territories of Difference: Place, Movement, Life, Redes*. Durham, NC: Duke University Press.

Escobar, Arturo, and Eduardo Restrepo. 2005. '"Other Anthropologies and Anthropology Otherwise": Steps to a World Anthropologies Framework', *Journal of the World Anthropology Network* 1: 81–107.

Fischer, Michael. 2009. 'Foreword: Renewable Ethnography', in J. Faubion and G. Marcus, (eds), *Fieldwork is Not What It Used to Be: Learning Anthropology's Method in a Time of Transition*. Ithaca, NY; London: Cornell University Press.

Gatt, Caroline. 2010. 'Serial Closure: Generative Reflexivity and Restoring Confidence in/of Anthropologists', in S. Keorner and I. Russel (eds), *Unquiet Pasts: Risk Society, Lived Cultural Heritage and Re-designing Reflexivity*. Farnham; Burlington: Ashgate, pp. 343–360.

Gatt, Caroline. 2011. 'By Way of Theatre: Design Anthropology and the Exploration of Human Possibilities', proceedings of the conference 'Participatory Innovation Conference', University of Southern Denmark.

Gatt, Caroline. 2015. 'The Anthropologist as Member of the Ensemble: Anthropological Experiments *with* Theatre Makers', in Alex Flynn and Jonas Tinius (eds), *Theatre as Change: The Transformative Potential of Performance*. New York: Palgrave, pp. 334–356.

Gatt, Caroline. 2017a. 'The Liveliness of Books', in *The Voices of the Pages*. Aberdeen: Knowing from the Inside, pp. 61–85.

Gatt, Caroline (ed.). 2017b. *The Voices of the Pages*. Aberdeen: Knowing from the Inside.

Gatt, Caroline. 2017c. *An Ethnography of Global Environmentalism: Becoming Friends of the Earth*. London: Routledge.

Gatt, Caroline. 2017d. 'Air: Becomes Breath, Becomes Song, Becomes Air', in R. Harkness (ed.), *An Unfinished Compendium of Materials*. Aberdeen: Knowing from the Inside, pp. 5–9.

Gatt, Caroline. 2017e. 'Living Atmospheres: Breath and Permeation through Song-action in Experimental Theatre', in S. Schmitt and S. Schroer (eds), *Exploring Atmospheres Ethnographically*. Farnham; Burlington: Ashgate, pp. 135–152.

Gatt, Caroline, Nazilihan Eda Ercin, Agnieszka Mendel, and Ben Spatz. 2017. 'He Almost Forgets There Is a Maker of the World', illuminated video essay. Submitted to the Arts and Humanities Research Council (AHRC) Research in Film Awards competition.

Gatt, Caroline, and Tim Ingold. 2013. 'From Description to Correspondence: Anthropology in Real Time', in Wendy Gunn, Ton Otto and Rachel Smith (eds), *Design Anthropology: Juxtaposing Theory and Practice*. London: Bloomsbury, pp. 139–58.

Geertz, Clifford. 1984. 'Distinguished Lecture: Anti Anti-relativism', *American Anthropologist* 86(2): 263–78.

Gough, Kathleen. 1968. 'Anthropology and Imperialism'. *Monthly Review* 19(11): 12–27.

Grosz, E. 1994. *Volatile Bodies: Toward a Corporeal Feminism*. Bloomington, IN: John Wiley & Sons.

Grotowski, J. [1968] 2002. *Towards a Poor Theatre*, 1st edn, ed. E. Barba. New York: Routledge.

Gunn, Wendy, Ton Otto, and Rachel Smith (eds). 2013. *Design Anthropology: Juxtaposing Theory and Practice*. London: Bloomsbury.

Gupta, Akhil, and James Ferguson. 1997. *Anthropological Locations: Boundaries and Grounds of a Field Science*. Berkeley, CA: University of California Press.

Hadot, P. 1995. *Philosophy as a Way of Life: Spiritual Exercises from Socrates to Foucault*. Ed. A. Davidson. Malden, MA: Wiley-Blackwell.

Hanson, Allan. 1997. 'Empirical Anthropology, Postmodernism, and the Invention of Tradition', in M. Mauzé (ed.), *Present is Past: Some Uses of Tradition in Native Societies*. Lanham, MD: University Press of America, pp. 195–214.

Haraway, Donna. 1991. *Simians, Cyborgs and Women: The Reinvention of Nature*. Oxford; New York: Free Association Books Ltd.

Harris, Mark. 2007. 'Introduction: "Ways of Knowing"', in *Ways of Knowing: New Approaches in the Anthropology of Learning and Experience*. New York: Berghahn Books, pp. 1–24.

Hendry, Joy, and C.W. Watson. 2001. 'Introduction', in *An Anthropology of Indirect Communication*. London: Routledge, pp. 1–16.

Herzfeld, Michael. 2007. 'Deskilling, "Dumbing Down", and the Auditing of Knowledge in the Practical Mastery of Artisans and Academics: An Ethnographer's Response to a Global Problem', in M. Harris (ed.), *Ways of Knowing: New Approaches in the Anthropology of Learning and Experience*. New York: Berghahn Books, pp. 91–110.

Holbraad, Martin. 2012. *Truth in Motion: The Recursive Anthropology of Cuban Divination*. London: Chicago University Press.

Ingold, Tim. 1993. 'The Art of Translation in a Continuous World', in G. Pálsson (ed.), *Beyond Boundaries: Understanding, Translation and Anthropological Discourse*. Oxford: Berg, pp. 210–230.

Ingold, Tim. 2000a. *The Perception of the Environment: Essays in Livelihood, Dwelling and Skill*. London; New York: Routledge.

Ingold, Tim. 2000b. 'Concluding Commentary', in A. Hornborg and G. Pálsson (eds), *Negotiating Nature: Culture, Power and Environmental Argument*. Lund: Lund University Press, pp. 213–224.

Ingold, Tim. 2007a. *Lines: A Brief History*. London: Routledge.

Ingold, Tim. 2007b. 'Anthropology Is *Not* Ethnography', Radcliffe-Brown Lecture at the British Academy.
Ingold, Tim. 2011. *Being Alive: Essays on Movement, Knowledge and Description*. London: Routledge.
Ingold, Tim. In press. 'One World Anthropology', *HAU: Journal of Ethnographic Theory*.
Ingold, Tim, with Ray Lucas. 2007. 'The 4 As (Anthropology, Archaeology, Art and Architecture): Reflections on a Teaching and Learning Experience', in M. Harris (ed.), *Ways of Knowing: New Approaches in the Anthropology of Learning and Experience*. New York: Berghahn Books, pp. 287–305.
Kelty, Chris. 2005. 'Geeks, Social Imaginaries and Recursive Publics', *Cultural Anthropology* 20(2): 185–214.
Lassiter, Luke. 2005. 'Collaborative Ethnography and Public Anthropology', *Current Anthropology* 46(1): 83–106.
Latour, Bruno. 2003. *Politics of Nature: How to Bring the Sciences into Politics*. Cambridge, MA: Harvard University Press.
Lave, Jean, and Etienne Wenger. 1991. *Situated Learning: Legitimate Peripheral Participation*. Cambridge: Cambridge University Press.
Layton, Robert. 1997. *An Introduction to Theory in Anthropology*. Cambridge: Cambridge University Press.
Lincoln, Amber. 2014. 'History Felt: Alaska Peninsula Reindeer Herding', installation and presentation at 'Ethnographic Terminalia', AAA, Washington DC, December.
Linnekin, Jocelyn. 1992. 'On the Theory and Politics of Cultural Construction in the Pacific', *Oceania* 62(4): 249–63.
Loovers, Jan Peter. 2016. '"Don't Write Bulls**t": Working with Gwich'in in the Canadian North', paper presented to the workshop 'Collaboration in the Making', Aberdeen, September.
Lucas, Ray. 2007. 'Towards a Theory of Notation as a Thinking Tool', Ph.D. diss. Aberdeen University.
Marcus, George. 1995. 'Ethnography in/of the World System: The Emergence of Multi Sited Ethnography', *Annual Review of Anthropology* 24: 95–117.
Marcus, George. 2001. 'From Rapport under Erasure to Theatres of Complicit Reflexivity', *Qualitative Enquiry* 7(4): 519–28.
Marcus, George, and Dick Cushman. 1982. 'Ethnographies as Texts', *Annual Review of Anthropology* 11: 25–69.
Marcus, George, and Michael Fischer. 1986. *Anthropology as Cultural Critique: An Experimental Moment in the Human Sciences*. Chicago, IL: University of Chicago Press.
Marcus, George, and Fernando Mascarenhas. 2005. *Ocasião: The Marquis and the Anthropologist*. Walnut Creek, CA: Altamira Press.
Marcus, George, and Fred Myers. 1995. 'The Traffic in Art and Culture: An Introduction', in *The Traffic in Culture: Refiguring Art and Anthropology*. Los Angeles, CA: University of California Press, pp. 1–52.

Miyazaki, Hirokazu. 2004. *The Method of Hope: Anthropology, Philosophy and Fijian Knowledge.* Stanford, CA: Stanford University Press.

Mol, Annelise, and John Law. 1994. 'Regions, Networks and Fluids: Anaemia and Social Topology', *Social Studies of Sciences*, 24(4): 641–671.

Moustakas, C. 1990. *Heuristic Research: Design, Methodology, and Applications*, 1st edn. Newbury Park, CA: SAGE Publications, Inc.

Neizen, Ronald. 2000. 'Recognizing Indigenism: Canadian Unity and the International Movement of Indigenous Peoples', *Comparative Studies in Society and History* 42(1): 119–48.

Okely, Judith. 1994. 'Thinking through Fieldwork', in A. Bryman and R.G. Burgess (eds), *Analyzing Qualitative Data.* London: Routledge, pp. 18–34.

Pels, Peter. 2000. 'The Trickster's Dilemma: Anthropological Ethics and Method as Liberal Technologies of Self', in M. Strathern (ed.), *Audit Cultures: Anthropological Studies in Accountability, Ethics and the Academy.* London: Routledge, pp. 135–72.

Petitmengin-Peugeot, C. 1999. 'The Intuitive Experience', in F. Varela (ed.), *The View from Within.* Thorverton: Imprint Academic, pp. 43–78.

Povinelli, Elizabeth. 2001. 'Radical Worlds: The Anthropology of Incommensurability and Inconceivability', *Annual Review of Anthropology* 30: 319–34.

Povinelli, Elizabeth. 2011. 'Routes/Worlds', *e-flux*, no. 27. Retrieved from http://www.e-flux.com/journal/routesworlds/#_ftn1.

Prattis, Ian (ed.). 1985. *Reflections: The Anthropological Muse.* Washington, DC: American Anthropological Association.

Rappaport, Joanna. 2008. 'Beyond Participant Observation: Collaborative Ethnography as Theoretical Innovation', *Collaborative Anthropologies* 1: 1–31.

Rodríguez, S. 2015. 'Mutuality and the Field at Home', in R. Sanjek (ed.), *Mutuality: Anthropology's Changing Terms of Engagement.* Philadelphia, PA: University of Pennsylvania Press, pp. 45–60.

Rothenberg, J., and D. Rothenberg (eds). 1983. *Symposium of the Whole: A Range of Discourses toward an Ethnopoetics.* Berkeley, CA: University of California Press.

Rutten, Kris, An van. Dienderen, and Ronald Soetaert. 2013a. 'Revisiting the Ethnographic Turn in Contemporary Art', *Critical Arts: South-North Cultural and Media Studies* 27(5): 459–73.

Rutten, Kris, An van Dienderen, and Ronald Soetaert. 2013b. 'The Rhetorical Turn in Contemporary Art and Ethnography', *Critical Arts: South-North Cultural and Media Studies* 27(6): 627–40.

Salmond, Amiria. 2013. 'Transforming Translations 1: "The Owner of These Bones"', *HAU: Journal of Ethnographic Theory* 3(3): 1–32.

Salmond, Amiria. 2014. 'Transforming Translations: Addressing Ontological Alterity', *HAU: Journal of Ethnographic Theory* 4(1): 155–87.

Sanjek, Roger. 2015. 'Deep Grooves: Anthropology and Mutuality', in Roger Sanjek (ed.), *Mutuality: Anthropology's Changing Terms of Engagement*. Philadelphia, PA: University of Pennsylvania Pres, pp. 1–7.

Sapir, David. 1988. 'Book Review of *Reflections: The Anthropological Muse*', *American Anthropologist* 90(2): 445–46.

Schechner, Richard. 1981. *Between Theatre and Anthropology*. Philadelphia, PA: University of Pennsylvania Press.

Schieffelin, Edward. 1998. 'Problematizing Performance', in F. Hughes-Freeland (ed.), *Ritual, Performance, Media*. London: Routledge, pp. 194–207.

Shore, Cris, and Susan Wright. 2000. 'Coercive Accountability: The Rise of Audit Culture in Higher Education', in M. Strathern (ed.), *Audit Cultures. Anthropological Studies in Accountability, Ethics and the Academy*. London: Routledge, pp. 57–89.

Skinner, Jonathan. 2012. *The Interview: An Ethnographic Approach*. London: Berg Publishers.

Ssorin-Chaikov, Nikolai. 2013. 'Ethnographic Conceptualism: An Introduction', *Laboratorium*, no. 2. Retrieved from http://www.soclabo.org/index.php/laboratorium/article/view/336/864.

Stoller, Paul. 2015. 'The Bureau of Memories: Archives and Ephemera', a review of 'Ethnographic Terminalia, 2014, Hierarchy, Washington, DC, December 3–7'. Retrieved from http://www.culanth.org/fieldsights/647-the-bureau-of-memories-archives-and-ephemera.

Stengers, Isabelle. 2011. 'Comparison as a Matter of Concern'. *Common Knowledge* 17(1): 48–63.

Strathern, Marilyn (ed.). 2000. *Audit Cultures: Anthropological Studies in Accountability, Ethics and the Academy*. London: Routledge.

Suchman, Lucy. 2000. 'Embodied Practices of Engineering Work', *Mind, Culture and Activity* 7(1/2): 4–18.

Suchman, Lucy. 2001. 'Building Bridges: Practice-Based Ethnographies of Contemporary Technology', in Michael Schiffer (ed.), *Anthropological Perspectives on Technology*. Dragoon, AZ: Amerind Foundation, pp. 163–177.

Todd, Zoe. 2015. 'Indigenizing the Anthropocene', in Heather Davis and Etienne Turpin (eds), *Art in the Anthropocene: Encounters among Politics, Aesthetics, Environments and Epistemologies*. London: Open Humanities Press, pp. 241–54.

Turner, Victor. 1979. 'Dramatic Ritual/Ritual Drama: Performative and Reflexive Anthropology', *Kenyon Review*, New Series, 1(3) (Summer 1979): 80–93.

Uzendoski, Michael. 2008. 'Somatic Poetry in Amazonian Ecuador', *Anthropology and Humanism* 33(1/2): 12–29.

Viveiros de Castro, Eduardo, Martin Holbraad, and Morten Axel Pedersen. 2014. 'The Politics of Ontology: Anthropological Positions', *Cultural Anthropology Online*, 13 January. Retrieved from http://www.culanth.org/fieldsights/462-the-politics-of-ontology-anthropological-positions.

Weiner, James. 2007. 'History, Oral History and Memoriation in Native Title', in B.R. Smith and F. Morphy (eds), *The Social Effects of Native Title: Recognition, Translation, Coexistence*. Canberra: ANU E Press, pp. 215–225.

Whitaker, M. 1996. 'Reflexivity', in A. Barnard and J. Spencer (eds), *Encyclopedia of Social and Cultural Anthropology*. London: Routledge, pp. 470–73.

Wikan, Unni. 1993. 'Beyond the Words: The Power of Resonance', in G. Pálsson (ed.), *Beyond Boundaries: Understanding, Translation and Anthropological Discourses*. Oxford: Berg, pp. 184–209.

Willerslev, Rane. 2004. 'Spirits as "Ready to Hand": A Phenomenological Analysis of Yukaghir Spiritual Knowledge and Dreaming', *Anthropological Theory* 4(4): 395–418.

Wright, Chris, and Arndt Schneider. 2006. 'The Challenge of Practice', in *Contemporary Art and Anthropology*. Oxford: Berg, pp. 1–28.

Wright, Chris, and Arndt Schneider. 2010. 'Between Art and Anthropology', in *Between Art and Anthropology: Contemporary Ethnographic Practice*. Oxford: Berg, pp. 1–22.

Wright, Chris, and Arndt Schneider. 2013. 'Ways of Working', in *Anthropology and Art Practice*. London; New York: Bloomsbury, pp. 1–24.

Chapter 7

TOWARDS AN ECUMENICAL ANTHROPOLOGY

João de Pina-Cabral

The growth of Anthropology as an academic discipline in the mid-nineteenth century was inspired by Darwin's major challenge to Christian principles of human exceptionalism, part of the project of an emergent Natural History. Nevertheless, an ethical awareness of the essential unicity of humankind never stopped being a central assumption. Without it, we would not have today's anthropology. As a matter of fact, one of the best-informed observers of our discipline sustains that the origins of social anthropology are to be found not in universities, where it later established itself with figures like Hatton, Tylor, and Boas, but in a series of private learning bodies that, in the second half of the nineteenth century, worked at conjoining natural history 'with a moral revulsion against slavery' (Needham 1981: 11). Modernist social anthropology was built upon this moral ground. The revulsion against the way in which modern slavery denied the uniqueness of the humanity of all humans remained a central consideration throughout, both in anthropology and in its sister discipline of history. For example, Franz Baermann Steiner's D.Phil. thesis, defended in Oxford in 1952, dealt precisely with slavery, and his humanist thinking on the notion of 'value' was central to the development of the work of some of the most influential thinkers in anthropology in the second half of the century: Mary Douglas, M.N. Srinivas, Louis Dumont, Julian Pitt-Rivers, Laura and Paul Bohannan.[1] Indeed, it is arguable that, in the latter quarter of the century, theoretical feminism was an heir to this same ethical drive (e.g. Ardener 1975).

For twentieth-century anthropology, then, the primary comparative task of the discipline was to understand the history of humankind by analysing its internal diversity. Frames of reference, however, shift in time and a discipline that was originally grounded on a deep moral affirmation of humanity's essential unicity ended up unmooring itself and, by hypostatizing diversity, turned it into a form of human incommensurability (e.g. Holbraad 2010). In my opinion, over the past decade, too many anthropologists of influence have played this dangerous game, trying to cash in on the schismogenic reflexes it can yield. To opt for a starting point such as Roy Wagner's 'man invents his own realities' (1975: ix) is to engage a dangerous truism, for while in one sense it is a verifiable observation, in another sense it leads us profoundly astray, pushing to secondary level the central fact that our existence (and all human communication) is predicated on the inhabiting of a world which is historically common.

In this chapter, I argue that today we are at risk of being misled by the rich crops anthropological modernism harvested from its fascination with exploring 'other' times, 'other' worlds, 'other' knowledges. Indeed, the problem is not recent, if we consider that Edwin Ardener was making a similar point in 1983 in 'Social Anthropology and the Decline of Modernism'.[2] Lest I should be misunderstood, I had better confirm from the start that I am not arguing in this chapter in favour of a re-encounter with the Christian humanist tradition, but I decidedly support a vision that sees human unicity as grounded on a common human history.[3]

In what follows, therefore, I assume that the world is an ecumene, that is, a dwelling space of intercommunicating humans (cf. Pina-Cabral 2017a) and that, consequently, we are entitled to pursue an 'anthropological' project (in the sense of a study of the human condition). This is the case even if we opt for questioning the nature of the boundaries between humanity and world, or to attribute 'agency' to things (see, for example, Connolly 2011 or Bennett 2010). The notion of anthropology as an ongoing analytical effort to understand all humans undertaken for the sake of all humans (past, present and future) will surely continue to be the basic background assumption of our disciplinary undertaking for many years to come.

Ever since the days of Emile Durkheim and Marcel Mauss, twentieth-century social science has relied on two basic theoretical dispositions inherited from nineteenth-century interpretations of Kantian thinking: representationism and sociocentrism. There have always been dissenting voices, of course (cf. Evans-Pritchard 1933, [1934]

1970, 1936), but the consensus was very broad. The conjoining of these two dispositions, however, has a peculiar but unavoidable corollary: if 'ours' is Western science, then 'others' have 'other sciences' that are just as valid. That being the case, then, there are as many 'anthropologies' as there are worlds![4] Note that what is at stake here is not just that anthropology (or world) will be plural in its manifestations (which is an observable fact), but that there are self-contained, separate, numerable 'anthropologies' (as many as there are 'worlds' – see Pina-Cabral 2017b). In one foul sweep, non-Western (or at least a-Western) anthropologists are simply pushed out of the anthropological arena and the imperial hegemony of the Western 'we' is perversely reinstalled.

Nevertheless, in the latter part of the century, both the representationist and sociocentric certainties have been slowly eroding. The process started with the Oxford poststructuralists in the 1970s (Needham 1972; Ardener 2007), but the best-known moments today are doubtlessly Marilyn Strathern's *The Gender of the Gift* (1988) and the series of debates that Ingold subsequently published in the mid 1990s (Ingold 1996). On the one hand, today, we are bound to reject the representationist disposition that sees all 'knowledge' as being essentially alike (see Pina-Cabral 2017b); on the other hand, we are bound to reject a proprietorial view of 'knowledge' as collectively owned, and a corresponding identification of 'science', and more particularly anthropology, with Westernness.

The present chapter advocates an *ecumenical anthropology*, one that grapples pluralism without abdicating from monism; one that rejects the *cogito* and sees worldly immanence as the starting point (see Toren 2002; Pina Cabral 2017a, 2017b). Instead of taking recourse to the sociocentric model of separate and unitary worlds, I defend here an ecumenist posture, one that sees collective projects of scientific understanding as being constituted in the occupation of world (cf. Ingold 1995) and that opens up the path for wider and wider dialogues, broader and broader ecumenes.

The Primitives and 'We'

I still own the copy of Mary Douglas's *Purity and Danger* (1966) that I bought in 1974 as an undergraduate student in South Africa, together with *Natural Symbols* ([1970] 1973). These two books had a big impact on me, as they addressed directly some of the perplexities concerning the relation between religion and sociocultural difference that had led me to study anthropology. But it was later on in 1980, in Oxford, that they inspired in me a kind of epiphany.

When I revisited them while searching for inspiration for writing on the symbolism of death among the peasant population of Northwest Portugal (Pina-Cabral 1986), I was struck by a feeling that there was in them some kind of subliminal message that made me deeply uncomfortable. As my reading went on, I started marking out with pencilled circles the authorial 'we/us/ours' that Mary Douglas peppered throughout the text. Then I suddenly understood with enormous vividness that I – that is, the historical João de Pina-Cabral – was not part of that collective whose vision the book addressed. Indeed, with hindsight, it is perhaps more correct to say that I was not *fully* part of it, but also that I *did not want* to be part of such a project of 'Westernness'. For that too surely counts: the life projects one lays out for oneself. This is the case, particularly, when one is as young as I was then and was raised in postcolonial Africa.

Mary Douglas's implicit 'we' was populated by urban, highly educated, well-off residents of one of the English-speaking capitals of the world (New York or London), most likely members of academic staff in one of the major English-speaking universities. With a push and some generosity, it might also have included other 'Westerners': French, German or Dutch intellectuals. But it certainly did not include Italians, Portuguese, Brazilians, Russians, South Africans or Indians. In order for these to be 'Western' by Mary Douglas's implicit standards, they would have had to perform a kind of distancing act, a kind of authorial splitting of their selves. Recently, Brazilian anthropologist Eduardo Viveiros de Castro, writing in French, claimed that he accepts the Western subject position *par courtoisie* (2009: 9n1). To the contrary, I found that my sense of rejection only increased as my own exploration of anthropology progressed.

Much later, in the 1990s, I discovered that postcolonial studies, in fact, did not help solve this problem any further; they only made it worse. In their writings, Edward Saïd, Talal Assad and their many disciples were implicitly occupying the same seat as Mary Douglas, albeit with radically different political standpoints. Nowhere in his books does Saïd address the issue of what Westernness really is and, as Aijaz Ahmad has compulsively detailed, the very idea that there could be such an epistemic construction that spans all those centuries, places and interests is deeply ahistorical (1992: 166). In Saïd's work, the ambiguities abound but they all serve to implicitly validate Westernness. For example, in the index of his book *Culture and Imperialism*, the words 'West' or 'Western' are absent, contrary to 'Oriental', which has a large number of entries. This is a curious aspect, in view of the fact that the author states, 'There are several varieties of domination and responses to it, but the "Western" one, along with the resistance it provoked, is the subject of this book' (1994: 10). This passage is particularly interesting for its ambiguity, since it follows on from a paragraph in which Saïd suggests, without actually putting it down precisely, that the empires of 'Spain, Portugal, Holland, Belgium, Germany, Italy and, in a different way, Russia and the United States' might not be included in his study of Western imperialism, as he is focusing mostly on the British and French forms.

By focusing on Orientalism, the postcolonialist writers were unwittingly validating Occidentalism (that is, the Western subject position – see Perez 2011: 42–43). They become simultaneously both the principal defining voice of Westernness and its critics. The price they paid for doing that, as Ahmad too has identified (1992: 162), was to reduce social existence to textuality and representation; the famous 'semiotic turn'. More recently, in his 2017 BBC Reith Lecture,[5] Kwame Anthony Appiah also develops a sharp critique of the contemporary uses of the concept of 'Western culture'. His call for a broader and more inclusive approach to human intellectual history is fully compatible with what I call in this chapter an ecumenical approach.

As the 1990s and 2000s unfolded – and I went on to carry out fieldwork in southern China among Portuguese-speaking Eurasians (Pina-Cabral 2002), and then in peri-urban Brazil (Pina-Cabral 2013) – the sense that the anthropology I wrote was not meant to be Western kept growing. I felt that I was just as Eurasian (being married to a Chinese lady), just as Latin American (as mine was every Brazilian's mother tongue), just as Portuguese as any and all of the people among whom I ever carried out fieldwork. For thirty years after I left Oxford, as I taught anthropology in Portuguese, Macanese, Mozambican, Spanish and Brazilian universities, I was constantly haunted by the question: what sort of anthropological 'we' am I fostering among my students?

At the time, I was happy to find that the problem was not uniquely my own. So distinguished an anthropologist as T.N. Madan had encountered it too. He claimed to experience a 'muted unease about the exclusivism of the idea of anthropology as the study of "other cultures"'. He insists that the critical process of breaking with the frontiers of Westernness has been an integral part of the tradition of anthropology for a very long time: 'anthropology is not a western discipline which is to be enriched . . . by feedback from other parts of the world. Nor is it the rhetoric of counterattack from the Third World. It is an empirical discipline, the data base of which has to be broadened to take in the whole world, without locating its centre today in the place of its historical origin' (Madan 1982: 268).

In fact, now that they are available online, I recently discovered in one of *JASO*'s early issues, that Mary Douglas's younger colleagues had responded with distaste to this very same aspect of her writing shortly after her book was published. One of Evans-Pritchard's closest disciples, Wendy James, published a note in 1970 in which she accuses Mary Douglas of fostering a 'colonialist' outlook. In those days, as African decolonization was still a fresh experience and most anthropologists supported it, this was no small accusation. It was perhaps still not clear then that the change from British colonialism to American imperialism during the second half of the twentieth century was not going to change matters significantly and was indeed going to take the suffering of African people to new, previously unimagined extremes.

I will paraphrase here Wendy James's summary of the argument as it is presented to us in *Purity and Danger* (James 1970: 82). There, in the famous Chapter 5, Mary Douglas concludes that 'we must attempt to phrase an objective, verifiable distinction between the two types of culture, primitive and modern', and she does so in terms closely related to those proposed by Lévy-Bruhl in his early works. She sees progress as 'differentiation', and in relation to thought, the relevant differentiation is, as she puts it, 'based on the Kantian principle that thought can only advance by freeing itself of its own subjective conditions'. The primitive world is therefore a pre-Copernican world, a subjective personal world in which the universe is turned in upon man, and which lacks 'self-awareness and conscious reaching for objectivity'. In conclusion, Mary Douglas asks, 'What is the objection to saying that a personal, anthropocentric, undifferentiated worldview characterizes a primitive culture?' (Douglas 1966: 93)

Wendy James finds this question 'ethnocentric', and I find it impossible to answer too, for it is ultimately circular. But, as it happens, the reference to Lévy-Bruhl in Douglas's argument turns out to be interesting, for Evans-Pritchard's youthful essay on that author, published originally in the 1930s in Cairo, is re-edited in the same volume of *JASO* (Evans-Pritchard [1934] 1970). Indeed, this is all the more fascinating since we know that Evans-Pritchard never quite managed to rid himself of the concept of primitive but, to the contrary, Lévy-Bruhl did, explicitly so. At the end of his long life, in his notebooks published posthumously as *Carnets* in 1949, the French philosopher rejected the notion that he was most responsible for popularizing: 'I have to show ... that, today more than ever, I do not believe that there is a *mentalité* which characterizes "primitives"' (1949: 164–65; see Pina-Cabral 2013).[6]

Following on Adam Kuper's history of the concept (1988, 2005), I have argued elsewhere that primitivism must be seen as a disposition within anthropological theory that goes beyond the mere ascription of an inferior mental condition to non-Western, technologically simpler, illiterate peoples (Pina-Cabral 2010, 2017a). The matter is far more momentous than the mere distaste for the attribution of inferiority to others, which is the principal reason why most anthropologists ended up abandoning the term in the post-Vietnam, post-May '68 era.

The fact is that, while rejecting many aspects of its evolutionistic legacy, twentieth-century anthropology remained tied to the modernist notion of the 'great divide' or, as Ernest Gellner also called it, 'the big ditch': 'The attainment of a rational, non-magical, non-enchanted world',[7] a positive definition of modernity which is of a seam with Mary Douglas's negative one quoted above. In this partition of the human condition between primitive/archaic and modern, anthropologists are postulated as being collectively and ontologically external to the human realities (the 'cultures') they describe – the latter, of course, being described as eminently collective. I argue that this disposition may be called primitivist principally because it associates essentiality with primordiality.

To be more specific: primitivism is a theoretical device that is at the very root of anthropology as an academic discipline and that has remained central to its development ever since those immediate post-Darwinian days. It operates as a kind of time machine: things that are most simple are automatically assumed to be also more essential, and, therefore, they are held to be anterior. The supposition that human life has evolved is associated with a view of progress as differentiation, as Mary Douglas highlights. Thus, one starts by postulating that the more essential aspects of the human condition will be more clearly manifested in the simpler forms of social living, for if they are essential then they are also indispensable to human social life. Then one goes on to posit that, as they are essential, they will also be anterior – not historically, but theoretically. In short, if one wants to know what is essential to human life, if one wants to lay down *an* 'anthropology', one will have to study primitives. In this way, primitivist ethnography cancels historical time and reveals the essence of the social, as so clearly set out in Durkheim and Mauss's essay on *Primitive Classification* ([1903] 1963). By denying coevalness, as

Johannes Fabian called it (2002), modernist anthropology reached for essentiality.

Sometime in the late 1990s, Lévi-Strauss, then in his nineties, gave an interview to Viveiros de Castro where he puts this matter in the clearest possible way:

> After all, one needs to state clearly that anthropology is a discipline that was born in the nineteenth century; it is the work of a civilization, ours, that possesses a crashing technical superiority over all others and that, conscious of the fact that it was going to dominate them and transform them, said to itself that it is urgently necessary to register all that can be registered, before this happens. Anthropology is that, nothing else. It is the work of a society about other societies. And when people tell us that these societies are not different from ours, that they have the same history as ours, etc., they are absolutely missing the point. What we were asking from those societies we were studying is that they should owe us nothing; that they should represent human experiences that are completely independent from ours. Aside from that, they can well have whatever history one may wish, but that is not the question. Do they or do they not owe us something? If they do, they interest us moderately; if they do not, then they interest us passionately. (Lévi-Strauss 1998: 120–21)[8]

In this quote, as indeed in Mary Douglas's *Purity and Danger*, and aside from the temporal manipulation that I highlighted above, two further aspects emerge that are very relevant to the present discussion: on the one hand, a representationist disposition that sees all 'knowledge' as being essentially alike; on the other hand, a proprietorial (sociocentric) view of 'knowledge' as collectively owned, that identifies 'science', and more particularly 'anthropology', with Westernness (i.e. 'us'). No wonder Durkheim and Mauss's essay on *Primitive Classification*, in which they explicitly propose that anthropology must adopt a strictly sociocentric attitude, became increasingly problematic as the 1970s progressed, as evidenced in Needham's and Ardener's revisitations of it.

In her brief comment, Wendy James already suggests that an answer to Mary Douglas's earlier question 'would include a rejection of the holistic concept of "a culture", of the assumption that "modern culture" is not in many ways personal and anthropocentric, and of the assumption that objectivity and differentiation are not found beyond the industrial world; and also a rejection of the accompanying theory that in "primitive cultures" thought is socially determined' (James 1970: 82). I guess we all agree that there is something almost visionary to this list, as it was written in 1970.

Wendy James's comments are in fact inspired by a quote from Edmund Leach who, in the introduction to *Dialectic in Practical Religion*, states: 'At one time anthropologists studied savages in contrast to civilized men; we now find ourselves studying the thought processes of practical, ordinary people as distinct from those of technical professionals. Among "civilized" practical people the distinction between primitive and sophisticated largely disappears . . . the similarities are more remarkable than the contrasts' (1968: 2). There is implicit in this quote a project for the anthropological endeavour as a part of the broadly defined scientific endeavour that is incompatible both with Mary Douglas's and Ernest Gellner's positions as well as with that of the radical relativists, today's ontologists (Pedersen 2012).

Leach's critical comment drives further the two quandaries raised above. Firstly, anthropologists today are indeed studying 'practical, ordinary people', but are they not also practical, ordinary people? Secondly, in what way are the thought processes of practical, ordinary people distinct from those of 'technical professionals' such as anthropologists?

The first question raises the problem of 'sociocentrism' in anthropological thinking, that is to say, the granting of priority to collective representations over personal thought processes, that Durkheim and Mauss defended ([1903] 1963: 86). But, in particular, it questions the assumed notion that, while anthropologists as Westerners are essentially individual, Others are essentially collective: that which Mary Douglas calls the 'greater differentiation' of modern persons. Thus, the opposition between the West and the Rest is not only one between different outlooks but also one between free-thinking individuals as opposed to collectively framed persons; according to Mauss, at the end of his famous essay, it was not before the work of Fichte that the universal truth that the individual self was 'the basic category of consciousness' was finally established (Durkheim and Mauss [1903] 1963: 22).

The second question raises an issue that anthropologists have been even less keen to discuss: in what way is what anthropologists write in their essays a manifestation of 'what goes on in their heads'? Is all 'knowledge' alike? Is what I write in this essay of the same nature as what goes through my head when I greet my child as I come home at the end of the working day? Ernest Gellner defended that modern society is uniquely critical of its beliefs. But in what sense is he using the word 'society' here? And what are the bounds of scientificity within modernity? I mean the actual scientific process, not the ideological use of some of its outcomes. Are the Han Chinese not modern? But can we say that they have been critical of their ethnic beliefs concerning Tibetans or Uighurs, or concerning democracy in Hong

Kong? What is 'not modern' about the caliphate that has been carving its boundaries in the Middle East? Is Mrs Merkel or was Mrs Thatcher critical concerning their neoliberal beliefs? If we accept too readily to say of any one of those that they are simply not modern, then we get to a concept of modern that is utterly indefensible. In any case, it would break the postulated association of modernity with 'science' that thinkers like Gellner and Douglas defended. As Gellner put it when he rejected it in his public debates, it would be a form of 'anti-caesurism'.

In the hope of contributing towards this discussion, in this chapter, I will present an example in order to try to clarify two questions: who is the 'we' of anthropology? – that is to say, what can one assume not only about the anthropological authors but also about their anthropological readership; and, what do 'we' do? – that is to say, what is the nature of ethnographic writing?

The Anthropologist and the Temple Dancers

More and more anthropology and ethnography is being written in English around the world. What do such texts tell us about the subject position of those who write them? In the light of current trends in ethnographic writing, which encourage explicit reference to authorial presence, one must assume that what one gathers about the project of collective positioning of the writer will be accessible to us both explicitly and subliminally.

The example I pick is an essay of historically inspired ethnography about the *devadasi* (the temple dancers) of Goa in India: *The Tulsi and the Cross: Anthropology and the Colonial Encounter in Goa* published in 2011 by Orient BlackSwan in New Delhi. Rosa Maria Perez, its author, is a Lisbon-trained professor of social anthropology whose initial inspiration was French structuralism, but who has spent long and repeated stays teaching at Brown University in the USA. There she was inspired mostly by the writings of anthropologists working in the postcolonial mode. Most of these writers, however, like Perez herself, originate from other parts of the world, from Edward Saïd to Veena Das, Aijaz Ahmad, Dipesh Chakrabarty, or her close collaborator at Brown University Lina Fruzetti. While her former work focused on untouchable women in Gujarat (2004), this present work focuses on Hindu temples in Goa, which was for many centuries a Portuguese colony. Indeed, we can take it that what unites both her field experiences is primarily her long-lasting preoccupation with femaleness and subalternity; the matter of untouchability and of acasteness, as she appropriately qualifies the condition of the Goan *devadasi* (see also Perez 2004).

Of late, however, Perez has been sharing her time between teaching at the Department of Anthropology of the University Institute of Lisbon, in Portugal, and as Visiting Professor of Anthropology (Spring) at the Indian Institute of Technology, Gandhinagar (Ahmadabad, Gujarat). Furthermore, her book is published in India and, as we read it, we become aware that it addresses an Indian readership in the social sciences, both in terms of the authors she quotes and in terms of that which she assumes the reader to know about India, for example about the long-term history of India's west coast, or about Hindu temple lore, aspects with which most Indian readers are familiar, but foreigners might not be.

I chose Perez's work for it seems to me to be characteristic of a kind of emerging anthropologist whose life experience does not allow her to sustain any clear boundary between the West and the Rest. It is written in English, but is it Anglo-American anthropology? Perez's intellectual history has three central moments: her encounter with French structuralism; her encounter with American postcolonialism; her lifelong engagement with India, not only as an ethnographer, but more recently as a teacher and colleague.

Yet she is writing about Goa, the core of Portuguese India from the early sixteenth century to 1961. Perez's association with Portugal is explicit in the book and, in fact, she makes good of it by bringing to bear on her analysis a wealth of historical knowledge concerning Portuguese imperialism in Asia that would be unavailable to someone who is not a fluent reader of Portuguese. In her essay, as much as she relies on her lifelong work as a scholar studying matters of caste in Gujarat, she also relies on her deep knowledge of Portuguese imperial history. This is a matter that cannot be taken for granted, since precisely one of the dominant characteristics of the postcolonial literature that so influences her intellectual outlook is its failure to deal satisfactorily with forms of imperialism and colonialism that are outside the Anglo-American mould (see Pina-Cabral 2005). Perez explicitly aims to bring together her two sources of expertise in her dialogue with her Indian anthropological readership in order to produce a new outlook on the relation between women and subalternity in India. For these are, after all, her explicit aims: to produce, as she says in her conclusion, 'another narrative of Goa . . . that goes beyond the colonial encounter' and that 'will give voice to those that history has removed from its writing: women, Dalits and (other) subalterns' (2011: 136).

The complexity of such an intellectual history and its cosmopolitan reach is not presented here as an exceptional case. Rather, to the contrary, I believe that this sense of engagement with those we study and this sense of crossing of intellectual entailments can be encountered just about everywhere in anthropology these days. To give yet another example, when our British-trained colleague Aya Ikegami goes on from writing about India's princely states (2013) to plan a research project on Japan's outcasts – the Bugakumin – she too is bringing some of her cosmopolitan luggage to bear upon topics that are close to her historical origins. Finally, when I undertook research in the 1990s on Macau's Eurasian population, publishing its results in Portuguese (1993), Chinese (1995) and English (2013), I was very conscious of the fact that my readership for each of these books was very different and that I had to adapt my writing to them, but that my research project somehow reached well beyond any of them.

For, indeed, the question of who 'we' are cannot be fully answered by merely considering what sort of persons the individual anthropologists are who write their books today. This matter is in many ways similar to the double meaning of the expression 'ethnographic present', the confusions of which I tried to unravel a while ago (Pina-Cabral 1994).

On the one hand, the term ethnographic present refers to the practice of mentioning ethnographic facts that happened in the past (and, often, in different moments of the past) as if they were actually ongoing. This rhetoric device was adopted in the early twentieth century by anthropologists whose notion of methodological holism was closely related to a synchronist view of sociocultural structuration. In short, they meant to show how things cohered in a determinable social context (a so-called 'culture') and they were not really interested in the minutiae of historical transformation. They aimed at capturing some sort of structuration that was temporally durable and that was essential to the collective entity (the 'culture') they aimed to represent.

The collective representations they wished to grasp were not those of this or that particular native, held in this or that time; they were generic and, while not atemporal, they were somehow permanent, for they structured the collective entity postulated to exist. Thus, the minutiae of history were seen as irrelevant when faced with the much more profound determinative value of the structure such anthropologists claimed to be able to identify. In this way, the presentation of the material would have remained the same, whether they had studied it three years ago, ten years ago, or whether most of it had actually come off the historical accounts of long-ago travellers (such as the notable case of Kathleen Gough's ethnography of the Nayars of the Malabar Coast, 1952, 1965).

However, seen from another perspective, anthropology is prone to forget that ethnographic fieldwork happens in an ethnographic present and that it cannot be dissociated from that present at the expense of proposing an ahistoricist version of sociocultural life of precisely the same nature as the one criticized above. If ethnographic fieldwork depends on a personal experience of intersubjectivity, then it is essentially historical, for it is dependent on processes of personal ontogeny (both in the ethnographer and in her interlocutors) that cannot be unravelled, postponed or generalized. This is one of the greatest difficulties with carrying out historically inspired anthropology such as Rosa Maria Perez is doing in her essay or such as I carried out when writing about Macau (2013).

Are there still *devadasis* dancing in the modern, tourist-oriented temples of Goa? When did they stop dancing and why? What has become of their descendants? These are questions that Perez attempts to answer. In fact, the more an anthropologist depends on historical records for her ethnography, the more important it is that she should declare carefully the conjuncture that lies behind her own personal acquaintance with the places and people she describes, for the greater is the danger of her pretending to achieve some sort of ahistorical knowledge. And the problem is not only with the information she passes on to us, it is also with the nature of the questions that her text addresses (her *problematique*, as the French would say). She must not pretend to escape the conjuncture that moved her very laying out of the issues she addresses.

Thus, on the one hand, the rhetorical device of the ethnographic present is a habit to be deplored, which anthropologists must get rid of, both when they write ethnography and when they report the ethnographies of their past peers; on the other hand, the conjunctural meaning of ethnographic present is absolutely essential to the writing of good ethnography, as it is one of the most important methodological instruments of ethnographic writing and anthropological comparison. One of the central challenges of so-called 'long-term' fieldwork or of fieldwork revisitation is precisely how to deal with this type of conjunctural dislocation of the ethnographic present. Signe Howell discusses this in her collected volume on the issue (Howell and Talle 2012).

A very similar argument might be made of 'holism', another deeply misused word. The atemporal, sociocentric use of holism that we became familiar with from the impact of Durkheimian thinking in twentieth-century anthropology should indeed be rejected. This is the sort of holism to which Wendy James refers in her critique of Mary Douglas. However, we must defend the methodological injunction to study sociocultural phenomena in their broader context, thus refusing to essentialize them, as if they could be the same for all time even when they are taken away from their historical context of occurrence. The explicitness of the ethnographic present must be safeguarded at all costs, for it is one of the main methodological instruments of our trade. Indeed, Jan Smuts' original botanical insight, which gave rise to the very word holism, pointed precisely in this direction. It suggested that the phenotype of a plant could not be assumed to be the same for all time and place, for it depended on its context of emergence and was not fully determined by the original genetic material.

Now, in the same vein, when we speak of the ethnographic 'we', we must not concern ourselves only with the mere reference to the characteristics and identifications of the ethnographer – that is to say, for example, whether he or she is a Portuguese national teaching in Ahmadabad, or an Indian national working at Columbia University in New York. These are, of course, important aspects but there is the further matter of knowing whom the ethnographer is convoking by that 'we', what company he or she is calling forth. And the matter is not passive, because such rhetorical devices place the reader. This was essentially the problem with Mary Douglas's use of the first-person plural when I first read it, for it assumed a project to which I was expected to adhere, it placed me, it determined a route in the world for my future practice as a budding young social anthropologist. In that case, this was a project that I explicitly rejected. And, fortunately for me, it turns out that I was not alone; Wendy James, T.N. Madan and so many other colleagues before me also rejected it. There was politics in that Western 'we' of Mary Douglas, a political position that I for one did not welcome.

But, just like with holism or the ethnographic present, Mary Douglas might only have been using the 'we' in the way that is unavoidable when one writes an anthropologically inspired text. That is to say, simply assuming that the readers know who wrote *The Elementary Structures of Kinship*, that the readers know what the relevance is of speaking of a cross-cousin or a mother's brother, or that they have read a minimum of Azande, Maori or Kwakiutl ethnography. That is to say, the collective we of the people who know or are supposed to know the history of such words as tabu, *hau*, *mana* or totem; structure, segmentation, semiotic turn, etc.

After all, the discipline has been going on for a very long time. So there is positively no sense in writing anthropological essays that pertain to explain everything that it takes to understand an anthropological argument. This is why one's first suggestion to one's undergraduate students who are confronted with the classical texts of the discipline is that they must read on without fear of misunderstanding. They must get the broad gist of what is being said in those essays; only later should they try to work out the precise meaning of the references. For, in the case of the better essays in the discipline, it may take them many years to do just that.

In short, anthropologists cannot but assume a community of information when they write their essays. It is to such a readership that they normally address their articles. Such a 'we' comprises people who regularly page through *JRAI*, *American Ethnologist*, *Current Anthropology* or *HAU*. To the contrary, to assume that anthropology is necessarily the task of Westerners; that Westerners are a category that is readily definable; and that Westerners are more differentiated than the Other with a capital O, etc., is an absurdity that anthropologists must fight against for the sake of their discipline, for the sake of their own complex engagements as citizens, and for the sake of respecting the subject positions of those they study.

What Knowledge?

Let us now focus on another aspect of Mary Douglas's defence of primitiveness: her adoption of 'the Kantian principle that thought can only advance by freeing itself of its own subjective conditions' or, in Gellner's words, 'the attainment of a rational, non-magical, non-enchanted world'. If, as so many of us have argued, Mary Douglas's books are manipulating her readers' subject position by proposing a political project, then it cannot be said that she achieved her own ideals. Without even having to enter into the specifics of her own particular life history (which, as it happens, would easily corroborate my argument – Fardon 1999), we can be quite certain that her subjective conditions are an integral part of what she wrote.

The question, then, is: is there a way of getting rid of politics in anthropological thinking? Is there a way of freeing anthropology from the social, personal and emotional engagements of the anthropologists? In the light of the history of the discipline of anthropology – which we have seen to be grounded on a fundamental rejection of slavery and oppression, an engagement with several styles of nationalism, and an association with colonialism and imperialism – can we really hope to achieve that aim? When a contemporary female ethnographer, such as Rosa Maria Perez, claims that her condition as a woman and her deep sympathy for those who are subaltern are driving aspects of her intellectual labours, is she in fact throwing the game down and admitting to being a bad anthropologist? Surely not! The question is even more poignant when it comes to ethnography. If ethnography is in some central way an exercise based on acquiring information through participating in a life world through intersubjectivity, how can we ever hope to free it from the subjective conditions of those who perform it?

We seem to be faced here with a radical choice: either anthropologists believe that they can produce science by ridding themselves of their 'subjective conditions', by knowing better than 'them'; or they have to opt for the radical relativist take, beat their own chests, and claim that they know no better than others ('man invents his own realities', as per Roy Wagner). In the second option, anthropology gives up on the ideal of science and becomes another suggestive but vaguely inoperative interpretative undertaking, a discourse among discourses. Many are those who have opted for this solution over the past decades.

However, while at first it may seem the simplest path out of the Kantian quandary, the fact is that this last solution is less easy to entertain than it promises to be. It should worry us, for it is an upside-down version of the Cretan Paradox. When a Cretan claims that all Cretans are liars, how can we trust him? Similarly, if all 'knowledges' are equally valid and if we find that they are contradictory, then no 'knowledges' are valid. Now the shadow part of this 'generosity' is that, if someone's anthropology is Western anthropology, then those who are not Western have other anthropologies (as per Restrepo and Escobar 2005). But that means that they no longer have the right to be 'anthropologists' in the sense of practitioners of a scientific discipline that has evolved globally over the past one and a half centuries. For surely we have to admit that there would be nothing more ethnocentric than to believe that all other anthropologies should think of themselves as being anthropological in the rather arcane sense anthropologists give the word (that is why we insist that our students spend years of learning to become anthropologists and why professional anthropologists are constantly making efforts to renew their scholarship). Amerindian perspectivism, trading nature with person, argues precisely this: that we cannot assume that humanity is the same for Amerindians as it is for Anglo-Americans (Viveiros de Castro 2012). In short, there would be no anthropology.

And that is precisely where I started this chapter: if by the standards of Mary Douglas or of Edward Saïd I am not a Western anthropologist, does that mean that I have no right to engage in anthropology? Worse still, if what I produce has no claim to some sort of exceptionality, if it is the same sort of thing that 'practical, ordinary people' do when they go home at the end of the working day, why should I trouble myself so much in order to produce it? It would seem that Leach had a point.

Then, in the contrary direction, there is that long line of arguments that attribute scientificity to activities that do not see themselves as scientific: the classical case is Robin Horton on African ritual;[9] but recently we have seen Ronald Dworkin in his tremendously influential book *Religion without God* (2013) arguing that theology is another science; etc. It is modernist caesurism (the proneness to argue in terms of all-or-nothing) that produces these basically defeatist approaches. It all starts by one's assumption that there must be a clear, determinable boundary of essence between what can be considered science and what cannot be so considered. If one takes this breach of essence for granted, then, when one confronts the myriad human endeavours that in the history of human thinking were placed in an intermediate position between what we today call science and other kinds of human intellectual engagement with the world, one is necessarily led to conclude that one's original breach was not valid. But if we had a historicist approach to science and saw it as an emergent human activity with strong historical links with the activities out of which it emerged, then the problem would not have existed in the first place.

I find all of these arguments (such as Horton's or Dworkin's) essentially anti-historicist and metaphysical. In all of its historical complexity, resulting from a wide variety of sources and inspirations, we have to recognize that there is today only one scientific tradition, and that is the science that emerged in the course of modern history. For a long time, Christian Europeans played a central role, then other imperial masters took on the leading seat; who knows what the future will bring? The scientific endeavour is not Western, neither is it one among various, for it is an exercise the aim of which is to be accessible to as many points of view as can possibly be imagined by any particular practitioner in any particular time and place.

The production of science is a very specific technical matter and those techniques were not all invented at the same time or just for the sake of making our lives difficult. Science has a history and it is omnivorous, in the sense that it will absorb all that it can from the past and all that it can from the future. Unlike the 'holistic cultures' that anthropologists used to describe, science is an ever-unfinished product, ever open to its own transformation. It is not out of a mean temper that we are forced to subject our theses to examination, our papers to peer review, that we have to study hard, that we have to confirm our findings, that we have to put in references, that we have to check our results, that we have to avoid plagiarism, that we are constantly checking for a flaw in the colleague's argument, etc. All of this is not just an exercise in interpretative entertainment to fight off Alzheimer's at the end of the day; we have seen what scientifically inspired technique has done to the world around us.

As far as anthropology is concerned, radical relativism as much as positivism are both best avoided. It is my conviction that the paradoxical situation concerning anthropology and science can be easily bypassed, for it is the result of the careless recourse to the all-or-nothing fallacy.[10] Suffice it to say that, if we adopt a minimal realist stance (see Lynch 1998), we can easily overcome such paradoxes and find ourselves again on the path to seeing anthropology as part of the broader scientific project without risking the sort of ethnocentrism of which Wendy James accused Mary Douglas.

There is, however, a further aspect that deserves our attention here. The unravelling of this conundrum will necessarily involve the casting into doubt of the validity of a set of metaphoric uses of concepts that were so central to our scholarly tool kit throughout the twentieth century that we no longer even contemplate their intellectual status. This is the case with the notion of 'knowledge' that is an intrinsic part of all of these debates. We seem to have forgotten that in many of the cases in which we use it, it is being used metaphorically. As a metaphor it has proved to be very useful, but it is nonetheless essential to distinguish its literal meaning from its metaphorical connotations if we are going to avoid the all-or-nothing rut.

The dictionary defines knowledge as 'awareness or familiarity gained by experience of a fact or situation', but 'awareness' or 'familiarity gained by experience' are occurrences that only apply to biological beings. Other definitions emphasise 'perception' and 'apprehension'. Yet, collectives do not perceive, they are not aware of or apprehend – when we use the word in that way, we are using it as a metaphor to say that, among the persons who comprise that collective, the perception, awareness or apprehension of a certain association is very common or even universal.

Moreover, we know that, in human thinking, indeterminacy and under-determination rule (cf. Davidson 2001). No two persons can ever hold precisely the same thought, as indeed there is no such thing as a separable, single thought. When we say that two persons hold the same knowledge, we mean that their thought processes concerning what is the case are very proximate when judged by a third party. So knowledge in that metaphorical sense depends on two exercises in triangulation, one with the world, the other with a third party. Yet we talk of knowledge as if it were a thing, an entity, an object. We claim that A attains a certain piece of knowledge that he communicates to B. In turn, B writes it down, and when C reads it, she too attains that same knowledge. Thus, we talk of knowledge as if it could be accumulated, produced, traded, corrected or improved. We confuse knowledge with information and with communication. A lot of suffering and many mistakes might have been avoided if we had remembered this, when discussing the economics of knowledge production along neoliberal lines (e.g. the bibliometric debates).

So we are back to Leach's insight. Anthropological 'knowledge' – in the sense of the ever-evolving set of associations that trained anthropologists who have access to the anthropological record would hold to be the case after serious and hard consideration – is not at all a process of the same nature as the sort of 'knowledge' that anthropologists describe in their notebooks as held by practical, ordinary people. But then the same is the case with the sort of theological exercise that St. Anselm of Canterbury carried out in the twelfth century when he wrote his theological treatises (1998) or what Muchona taught Victor Turner (1960). Why must we call that 'science' when it did not think of itself in that way and did not follow scientific procedure? The fact that St. Anselm's thoughts were important historically to the birth of modern science or that Muchona had a decisive impact on the history of anthropology seems to be beside the point.

In sum, my argument is that our current use of the word 'knowledge' naturalizes a metaphor (the notion of collective representations) and depends on a representationist view of mind that, judging by present scientific debate, is best avoided.

Conclusion: An Ecumenical Anthropology

Anthropology, in all of its different angles, is a product of human history. The anthropology of the past was a daughter of the past, as much as the anthropology of the present navigates the present. For a while, during those heady postcolonial days, it seemed to many like they could abdicate from the imperial present in order to understand critically the conjunctural immersion of the anthropology of the colonial past. This, however, was yet another manifestation of the historical immersion of all scientific discourse; indeed, of all human acts of communication. It was another ideological gambit at global elite status on the part of academics who thought that, by exorcizing the past masters, they could obtain rights of citizenship from the new masters.

History is in the making. As Edwin Ardener long ago reminded us, in the course of his own poststructuralist bereavement, '"comprehending others" cannot be a kind of passive act leaving one or both sides unchanged' (2007) – those are the wages of all attempts at inscribing history. The practitioners of anthropology in the past were essentially as capable of arising out of history as the practitioners of the present, which should give us a sense of humility in the face of the passing of yet another anthropological fashion, yet another theoretical cargo cult.

To conclude, therefore, I would like to argue for what I call an *ecumenical anthropology*, that is, one that builds on the ever-widening nature of the information and analysis that the social sciences produce about the world and that is open to an ever-wider range of practitioners. The concept of ecumene as proposed by people like Sidney Mintz (1996) or Ulf Hannerz (1991) was originally inspired by the work of Kroeber (e.g. Kroeber and Kluckhohn 1963). It describes a space or an ambit of human communication – not a place or a group, but a communicational environment structured by a *habitus*. Thus, there may be ecumenes within ecumenes, in much the same way as it is possible to identify a more local *habitus* within a more broadly defined *habitus*. Human communication is seen as historical and localized and as built on the very process of constitution of its interveners (see Pina-Cabral 2017b). Like all good science, ecumenical anthropology will be an unfinished project, for humans are constantly revealing themselves in history, as much in the past as in the future.

In the above discussion about who comprises the first-person plural to which anthropological analyses are addressed, I started by noting that most anthropologists today exist within a cosmopolitan condition. In my own lifetime, the discipline has expanded immensely, way beyond the range of the few colonial outposts that were its furthest outreaches until the 1970s; places such as the illustrious department where I was trained in Johannesburg. Today, there are universities with anthropology departments in many unsuspected parts of the world. Anthropology gets taught to just about every kind of person from China and Australia to Venezuela and Canada. The development of the discipline in South America, for example, can be held as a good example. In Brazil, Argentina, Peru, Columbia, anthropology is a lively discipline that has opened itself to a broad diversity of student publics and that participates actively in the civic debates concerning local social issues and their relations to the broader world.

But anthropology today is deeply cosmopolitan in yet another sense. The old distinction between anthropology abroad and anthropology at home no longer makes any sense in such a context (see Hannerz 2010). There are an increasing number of anthropologists whose subject position can hardly be described as Western. Moreover, the four old imperial traditions have irremediably lost their singularity (cf. Barth et al. 2010). A fifth tradition has arisen, the one that is entertained by people such as myself, Rosa Maria Perez, and most of the Brazilian and Indian anthropologists we collaborate with, which results from a largely eclectic inspiration derived from all previously available anthropologies, wherever we can find them. I insist, however, that such a view of anthropology is not new; it is echoed in a long line of anthropological thinkers, from Fei Xiaotong and Franz Baermann Steiner to Carmelo Lisón Tolosana or Ricardo Cardoso de Oliveira, people who, much like myself, do not see the imperial subject as a project they can entertain. T.N. Madan, for instance, defended just this in the early 1980s, as we have seen.

Contrary to those who are trapped in the all-or-nothing dilemma, we have to realize that the option is not between relativism and positivism, but rather the work of anthropology is realized by a series of triangulations that, while each retaining one's insertion in the world, relocate one in an ever-widening process of critical analysis – an ever-unfinished process that Julian Pitt-Rivers used to call de-ethnocentrification (1992). Similarly, sociocentric holism and the rhetoric use of the ethnographic present must be rejected, but method ological holism and an attention to conjunctural ethnographic present are central tools of the anthropological trade. Thus, while epistemic relativism means an abdication from anthropology, methodological relativism must be defended, as anthropology's indispensable tool.

Acknowledgements

I am grateful to Liana Chua and Nayanika Mathur for their invitation to participate in this discussion and to all the colleagues present in our meeting in Cambridge for the very exciting debate. I also wish to thank Minnie Freudenthal for all those marvellous conversations during our lengthy perambulations which have so influenced my view of the world and of science.

João de Pina-Cabral is Professor of Social Anthropology at the School of Anthropology and Conservation of the University of Kent at Canterbury, UK, and Research Professor at the Institute of Social Sciences, University of Lisbon, Portugal. He was co-founder and president both of the Portuguese Association of Anthropology and of the European Association of Social Anthropologists. He has published extensively on matters related to kinship and the family, personhood, and ethnicity in postcolonial contexts. He has carried out extensive ethnographic fieldwork on the Alto Minho (Northwest Portugal), Macau (South China) and Bahia (Northeast Brazil). His principal academic publications in English are *Sons of Adam, Daughters of Eve: The Peasant Worldview of the Alto Minho* (Clarendon Press, 1986), *Between China and Europe: Person, Culture and Emotion in Macau* (LSE Monographs, Berg, 2002) and *World: An Anthropological Examination* (HAU/University of Chicago Press, 2017). He co-edited with Antónia Lima *Elites: Choice, Leadership, and Succession* (Berg, 2000), with F. Pine *On the Margins of Religion* (Berghahn, 2008), and with Christina Toren *The Challenge of Epistemology: Anthropological Perspectives* (Berghahn, 2011).

Notes

1. See the introductions to Steiner's work by Mary Douglas, M.N. Srinivas, Jeremy Adler and Richard Fardon (1999a: 3–102 and 1999b: 3–106).
2. Written at the demand of Hermínio Martins and Jonathan Webber (Ardener 2007: 191–210).
3. Of late, people advocating visions akin to this one have been emerging out of the woodwork in all sorts of places. See, for example, David Christian's Big History pedagogic project (2007).
4. For example, Restrepo and Escobar 2005; see also the response (Pina-Cabral 2006).
5. 'There Is No Such Thing as Western Civilisation', https://www.theguardian.com/world/2016/nov/09/western-civilisation-appiah-reith-lecture (accessed 3 August 2017).
6. But then again, the English translation of this book, oddly entitled *Notebooks on Primitive Mentality*, was only published in Oxford by Peter Rivière in 1975 (Lévy-Bruhl 1975).
7. In *The Legitimation of Belief*, he claims: 'The attainment of a rational, non-magical, non-enchanted world is a much more fundamental

achievement than the jump from one scientific vision to another' (Gellner 1979: 182).
8. My translation from Viveiros's Portuguese version.
9. Cf. Robin Horton: 'African religious systems, then, can be seen as the outcome of a model-making process which is found alike in the thought of science and in that of pre-science' (1964: 99).
10. Inspired by the thought of Donald Davidson, I have argued this point at length elsewhere (Pina-Cabral 2010, 2011, 2017b).

References

Ahmad, Aijaz. 1992. *Theory: Classes, Nations, Literatures*. London: Verso.
Anselm, Saint. 1998. *The Major Works*. Oxford: Oxford University Press.
Ardener, Edwin. 2007. 'Social Anthropology and the Decline of Modernism', in Malcolm Chapman (ed.), *The Voice of Prophecy and Other Essays*. Oxford: Berghahn, pp. 191–210.
Ardener, Shirley. 1975. *Perceiving Women*. London: Malaby Press.
Barth, Fredrik, Andre Gingrich, Rober Parkin, and Sydel Silverman. 2010. *One Discipline, Four Ways: British, German, French, and American Anthropology*. Chicago, IL: University of Chicago Press.
Bennett, Jane. 2010. *Vibrant Matter: A Political Ecology of Things*. Durham, NC: Duke University Press.
Christian, David. 2007. *This Fleeting World: A Short History of Humanity*. Great Barrington, MA: Berkshire Publishing.
Connolly, William E. 2011. A World of Becoming. Durham, NC: Duke University Press.
Davidson, Donald. 2001. *Subjective, Intersubjective, Objective*. Oxford: Oxford University Press.
Douglas, Mary. 1966. *Purity and Danger: An Analysis of Concepts of Pollution and Taboo*. London: Routledge and Kegan Paul.
Douglas, Mary. [1970] 1973. *Natural Symbols: Explorations in Cosmology*. London: Pelican.
Durkheim, Émile, and Marcel Mauss. [1903] 1963. *Primitive Classification*, trans. and introduction by Rodney Needham. Chicago, IL: University of Chicago Press.
Dworkin, Richard. 2013. *Religion without God*. Cambridge, MA: Harvard University Press.
Evans-Pritchard, E.E. 1933. 'The Intellectualist (English) Interpretation of Magic', *Bulletin of the Faculty of Arts* 1(2): 282–311.
Evans-Pritchard, E.E. [1934] 1970. 'Lévy-Bruhl's Theory of Primitive Mentality', *Journal of the Anthropological Society of Oxford* 1(2): 39–60.
Evans-Pritchard, E.E. 1936. 'Science and Sentiment: An Exposition and Criticism of the Writings of Pareto', *Bulletin of the Faculty of Arts* 3(2): 163–92.

Fabian, Johannes. 2002. *Time and the Other: How Anthropology Makes Its Object*. New York: Columbia University Press.
Fardon, Richard. 1999. *Mary Douglas: An Intellectual Biography*. London: Routledge.
Gellner, Ernest. 1979. *The Legitimation of Belief*. Cambridge: Cambridge University Press.
Gough, E. Kathleen. 1952. 'Changing Kinship Usages in the Setting of Political and Economic Change among the Nayars of Malabar', *Journal of the Royal Anthropological Institute of Great Britain and Ireland* 82(1): 71–88.
Gough, E. Kathleen. 1965. 'A Note on Nayar Marriage', *Man* 65: 8–11.
Hannerz, Ulf. 1991. 'The Global Ecumene as a Network of Networks', in Adam Kuper (ed.), *Conceptualizing Societies*. London: Routledge, pp. 34–56.
Hannerz, Ulf. 2010. *Anthropology's World: Life in a Twenty-First-Century Discipline*. London: Pluto Press.
Holbraad, Martin. 2010. 'Ontology Is Just Another Word for Culture', *Critique of Anthropology* 30(2): 152–200.
Horton, Robin. 1964. 'Ritual Man in Africa'. *Africa: Journal of the International African Institute* 34(2): 85–104.
Howell, Signe, and Aud Talle. 2012. *Returns to the Field: Multitemporal Research and Contemporary Anthropology*. Bloomington, IN: Indiana University Press.
Ikegami, Aya. 2013. *Princely India Re-imagined: An Historical Anthropology of Mysore from 1799 to the Present*. New York: Routledge.
Ingold, Tim. 1995. 'Building, Dwelling, Living: How Animals and People Make Themselves at Home in the World', in Marilyn Strathern (ed.), *Shifting Contexts: Transformations in Anthropological Knowledge*. London: Routledge, pp. 57–80.
Ingold, Tim (ed.). 1996. *Key Debates in Anthropology*. London: Psychology Press.
James, Wendy. 1970. 'Are "Primitives" Necessary?' *JASO* 1(2): 82–83.
Kroeber, Alfred, and Clyde Kluckhohn. 1963. *Culture: A Critical Review of Concepts and Definitions*. New York: Vintage Books.
Kuper, Adam. 1988. *The Invention of Primitive Society: Transformations of an Illusion*. London: Psychology Press.
Kuper, Adam. 2005. *The Reinvention of Primitive Society: Transformations of a Myth*. New York: Taylor and Francis.
Leach, Edmund. 1968. 'Introduction', in *Dialectic in Practical Religion*. Cambridge: Cambridge University Press, pp. 1–6.
Lévi-Strauss, Claude. 1998. 'Lévi-Strauss nos 90: A Antropologia de Cabeça para Baixo'. Interview with Eduardo Viveiros de Castro, *Mana* 4(2): 119–26.
Lévy-Bruhl, Lucien. 1949. *Carnets*, 1st edn, ed. Bruno Carsenti. Paris: PUF.
Lévy-Bruhl, Lucien. 1975. *Notebooks on Primitive Mentality*, preface by M. Leenhardt, trans. P. Rivière. London: Harper & Row.

Lynch, Michael P. 1998. *Truth in Context: An Essay on Pluralism and Objectivity.* Cambridge, MA: MIT Press.

Madan, T.N. 1982. 'Indigenous Anthropology in Non-Western Countries: An Overview', in Hussein Fahim (ed.), *Indigenous Anthropology in Non-Western Countries.* Durham, NC: Carolina Academic Press, pp. 4–17.

Mintz, Sidney W. 1996. 'Enduring Substances, Trying Theories: The Caribbean Region as Oikoumenê', *Journal of the Royal Anthropological Institute* (N.S.) 2: 289–93.

Needham, Rodney. 1972. *Belief, Language and Experience.* Chicago, IL: University of Chicago Press.

Needham, Rodney. 1981. *Circumstantial Deliveries.* Berkeley, CA: University of California Press.

Pedersen, Morten Axel. 2012. 'Common Sense: A Review of Certain Reviews of the "Ontological Turn"', *Anthropology of this Century* 5, http://aotcpress.com/articles/common_nonsense/#sthash.1yvGKe2k.dpuf.

Perez, Rosa Maria. 2004. *Kings and Untouchables: A Study of the Caste System in Western India.* New Delhi: Orient BlackSwan.

Perez, Rosa Maria. 2011. *The Tulsi and the Cross: Anthropology and the Colonial Encounter in Goa.* New Delhi: Orient BlackSwan.

Pina-Cabral, J. 1986. *Sons of Adam, Daughters of Eve: The Peasant Worldview of the Alto Minho.* Oxford: Clarendon Press.

Pina-Cabral, J. 1993 (Chinese ed. 1995). *Em Terra de Tufões: Dinâmicas da Etnicidade Macaense.* Macau: Instituto Cultural de Macau.

Pina-Cabral, J. 1994. 'Personal Identity and Ethnic Ambiguity: Naming Practices among the Eurasians of Macau', *Social Anthropology/ Anthropologie Sociale* 2(2): 115–32.

Pina-Cabral, J. 2002. *Between China and Europe: Person, Culture and Emotion in Macao.* LSE Anthropology Series 74. London: Berg.

Pina-Cabral, J. 2005. 'New Age Warriors: Negotiating the Handover on the Streets of Macao', *Journal of Romance Studies* 5(1): 9–22.

Pina-Cabral, J. 2006. 'Responses to "Other Anthropologies and Anthropologies Otherwise: Steps to a World Anthropologies Framework" by Eduardo Restrepo and Arturo Escobar (2005)', *Critique of Anthropology* 26(4): 467–70.

Pina-Cabral, J. 2010. 'The Door in the Middle: Six Conditions for Anthropology', in Deborah James, Evie Plaice, and Christina Toren (eds), *Culture Wars: Context, Models and Anthropologists' Accounts.* New York: Berghahn, pp. 152–69.

Pina-Cabral, J. 2011. "Afterword: What Is an Institution?" *Social Anthropology,* 19(4): 477–494.

Pina-Cabral, J. 2013. 'The Core of Affects: Namer and Named in Bahia (NE Brazil)', *Journal of the Royal Anthropological Institute* 19(1): 75–101.

Pina-Cabral, J. 2017a. 'Lusotopy as Ecumene', in T.H. Eriksen, C. Garton, and S. Randeria (eds), *Anthropology Now and Next: Essays in Honor of Ulf Hannerz.* London: Berghahn Books, pp. 241–63.

Pina-Cabral, J. 2017b. *World: An Anthropological Examination*. Chicago, IL: HAU Books.
Pitt-Rivers, Julian. 1992. 'The Personal Factors in Fieldwork', in J. Pina-Cabral and John K. Campbell (eds), *Europe Observed*. London: Macmillan/St. Antony's, pp. 133–47.
Restrepo, Eduardo, and Arturo Escobar. 2005. '"Other Anthropologies and Anthropologies Otherwise": Steps to a World Anthropologies Framework', *Current Anthropology* 25(2): 99–129.
Saïd, Edward W. 1994. *Culture and Imperialism*. New York: Vintage Books.
Steiner, Franz Baermann. 1999a. *Selected Writings I: Taboo, Truth, and Religion*. New York: Berghahn Books.
Steiner, Franz Baermann. 1999b. *Selected Writings II: Orientpolitik, Value, and Civilisation*. New York: Berghahn Books.
Strathern, Marilyn. 1988. *The Gender of the Gift*. Berkeley, CA: University of California Press.
Toren, Christina. 2002. 'Anthropology as the Whole Science of What It Is to Be Human', in Richard Fox and Barbara King (eds), *Anthropology beyond Culture*. Oxford: Berg, pp. 105–24.
Turner, Victor W. 1960. 'Muchona the Hornet, Interpreter of Religion (Northern Rhodesia)', in Joseph Casagrande (ed.), *In the Company of Men: Twenty Portraits of Anthropological Informants*. New York: Harper, pp. 333–56.
Wagner, Roy. 1975. *The Invention of Culture*. Chicago, IL: University of Chicago Press.
Viveiros de Castro, Eduardo. 2009. *Métaphysiques Canibales*. Paris: PUF.
Viveiros de Castro, Eduardo. 2012. *Cosmological Perspectivism in Amazonia and Elsewhere*, introduction by Roy Wagner. HAU Masterclass Series. HAU Books, http://haubooks.org/cosmological-perspectivism-in-amazonia/.

AFTERWORD

Mwenda Ntarangwi

Is there enough room at the anthropology table for multiple ways of knowing and carrying out research that reflect and are informed by the diversity of its practitioners? Is there a discipline we can call anthropology or are there multiple versions of it? When students get trained in the discipline in different institutions located in different regions and countries, do they receive similar skills and perspectives that help them produce a singular entity we can call anthropology? Despite its short life as a professional discipline (starting only at the turn of the twentieth century), anthropology is now part of the training and vocation of individuals located in Africa, Antarctica, Asia, Australia, Europe, North America and South America. Its methods and ways of knowing that primarily focus on local sociocultural ways of living, thinking and being lead to its inevitable influence from the practitioner's own subject position, anthropology that in turn produces a wide variety of works and theoretical positions. One expects, for instance, that an anthropological project carried out in India by an Indian anthropologist or in Japan by a Japanese anthropologist will be different from one carried out in the same locations by an African or European anthropologist. The questions asked, the emphasis laid, the relations and interpretations of those relations and the interactions that the anthropologist ends up having with his/her interlocutors are increasingly shaped by, among other factors, the anthropologist's subject position, their lived experiences, the perceptions the interlocutors have of the anthropologist, and the kind of training received by the anthropologist. Therein lies anthropology's dilemma: if there exist all these pointers to the discipline's multiple identities reflecting the diversity of its practitioners, are there shared traits or practices that anthropologists bring to the table that form some kind of coherent and shared identity?

In a recent conversation, a close friend remarked that one of the traits she has observed among the anthropologists she knows is their habit to always take notes at meetings and other social gatherings involving some element of learning or training. Two years earlier, a friend trained in philosophy made a similar comment about me during a scholarly gathering in Dakar, Senegal that we were both attending. Constantly taking notes, it seems, is the one thing we may share as anthropologists. This observation got me thinking. Are there some shared traits that anthropologists bring to their professional practices despite our varied experiences, training styles and contexts of practice? Do we have something in common that we can identify as part of what it means to be an anthropologist? Can we have shared characteristics or even practices and yet remain unique and produce multiple anthropologies? It is not hard to imagine most anthropologists as perpetual learners and each cultural context providing an opportunity for learning. This would explain the shared practice of taking notes. Ethnography is after all about ongoing observation, interpretation and analysis. And yet I find myself constantly asking whether anthropologists find themselves taking notes in all social contexts due to their training in carrying out ethnographic fieldwork. Do they share this practice because of their shared training methods or does anthropology as a discipline attract curious individuals whose first step to respond to their curiosity is note taking? Do those individuals always find that whatever contexts they are in provide for them important opportunities for learning something new? The answer may be a mixture of these two suggestions. Anthropology as a discipline has attracted a number of practitioners because of its methodological approaches and the potential that data collected through those methods has for addressing critical social and personal issues. It also, I may add, draws heavily on records of observed phenomena to sustain its data presentation in the form of writing (at least for the sociocultural variety). Moreover, the very nature of fieldwork trains us to not rely on memory, especially when in unfamiliar social spaces or in places where whatever is going on at that moment is important for our full comprehension of its meaning. As Stutz notes of anthropologists' shared trait,

> All anthropologists utilize methodologies that involve zooming out and studying aspects of humanity that we can't easily grasp within the myopic experiences that we usually have of our lives and surroundings, as we constantly work to discipline our emotions and actions in responding to daily challenges, in setting goals, and juggling competing obligations.[1]

This idea of 'juggling competing obligations' that our research field presents us with is what may lead to our shared identity as anthropologists. Anthropology, I would also suggest, attracts individuals who have a specific desire to change the way things are in their worlds and see the discipline's methods and perspectives as helpful towards that goal. African-American educator, scholar and researcher Allison Davis, for instance, 'wanted to dismantle racism and saw anthropology as a source of potentially useful weapons in that struggle for justice-seeking change' (Harrison 2008: 13). Faye Harrison, another African-American scholar, was drawn to anthropology because, as she notes, 'Anthropological analysis played an important role in offering me the concepts, vocabulary, and comparative perspective for articulating a critique of racism and the culture of race in which I lived. That critique has been an invaluable resource in helping me gain an enabling and affirmative sense of my full humanity' (ibid.: 22).

I too have a similar story about my interest and entry into anthropology. I chose anthropology because it had the promise of equipping me with tools to analyse and understand complex social and cultural issues in ways that my training in other disciplines could not. Anthropology provided me with methodological approaches that promised to guide me towards a well-rounded understanding of what makes us human through holistic, contextual and comparative analyses (see Ntarangwi 2010). This embrace of anthropology for its methods, which attracted these three different scholars, points to a shared set of tools that those trained in the discipline bring to their practice. What stands out in these three cases is the value placed on anthropology's methods, analyses and application of those tools in response to pressing social challenges. Moreover, many scholars from other disciplines have embraced and even adopted anthropology's signature methodological approaches encapsulated in fieldwork. Scholars from these other disciplines adopt ethnographic methods for their work because of the utility that such a tool offers in understanding whatever aspect of human life they seek to explore and the potential for providing real solutions to the phenomenon. Corporations seek out the services of anthropologists not only to expand their reach internationally but also to better serve their clients and customers, and medical teams involve anthropologists to help understand health-seeking behaviour and plan medical interventions for communities.[2] Many scholars from other disciplines are particularly drawn to anthropology because of ethnography and fieldwork. Elevating fieldwork and even ethnography to represent the quintessential mark of anthropology's *modus operandi*, however, has drawn the critique of fellow anthropologist Tim Ingold, who argues that anthropology is not ethnography (see Ingold 2006). Ingold further notes that the term ethnographic 'appears to be a modish substitute for qualitative' but ends up offending 'every principle of proper, rigorous anthropological inquiry' that we associate with anthropology (2014: 384).

A shared set of tools does not guarantee a shared set of products or even analyses. Simply taking up fieldwork or pursuing ethnography does not turn these members of other disciplines into anthropologists. Anthropology, I believe, is a way of being. It is, as Ingold rightly observes, a discipline that enables its practitioner to 'study with people' and 'educates our perception of the world' (2006: 82). It is this engagement with others that makes anthropology such a diverse and complex discipline. Each anthropologist brings to the discipline his/her own individual identity as well as the culture of the institution and country at which the training took place. How, then, do we explain this tendency for the discipline to be conceived of as a singular entity? As Chua and Mathur show in the introduction to this volume, there is a tendency to apply the notion of 'we' in anthropology, imagining a unified group of practitioners who share 'a collective disciplinary identity'. Such a totalizing identity erases the multiple identities of all those trained and practising as anthropologists.

In 1969, Dell Hymes had anticipated this erasure of the differences inherent in the identity of the discipline when he asked, 'If it [anthropology] has a natural unity, why does its makeup differ so much from one country and national tradition to another, even from one department to another?' (Hymes 1969: 3). Contributors to the current volume provide good examples of how problematic the notion of 'we' in anthropology can be, especially when we ignore the distinct traditions observable in other countries as well as individual group differences observable among different anthropologists. Ang and Gatt (this volume), for instance, wonder why this notion of 'we' in anthropology does not include 'the people anthropologists conventionally work with during fieldwork'. By exploring their collaborative work as an anthropologist and a theatre maker, they challenge conventional understandings of anthropological work that tends to form hierarchical relationships between the anthropologist(s) and interlocutors.

Other examples of the diversity of anthropological traditions, practices and identities abound (see Bošković 2008; Restrepo and Escobar 2005; and Ribeiro and Escobar 2006, among others), pointing to the discipline's complexity and diversity that defies any attempt to fit it into a 'we' narrative. What, then, leads to this collective 'we' that Chua and Mathur so competently identify? My sense is that it has to do with ethnography and the consequence of capturing anthropological work through the writing process. Here I again agree with Tim Ingold when he argues that there is an important difference between anthropology and ethnography. Ingold states, 'Ethnographers describe, principally in writing, how the people of some place and time perceive the world and how they act in it' (2006: 90). The very act of writing freezes life into slices that are manageable and easily manipulatable to form a coherent and understandable story. Freezing or containing life entails certain practices that can be easily learned and replicated. Ethnography is one such practice because it entails some form of storytelling, with its own style, language, forms of self-regulation and perpetuation. Those who can tell these stories well become models to be emulated (often considered the discipline's gatekeepers). Their ethnographies become popularized by being assigned as required texts for courses taught to those being prepared to enter into the discipline; they are sought after to give public lectures at important forums that carry academic clout, and are appointed to prestigious positions that showcase their valued presence in the discipline or academy.

New anthropologists soon start to realize that to survive in the discipline they have to emulate these 'stars' or be completely forgotten. In the quest to be relevant, certain ways of writing are preferred. Such preference can easily lead to archetypes that in turn produce singular identities that can be easily represented by a 'we' narrative. If anything, telling stories through ethnography has not always been an open terrain that invites and accommodates multiple voices and identities among practitioners. As Faye Harrison shows, there has always been a struggle 'for a more democratized anthropology wherein Westerners and non-Westerners, men and women, class privileged and class oppressed can engage on more leveled terrain in an anthropology enterprise that no longer objectifies, appropriates, or nativizes ethnographic others' (2008: 112). The crisis in anthropology that was attributed to postmodernist challenges of the discipline's identity and practice (mostly focused on forms of writing) almost provided a way out of this exclusion. Unfortunately, the critiques did not bring much change because even as the whole enterprise of anthropological writing was challenged through postmodernist critiques by authors such as George Marcus and James Clifford, the centre of the discipline predominantly occupied by white Western males was not threatened. How else do we explain the emergence of this critique of anthropological writing and representation of others at the same time that women and minorities start to challenge anthropology and its representation of others (Harrison 2008)? It is no wonder that the discipline could adopt an identity encapsulated in a 'we' narrative. When a select few become the voice of the discipline, a common and singular language and identity emerges.

Such exclusion is further perpetuated by carefully controlled forms of membership into this exclusive club. Publications become tools of marking club membership as entry and participation are carefully controlled and monitored. Virginia Dominguez provides a window into this exclusionary practice when she critiques US anthropologists' intellectual parochialism in authorship and readership. In her 2012 presidential address for the American Anthropological Association, Dominguez notes, 'it is clear that we privilege a small number of scholarly journals over many others' (2012: 401). These 'preferred' journals become gates that anthropologists use to maintain a certain level of exclusivity. English-speaking US anthropologists dominate such journals, partly because of the influence of the US in world affairs; that influence is transferred to anthropology (Ntarangwi 2010), as well as the use of English. As Bošković and Eriksen note, 'the fact remains that the most influential anthropological works today are published in English' (2008: 3). US scholars and their use of English, therefore, carry double advantage. As Brodkin, Morgen and Hutchinson show, however, even these exclusive and dominant clubs have their own differences and levels of exclusion. Brodkin, Morgen and Hutchinson point out that US anthropology is primarily a white space, with its mechanisms for maintaining the status quo. They state, for instance, that 'departmental labor is divided in ways that assign to faculty and graduate students of color responsibilities that have lower status and rewards than those of their white counterparts' (2011: 545), ensuring that the machine reproduces itself.

What, then, is anthropology's identity as a discipline? Is it a conglomeration of multiple anthropologies as exemplified by the emerging field of world anthropologies, or is it a singular discipline with multiple versions that are reflective of the diversity of its practitioners? The contributors to this current volume have shared multiple answers to this question, and I am privileged to have had the opportunity to peek into them.

Mwenda Ntarangwi is an Associate Professor of Anthropology and currently Commission Secretary and CEO of Commission for University Education in Kenya. His research interests lie in the intersection between popular culture and social practices as well as in the practice of anthropology as a discipline. He is the author of *The Street Is My Pulpit: Hip Hop and Christianity in Kenya* (University of Illinois Press, 2016), *Annotated Bibliography on Children and Youth in Africa, 2001–2011* (CODESRIA Books, 2014), *Reversed Gaze: An African Ethnography of American Anthropology* (University of Illinois Press, 2010), *East African Hip Hop: Youth Culture and Globalization* (University of Illinois Press, 2009), and *Gender Identity ad Performance: Understanding Swahili Culture through Songs* (Africa World Press, 2003), co-editor of several volumes and author of numerous peer-reviewed scholarly journal papers and book chapters. He holds a doctorate in cultural anthropology from the University of Illinois in Urbana-Champaign and a Masters in Swahili Cultural Studies from Kenyatta University, Kenya.

Notes

1. See Aaron Stutz, 'What Do Anthropologists Have in Common?', blog post, 16 August 2013, https://bioculturalevolution.net/2013/08/16/what-do-anthropologists-have-in-common/ (accessed 2 February 2017).
2. See the American Anthropological Association website (http://www.americananthro.org/AdvanceYourCareer/Content.aspx?ItemNumber=1783) for more information on the various ways in which anthropologists get involved in different jobs and teams.

References

Bošković, Aleksandar (ed.). 2008. *Other People's Anthropology: Ethnographic Practice on the Margins*. New York: Berghahn Books.
Bošković, A., and T.H. Eriksen. 2008. Introduction to A. Bošković (ed.), *Other People's Anthropologies: Ethnographic Practice on the Margins*. New York: Berghahn Books, pp. 1–19.
Brodkin, Karen, Sandra Morgen, and Janis Hutchinson. 2011. 'Anthropology as White Public Space?', *American Anthropologist* 113(4): 545–56.

Dominguez, Virginia. 2012. 'Comfort Zones and Their Dangers: Who Are We? Qui Sommes-Nous?', *American Anthropologist* 114(3): 394–405.

Harrison, Faye. 2008. *Outsider Within: Reworking Anthropology in the Global Age*. Urbana, IL: University of Illinois Press.

Hymes, Dell. 1969. 'The Use of Anthropology: Critical, Political, Personal', in *Reinventing Anthropology*. New York: Vintage Books, pp. 3–79.

Ingold, Tim. 2006, 'Anthropology Is Not Ethnography', in R. Johnson (ed.), *Proceedings of the British Academy 154*. London: Oxford University Press, pp. 69–92.

Ingold, Tim. 2014. 'That's Enough about Ethnography!', *HAU: Journal of Ethnographic Theory* 4(1): 383–95.

Ntarangwi, Mwenda. 2010. *Reversed Gaze: An African Ethnography of American Anthropology*. Urbana, IL: University of Illinois Press.

Restrepo, Eduardo, and Arturo Escobar. 2005. 'Other Anthropologies and Anthropology Otherwise: Steps to a World Anthropologies Framework', *Critique of Anthropology* 25(2): 99–129.

Ribeiro, Gustavo Rins, and Arturo Escobar. 2006. *World Anthropologies: Disciplinary Transformations within Systems of Power*. Oxford: Berg Publishers.

INDEX

AAA. *See* American Anthropological Association
Abu-Lughod, Lila, 163
Academia; patronage in, 14–15; politics of, 14; WOC in, 12
academic epistemology, 181–82
affinity, 24–28; alterity and, 95–124, 179–99; celebration of, 128–29; experiential practice and, 192–94; imaginaries of, 118–24; indigenous media and, 143; performance and, 179–99; with research subjects, 129; risks of, 129–32; search for, 129; as similarities, 102–3; theory of, 12; value of, 84
Africa, 79
Africa, 48
African Political Systems (Evans-Pritchard and Fortes), 61, 79–80
agnatic descent, 70
Ahmad, Aijaz, 210–11
Ahmed, Sara, 11–13, 14
Allegra Lab, 28–29
alterity, 27–28; affinity and, 95–124, 179–99; in anthropology, 130, 198n4; as differences, 102–3; distances through, 143–44; identifying, 199n5; imaginaries of, 118–24; inescapability of, 129–32; performance and, 179–99; planes of, 117; potential, 165; self and, 95–124; theory of, 12
American Anthropological Association (AAA), 158, 238
American Ethnological Society, 10

Amerindian perspectivism, 222–23
The Andaman Islanders (Radcliffe-Brown), 41
Ang, Gey Pin, 27–28, 197, 236–37; approach of, 192–93; background of, 183–84; career of, 184–88; on experiential practice, 193; on performance studies, 193–94
anglophone mainstream, 19–20, 22–23
anthropological imaginarium, 102–6; of affinity, 118–24; editing, 112–14; impact of, 119; shooting of, 107–12
anthropologists; amateur, 163; anglophone, 10; for corporations, 235–36; feelings of, 179–80; on film, 107–12; freedom of, 180–81; Hau'ofa on, 168–69; heterogeneous, 187; homework for, 10–11; Indigenous Australian, 172; linguistic, 161–62; native, 144; obligation of, 53; political, 66; standardization of, 181; temple dancers and, 216–21
anthropology; academic, 187; alterity in, 130, 198n4; anglophone, 5, 130; approaches of, 234–35; Asian, 20–21; bounded, 30n4; British, 12–13, 24–25; career-complex of, 180; citizenship in, 16–17; collaborations in, 181–89; contemporary, 4; contributions to, 143; craft of, 194–95; as cultural translation, 83; debates

anthropology (*cont.*)
of, 2, 182, 197, 233–39; in dialogue, 28; differences within, 28; diversity in, 233; domestic, 227; dominant, 145; dynamic of, 6; ecumenical, 207–27; epistemic problems with, 21; on equality, 80; ethics in, 196–97; Euro-American, 2; evolutionist-era, 66; experimental approaches of, 181, 195; gatekeepers of, 15–16; global landscape of, 4; global multiplicity of, 22; good, 4, 10, 13–17, 22; heterogeneous, 180; hierarchies in, 143; as human history, 225–26; identity of, 238–39; imagination in, 102–7; Indian, 22; indigenous, 21; influences on, 24; as inheritance, 25; intellectual discontinuity in, 15; interlocutors and, 95–96; international, 14; layers of, 112–14; multiple existence of, 20–23; mythic charter in, 5–6; Native, 21, 154; object of, 144; ontologically inflected, 30n2; ontological turn in, 5–7; original sin of, 84; other in, 12, 21, 144–45; peripheral, 21; persona of, 9–10; pluralism in, 23; radical, 145; reflexive turn in, 18–19; regional, 21; reimagination of, 23–30; relevant, 48; reproduction of, 11; revisionist, 85; scrutiny of, 1; self-other in, 95; social constitution of, 10; sociocultural, 1; spectrum of, 9; structural-functionalist, 65, 72–73; terminology in, 82–83; theoretical fetishism in, 15–16; traditions in, 8; twentieth-century, 208; US, 11; world, 17, 21
Appiah, Kwame Anthony, 211
Ardener, Edwin, 226
Argonauts, 8
Argonauts of the Western Pacific (Malinowski), 5–7
aristocracy; in Africa, 79–80; differences in, 82; hereditary elite, 83; of Nuer tribe, 66–72 power of, 86n11; Tocqueville on, 80–81; tribes and, 75; of Trobriand Islanders, 72–79. *See also diel*
Aristotle, 87n14
Asad, T., 20
ASAO. *See* Association for Social Anthropology in Oceania
Asia, 20–21
Association for Social Anthropology in Oceania (ASAO), 152, 160, 165
audit culture, 195–96
Austen, Leo, 73
Australian and New Zealand Association for the Advancement of Science, 151
authority, 3. *See also Herrschaft*
avunculocal residence, 78

Barragán, Rossana, 130
Bassnett, S., 83
Beck, Ulrich, 60
Ben-Ari, E., 1
Benedict, Ruth, 22, 87n12
Beteille, Andre, 14
block grants, 37
Boas, F., 79–80
Bolivia; economy of, 142; ethnography in, 146n4; film production in, 128–46; indigenous media initiative of, 131. *See also* indigenous media
Bošković, Aleksandar, 238
Bourdieu, P., 82
Britain; anthropology in, 12–13; China and, 97–98
British Association for the Advancement of Science in Australia, 40, 47
A Briton in the Cool Mountains of China; challenges in, 112–13; editing of, 112–14; fifth stop

Index 243

in, 123; gratitude for, 115–16; impact of, 115; introduction of, 119; map from, 121; as Orientalist, 116–17; perspective of, 116–17; premiere of, 115; production of, 107–12; slaves in, 120; storyboard of, 112–14; villagers in, 121; Winnington in, 120
Brodkin, Karen, 11
Brunton, Annie, 47
Buchowski, Michał, 15–16

Cambridge University Press, 13
Canessa, A., 133
canoes, 6
Cape Peninsula Native Welfare Society, 45
Cartesian society, 2–3
Castaneda, Quetzil, 188
CEFREC. See Centro de Formación y Realización Cinematográfica
centralization, 67
Centro de Formación y Realización Cinematográfica (CEFREC), 136
Chakrabarty, Dipesh, 11
Chao, Emily, 101
chief (*guya'u*), 63, 71
children of girls. See *gaat nyiet*
China, 25; Britain and, 97–98; media in, 100–101. See also Ninglang; Southwest China
Chinese Visual Festival Club, 117
Christianity; Catholic Church, 103; conversion in, 81; principles of, 207
The Chrysanthemum and the Sword (Benedict), 22
Chua, Liana, 29–30, 96, 117, 182, 236–37
citizenship, 16–17; acts of, 190; Malinowski on, 73–75
CLACPI. See Latin American Council of Indigenous Peoples' Film and Communication
clan. See *gens*

Clifford, James, 18–19, 83, 118–19, 159, 169, 238; essays of, 172n8; on Indigenous peoples, 160–61
collaboration; in anthropology, 181–89; challenges of, 138–43; in fieldwork, 192; in heterogenous discipline, 190–92; in indigenous media, 134, 138–43
colonial administration, 74, 76–77
colonial domination, 65–66
colonialism, 24, 221–22
Coming of Age in Samoa (Mead), 163
commodity, 2
commoners, 77
communication, 196; human, 198n2; multiple modes of, 199n6
communism, 65, 97–98
community; division of, 75–76; information of, 221; researchers in, 190
Consejo Latinoamericano de Cine y Comunicación de Pueblos Indígenas. See Latin American Council of Indigenous Peoples' Film and Communication
Constituent Assembly, 128
copyrights, 13–14
Cretan Paradox, 222
critiques, 30nn5–6
Crocombe, Ronald, 169–70
Cultural Anthropology, 12–13
culture; of Hawaii, 162–63; institutional, 30n3; of Nuosu group, 95–124; writing, 4–5, 17
Culture and Imperialism (Saïd), 210–11

dala (Matrilineage), 72, 79
Dalsgaard, Steffen, 103–4
Dartmouth College, 162–63
Das, Veena, 14
death, 152, 210
decolonization, 212
Deger, Jennifer, 104
Deleuze, Gilles, 106–7
Delhi University, 13

Democracy in America (Tocqueville), 80
Democratic Reforms, 99, 102
descent groups, 64
destabilization, 4–5; others in, 20–23; reflexive challenges, 17–20
devadasi (the temple dancers), 216, 219
Dialectic in Practical Religion (Leach), 214–15
diel (aristocracy), 68
Dinka tribe, 68–69
Dirlick, Arif, 181
disciplinary models, 3–4
discover. *See heuriskein*
diversity, 11–12. *See also* gender; race; women
dominant lineage, 68
Dominguez, Virginia, 238
Dongba Cultural Research Institute in Lijiang city, 99
Douglas, Mary, 209–16, 220–25
dualism, 2
Dufrenne, Mikel, 193
Dumont, Louis, 80–81
Durkheim, Emile, 208–9, 213–15
Durkheimian sociology, 85
Dworkin, Ronald, 223
The Dynamics of Culture Change (Malinowski), 54

Economic and Social Research Council (ESRC), 37
economy; of Bolivia, 142; commodity compared to, 2
education, 46–47; Malinowski on, 51–54; of Radcliffe-Brown, 40; sex, 52–53; in South Africa, 51–54; structure of, 30n3
The Elementary Structures of Kinship (Lévi-Strauss), 220
elite theory, 67
equality, 80
Eriksen, T.H., 63, 70, 86n1, 238
Escobar, Arturo, 181, 186–87, 191

ESRC. *See* Economic and Social Research Council
ethics, 37–38; in anthropology, 196–97; awareness in, 207; of nobility, 82
ethnic affiliation, 133–34
ethnodramatics, 179
ethnographic filmmaking; crisis in, 137; as imaginarium, 118–19; impact of, 118–19; in Southwest China, 95–124
ethnographic publications, 188
ethnography, 5–7; aristocracy of, 24–25; authority in, 26; in Bolivia, 146n4; fieldwork in, 219; goals of, 234; methodological holism in, 219; politgraphy and, 84–86; in present, 220; reflexivity of, 18–19; revelations of, 8–9; of Trobriand Islands, 67, 72; writing in, 181
ethno-history; images of, 100–102; layers of, 112–14
ethnology, 41–42
ethno-politics, 100–102
European Association of Social Anthropologists, 29
Evans-Pritchard, E.E., 24–25, 61, 65–66; McKinnon on, 86n5; on Nuer, 68–72, 84
evolutionary distance, 64–67
evolutionism, 61–63; Malinowski on, 72; as social science, 64
experiential practice; affinity and, 192–94; Ang on, 193
experimental online spaces, 28–29

Fabian, Johannes, 213–14
Fahim, Hussein, 21
fieldwork, 96; collaborators in, 192; ethnographic, 219
filmmaking; experimentation in, 135–36; montage in, 104–5; observational cinema, 105, 118; at Plan Nacional Indígena Originario de Comunicación Audiovisual, 133; politics in,

137–38; revolutionary, 135–36; techniques of, 103–6. *See also* ethnographic filmmaking; indigenous media
films. *See* ethnographic filmmaking
Finney, Ben, 163
Fortes, Meyer, 61
Foucault, M., 67
Fraser, James, 42

gaat nyiet (children of girls), 69
Gatt, Caroline, 27–28, 183–88, 198, 236–37
Geertz, Clifford, 195–96
Gellner, Ernest, 47, 215–16
Gemeinschaft communality, 65
gender, 11–12
gens (clan), 64
George, Lila, 163–64
Gerholm, T., 21
Gilliam, Terry, 106–7, 118
Ginsburg, F., 134, 139
global inequalities; asymmetrical ignorance due to, 15; in representation, 13–17
Gluckman, Max, 38
Goldman, Irving, 80
Goodyear-Ka'opua, Noelani, 159
Gough, Kathleen, 218–19
Greece, 64–65
Grote, George, 64
Grotowski, Jerzy, 183
Gusterson, Hugh, 10–11
guya'u (chief), 76–77

Hall, Lisa Kahaleole, 155
Hannerz, Ulf, 21, 226
Harrison, Faye, 237–38
HAU: Journal of Ethnographic Theory, 15
Hau'ofa, Epeli, 26–27, 86n11; on anthropologists, 168–69; background of, 151; career of, 151–52; death of, 152; on Indigenous peoples, 154–55; on Oceania, 155–56; poetry of, 169–71; on time, 158–59; on traditions, 159–60
Hawaii, 158–59; culture of, 162–63; language of, 173n13
hegemony, 66
Hereniko, Vilsoni, 163
Herrschaft (authority), 65
Hertzog, J.B.M, 38, 45
heterogenous discipline, anthropology as; anthropologists in, 187; anthropology and, 180; challenges for, 194–97; collaboration in, 190–92
heuriskein (discover), 185–86
hierarchy; in anthropology, 143; Dumont on, 80–81
Hoernlé, Winifred, 41–43, 50, 52
Homo Hierarchicus (Dumont), 80
Horton, Robin, 223
house. *See tabinau*
human difference, 38
human incommensurability, 208
humanity, 180; planes of, 117; savage, 6; thinking in, 224–25; world and, 208
Hutchinson, Sharon, 11, 71, 84
Hviding, Edvard, 165–66
Hymes, Dell, 186, 195, 236

I, 17–20, 25
IAI. *See* International Africa Institute
identity; of anthropology, 238–39; collective, 9; disciplinary, 1, 9–10; self-, 9
identity politics, 139
Ikegami, Aya, 218
imaginaries. *See* anthropological imaginarium
The Imaginarium of Doctor Parnassus, 106–7
imagination, 4, 102–7
imperialism, 221–22
Inalienable Possessions: The Paradox of Keeping-While Giving (Weiner), 81–82
India, 20, 22

Indigenista National Institution (INI), 138–39
Indigenous Anthropology in Non-Western Countries (Fahim), 21
indigenous media; affinity and, 143; collaboration in, 134, 138–43; debates in, 140–42; ethnic affiliation in, 133; features of, 141; goals of, 139–40; languages in, 139; in Latin America, 144; perspectives in, 135; politics in, 138; production of, 131; technical training in, 136; techniques in, 134–35; tensions in, 130, 140–42; visual representations in, 132; women in, 131
Indigenous Media Transference to Indigenous Communities in Mexico, 138–39
Indigenous peoples; alliances in, 156; claims to, 171n3; Clifford on, 160–61; determining, 146n1; Hau'ofa on, 154–55; as sovereign, 153–55. *See also* Native; Pacific Islander
individualism, 2
Ingold, Tim, 198, 236
INI. *See Indigenista* National Institution
institutional structures, 10–13
interlocutors, 95–96; Baluan, 104; in Nuosu group, 101–2
International Africa Institute (IAI), 48
international bodies, 30n7
intuitive listening, 193–94
The Invention of Primitive Society (Kuper), 62

Jabavu, J.D., 44–45
James, Wendy, 212–15, 220
Jiarimuji (anthropologist), 107–8, 116

Kahnawà:ke, 154
Ka'ili, Tevita O, 155–56
Kame'eleihiwa, Lilikala, 159–60

Kapferer, Bruce, 106–7
Kelty, Chris, 192
KFI. *See Knowing from the Inside*
Kingdom of Tonga, 171n3
King Kamehameha's Kona Beach Hotel, 166
kinship society, 24–25
kinship systems, 42, 61–62; links of, 71–72; pre-class and, 67; structural-functionalist schemes for, 63; totemic, 72–73; zombie, 84
Knowing from the Inside (KFI) project, 187–88
Kroeber, Alfred, 226
Krotz, E., 143–44
Kubrick, Stanley, 106–7
Kuklick, H., 38
Kuper, Adam, 62, 213
Kuwayama, Takami, 23–24

labour division, 11
land; manager of, 75; as property, 82; tenure of, 73; use-rights of, 79
Lassiter, Luke, 195
Latin America, 26, 128; indigenous media in, 144; media initiatives in, 129, 133–34; struggles in, 129. *See also* Bolivia
Latin American Council of Indigenous Peoples' Film and Communication (CLACPI) *(Consejo Latinoamericano de Cine y Comunicación de Pueblos Indígenas)*, 136–37
Latin etymology, 191
Leach, Edmund, 214–15, 225
Lee, Helen, 168
Lefevere, 83
Lévi-Strauss, 214, 220
Lévy-Bruhl, Lucien, 212
Lintott, A., 87n15
Lugard, Frederick, 47
Lyons, Paul, 158–61

MacDougall, David, 104, 139
Macht (power), 65
Madan, T.N., 211–12, 220

Mahina, Hufanga 'Okusitino, 155–56
Malinowski, Bronislaw, 5, 24–25; background of, 46; on canoes, 6; career of, 47–53; character of, 49–50; on citizenship, 73–75; on differences, 7; on education, 51–54; education of, 46–47; Ethnographer of, 6–7, 9; on evolutionism, 72; on family, 50–51, 77; ideological commitment of, 53–54; on integration, 48; on labour, 48–49; monographs of, 47; on nobility, 77; on Noble Savage, 85; politics of, 47–50; on race, 49; Radcliffe-Brown and, 53–54; Smuts and, 49, 51; on social order, 74–75; strategy of, 6–7, 38–39; sympathy of, 84; on Trobriand Islanders, 72–79; Weiner on, 82; on women, 50
Maori peoples, 164–65
Marcus, George, 18, 118–19, 190–91, 238
marriage, 61–62
Marsh, Selina Tusitala, 170
Marxism, 136
Mathews, Gordon, 15–16
Mathur, Nayanika, 29–30, 117, 182, 236–37
Matrilineage (*dala*), 72, 79
Mauss, Marcel, 208–9, 213–15
Mawyer, Alex, 167–68
McGavin, Kirsten, 155
McKinnon, S., 86n5
Mead, Margaret, 153, 163
Merleau-Ponty, Maurice, 104
methodological holism, 218–19
Mexico, 131–32
Mills, David, 45
minority dominance, 70
minority groups, 98–99
Mintz, Sidney, 226
Mitsu (ethnologist), 97–98, 100
Mohawk peoples, 153–54
monographs, 191

Morgan, L.H., 61, 64–65
Morgen, Sandra, 11
movements, 17–18; decolonizing, 20; renewed, 28–29
Muru-Lanning, Marama, 164–65, 173n15
Mutman, Mahmut, 19–20

nationalism, 221–22
National Plan of Indigenous Audiovisual Communication. *See* Plan Nacional Indígena Originario de Comunicación Audiovisual
Native, 154; 'primitive', 163; of South Africa, 38, 51
Native American peoples, 162–63
Native American Studies, 163
Navarro, T., 12–13
Naxi group, 98–99
neo-liberalism, 10–11
New Education Fellowship, 50
Ngat Is Dead – Studying Mortuary Traditions, 103–4
NGO. *See* non-governmental organization
Nickolov, Nickolai D., 194
Niehaus, Isak, 24–25
Ninglang, 97–101, 109
nobility; ethics of, 82; Malinowski on, 77; privileges of, 76–77
Noble Savage, 85
non-governmental organization (NGO), 128
Norton, William, 41–43
Ntarangwi, Mwenda, 22–24, 28, 239
Nuer, 24–25, 61; aristocracy of, 66–72; Evans-Pritchard on, 68–69, 84; structure of, 68–69
#xcol, 29
Nuosu (Yi); culture of, 95–124; fame of, 99;interlocutors in, 101–2; slavery of, 99; Winnington on, 97–99. *See also A Briton in the Cool Mountains of China*

objectivism, 18
observational cinema, 105, 118
Occidentalism, 211
Oceania, 166–67
Oceanian anthropologists, 151; Hau'ofa on, 155–56; Indigenous, 156–58
Oceanian anthropology, 26–27, 151–53
Oceanian peoples, 158
ontological shift, 159
ontological turn, 5–6; challenges of, 8; pluralities of, 7; premise of, 7–8
ontology, 80
Orientalism, 211
Orientalism (Said), 17–18, 117
others; in anthropology, 12, 21, 144–45; indigenous peoples as, 143
Otto, Ton, 103–4, 106
Ottomans, 81
Oxford University Press, 13

Pacific Islander, 154
Pacific Studies, 157
'para-site' experiments, 199n8
patrilineal genealogy, 61
patrimonialism, 81
People's Liberation Army (PLA), 99–101
Perez, Rosa Maria, 216–18, 222
performance studies, 186–87, 193–94
phyle (tribe), 65
Pina-Cabral, João de, 27–28, 60, 196, 228
Piper, A., 14
Pitt-Rivers, Julian, 227
PLA. *See* People's Liberation Army
Plan Nacional Indígena Originario de Comunicación Audiovisual (National Plan of Indigenous Audiovisual Communication), 131–32, 146nn2–3; Communication Strategy of, 147; filmmaking at, 133; research on, 133

Pobłocki, Kacper, 15
politgraphy, 84–86
political commitment, 135–38
politics; of academia, 14; ethnopolitics, 100–102; in filmmaking, 137–38; in indigenous media, 138; Malinowski on, 47–50; of Radcliffe-Brown, 40–41. *See also* identity politics
Poole, D., 142–43
Portugal, 217
positivism, 224
postcolonial critiques, 2
postmodernism, 18
postmodernist critiques, 2
poststructuralism, 18
poststructuralists, 209
pouvoir-savoir (power-knowledge), 65–66
Powell, Harry, 74
power. *See Macht*
power-knowledge. *See pouvoir-savoir*
power relations, 71–72; naturalization of, 64–67; tradition and, 66; in tribes, 64
primitives, 209–16; defense of, 221–25; Douglas on, 221–25; Native peoples as, 163; society of, 60; study of, 64
process risk, 196
professionalization, 195
Provincialising Europe (Chakrabarty), 11
Pukui, Mary Kawena, 167
Purity and Danger (James), 212–14

Quality Assurance Agency (QAA), 195–96

race, 235; labour division of, 11; Malinowski on, 49
Radcliffe-Brown, Alfred, 24, 38; background of, 39–46; career of, 40–43; criticism of, 44; education of, 40; on ethnology, 41–42;

health of, 40–41; influences of, 39; interventions of, 53–54; Malinowski and, 53–54; politics of, 40–41; on religion, 44; on retribalization, 45–46; on science, 43–44; on segregation, 45–46
rank; evolutionist terminology of, 80; of women, 76
Rappaport, Joanna, 190–91
Refiti, Albert, 168–69
reflexive complicity, 190
reflexive turn, 18–19
relativism, 224
religion, 44. See also Christianity
Religion without God (Dworkin), 223
research; funds for, 37, 53–54; on Plan Nacional Indígena Originario de Comunicación Audiovisual, 133
research subjects, 129, 132
resources, 13–14
Restrepo, Eduardo, 181, 186–87, 191
revelations, 4–10
Richards, Thomas, 183
Rock, Joseph, 98–99
Rockefeller Foundation, 50
Rodríguez, Marta, 135–36
Rouch, Jean, 134–35, 139
Roy, Lamaku Mikahala, 166–67

Sabiston, Leslie, 172n7
Sahlins, Marshall, 61–63, 80
Saïd, Edward W., 17–18, 117, 210–11
Salmond, Amiria, 30, 163–64, 165, 172n9
Sanjinés, Iván, 136–37
Sanjinés, Jorge, 135–36
Schechner, Richard, 187
Schneider, David, 61
scholarship; anthropological, 180–81; feminist, 62; foreign, 97–99; global anthropological, 23; postcolonial, 17–18; validity of, 15

science; in modern history, 222–23; within modernity, 215–16; Radcliffe-Brown on, 43–44
segmental organization, 65
Seligman, G., 73
Seminar, 20
Sharp, J., 62–63
Shore, Cris, 195–96
Silva, Jorge, 135–36
Silva, Noenoe, 163, 173n11
Silverstein, 161–62
Simpson, Audra, 153–54
slavery; in *A Briton in the Cool Mountains of China*, 121; defending of, 207; of Nuosu group, 99
The Slaves of the Cool Mountains (Winnington), 97–99, 107–12
Smith, Linda Tuhiwai, 163
Smuts, Jan, 38, 40–41, 49, 51
Sneath, David, 24–25, 85–86
social constitution, 10
social evolution; theories of, 84; zombie theory of, 60–63
social movements, 182
social order, 74–75
social science, 64
social theory, 59–60
social value, 43
society; Cartesian, 2–3; kinship, 24–25; primitive, 60; structure of, 40; Western, 1–3
sociocentrism, 215
sociology; Indian, 22; local, 223
solidarity, 85
Sourcing Within Worksessions, 183, 188–89, 197
South Africa, 24; colour bar in, 38; education in, 51–54; equality in, 54; government in, 38; Natives of, 38, 51; University of Cape Town, 39, 41; war in, 38
Southwest China; ethnographic filmmaking in, 95–124; media in, 100
stakeholders, 38
Steiner, Franz Baermann, 207

Stengers, Isabelle, 191
strategy; diplomatic, 19; of Malinowski, 6–7, 38–39of representation, 19–20 study, 64
Stultz, Aaron, 234–35
Subaltern Studies collective, 17–18
Suhr, Christian, 103–6, 116–17
Swancutt, Katherine, 25–26, 124–25

Tabalu tribe, 76
tabinau (house), 62
Taller de Historia Oral Andina in Bolivia (THOA), 144
Taylor & Francis, 13
Teaiwa, Katerina, 157–58
the temple dancers. *See devadasi*
temporary crystallization, 189
Tengan, Ty, 26–27, 108, 171
Theatre Artist Award, 183
Third World, 211–12
THOA. *See Taller de Historia Oral Andina in Bolivia*
Tocqueville, A., 80–81
Tonga, Kingdom of, 171n3
Torres Strait Islanders, 171n4
traditions; in anthropology, 8; Hau'ofa on, 159–60; nation-based, 21; power relations and, 66
Trask, Haunani-Kay, 153
tribal, 61–62
tribal law, 77–78
tribe. *See phyle*
tribes; aristocracy and, 75; chief and, 63; criticism of, 62–63; formation of, 60–61; power relations of, 64; Tsonga, 42
Tribesmen (Sahlins), 61
Trobriand Islanders, 7, 24–25; aristocracy of, 72–79; ethnography of, 67, 72; hierarchy of, 75–76; Malinowski on, 72–79; non-citizens of, 74
Trobriand Islands, 67

Tupuna Awa: People and Politics of the Waikato (Muru-Lanning), 164
Turner, Edith, 187
Turner, Victor, 179, 187
2001: A Space Odyssey, 106–7

Uberoi, J.P.S., 14, 20
United Kingdom, 11
United States (US), 11
universities, 10–11, 37
University of Aberdeen, 184–85
University of California's Museum of Anthropology, 162
Uperesa, Lisa, 153, 163, 165–68
US. *See* United States
Uzendoski, Michael, 198

villages, 71–72, 74
Villarreal, Gabriela Zamorano, 26, 105–6, 145–46
Vitebsky, Piers, 96
Viveiros de Castro, Eduardo, 214

Wagner, Roy, 208
WCAA. *See* World Council of Anthropological Associations
We Are the Ocean (Hau'ofa), 152
Weber, M, 81–82
Weiner, Annette, 75, 78, 81–82, 86n8
Wellens, Koen, 102
Wellman, C., 14
West, Paige, 2–3, 165–68
Western society, 1–3
West vs. the rest, 2–3
White, Geoffrey, 153, 156
Willerslev, Rane, 104–6, 116–17
Williams, B., 12–13
Winnington, Alan, 107–12; network of, 117–18; on Nuosu group, 97–99; photos of, 100. *See also A Briton in the Cool Mountains of China*
WOC. *See* women of colour
women, 11; in academia, 12; feminism, 18, 62; in indigenous

media, 131; Malinowski on, 50; rank of, 76; subalternity, 216–17; untouchable, 216–17
women of colour (WOC), 12
Wood, D.M.J., 135–36
World Council of Anthropological Associations (WCAA), 21
Wortham, Erica, 138–39
Wright, Sue, 195–96

writing culture, 4–6; as composition, 192; ethnographic, 181; reflexive, 17–20
Writing Culture (Clifford and Marcus), 18

Yano, Christine, 163
Yi. *See* Nuosu
Young, Kalaniopua, 172n7
Yunnan Minzu University, 116

Methodology and History in Anthropology

Series Editors:
David Parkin, Fellow of All Souls College, University of Oxford
David Gellner, Fellow of All Souls College, University of Oxford

Just as anthropology has had a significant influence on many other disciplines in recent years, so too have its methods been challenged by new intellectual and technical developments. This series is designed to offer a forum for debate on the interrelationship between anthropology and other academic fields but also on the challenge to anthropological methods of new intellectual and technological developments, and the role of anthropological thought in a general history of concepts.

Volume 1
Marcel Mauss: A Centenary Tribute
Edited by Wendy James and N.J. Allen

Volume 2
Franz Baerman Steiner: Selected Writings Volume I: Taboo, Truth and Religion. Franz B. Steiner
Edited by Jeremy Adler and Richard Fardon

Volume 3
Franz Baerman Steiner: Selected Writings Volume II: Orientalism, Value, and Civilisation. Franz B. Steiner
Edited by Jeremy Adler and Richard Fardon

Volume 4
The Problem of Context: Perspectives from Social Anthropology and Elsewhere
Edited by Roy Dilley

Volume 5
Religion in English Everyday Life: An Ethnographic Approach
By Timothy Jenkins

Volume 6
Hunting the Gatherers: Ethnographic Collectors, Agents and Agency in Melanasia, 1870s–1930s
Edited by Michael O'Hanlon and Robert L. Welsh

Volume 7
Anthropologists in a Wider World: Essays on Field Research
Edited by Paul Dresch, Wendy James and David Parkin

Volume 8
Categories and Classifications: Maussian Reflections on the Social
By N.J. Allen

Volume 9
Louis Dumont and Hierarchical Opposition
By Robert Parkin

Volume 10
Categories of Self: Louis Dumont's Theory of the Individual
By André Celtel

Volume 11
Existential Anthropology: Events, Exigencies and Effects
By Michael Jackson

Volume 12
An Introduction to Two Theories of Social Anthropology: Descent Groups and Marriage Alliance
By Louis Dumont

Volume 13
Navigating Terrains of War: Youth and Soldiering in Guinea-Bissau
By Henrik E. Vigh

Volume 14
The Politics of Egalitarianism: Theory and Practice
Edited by Jacqueline Solway

Volume 15
A History of Oxford Anthropology
Edited by Peter Rivière

Volume 16
Holistic Anthropology: Emergence and Convergence
Edited by David Parkin and Stanley Ulijaszek

Volume 17
Learning Religion: Anthropological Approaches
Edited by David Berliner and Ramon Sarró

Volume 18
Ways of Knowing: New Approaches in the Anthropology of Knowledge and Learning
Edited by Mark Harris

Volume 19
Difficult Folk? A Political History of Social Anthropology
By David Mills

Volume 20
Human Nature as Capacity: Transcending Discourse and Classification
By Nigel Rapport

Volume 21
The Life of Property: House, Family and Inheritance in Béarn, South-West France
By Timothy Jenkins

Volume 22
Out of the Study and Into the Field: Ethnographic Theory and Practice in French Anthropology
Edited by Robert Parkin and Anne de Sales

Volume 23
The Scope of Anthropology: Maurice Godelier's Work in Context
Edited by Laurent Dousset and Serge Tcherkézoff

Volume 24
Anyone: *The Cosmopolitan Subject of Anthropology*
By Nigel Rapport

Volume 25
Up Close and Personal: On Peripheral Perspectives and the Production of Anthropological Knowledge
Edited by Cris Shore and Susanna Trnka

Volume 26
Understanding Cultural Transmission in Anthropology: A Critical Synthesis
Edited by Roy Ellen, Stephen J. Lycett and Sarah E. Johns

Volume 27
Durkheim in Dialogue: A Centenary Celebration of The Elementary Forms of Religious Life
Edited by Sondra Hausner

Volume 28
Extraordinary Encounters: Authenticity and the Interview
Edited by Katherine Smith, James Staples and Nigel Rapport

Volume 29
Regimes of Ignorance: Anthropological Perspectives on the Production and Reproduction of Non-Knowledge
Edited by Roy Dilley and Thomas G. Kirsch

Volume 30
Human Origins: Contributions from Social Anthropology
Edited by Camilla Power, Morna Finnegan and Hilary Callan

Volume 31
The Ethics of Knowledge Creation: Transactions, Relations and Persons
Edited by Lisette Josephides and Anne Sigfrid Grønseth

Volume 32
Returning Life: Language, Life Force and History in Kilimanjaro
Knut Christian Myhre

Volume 33
Expeditionary Anthropology: Teamwork, Travel and the 'Science of Man'
Edited by Martin Thomas and Amanda Harris

Volume 34
Who Are 'We'? Reimagining Alterity and Affinity in Anthropology
Edited by Liana Chua and Nayanika Mathur

www.ingramcontent.com/pod-product-compliance
Lightning Source LLC
Chambersburg PA
CBHW051534020426
42333CB00016B/1922